CONTESTI
AUSTRALI

States, Markets and Civil Society

EDITED BY
PAUL SMYTH and BETTINA CASS

CAMBRIDGE UNIVERSITY PRESS

PUBLISHED BY THE PRESS SYNDICATE OF THE UNIVERSITY OF CAMBRIDGE
The Pitt Building, Trumpington Street, Cambridge, United Kingdom

CAMBRIDGE UNIVERSITY PRESS
The Edinburgh Building, Cambridge CB2 2RU, UK   http://www.cup.cam.ac.uk
40 West 20th Street, New York, NY 10011–4211, USA   http://www.cup.org
10 Stamford Road, Oakleigh, Melbourne 3166, Australia

© Cambridge University Press 1998

This book is in copyright. Subject to statutory exception
and to the provisions of relevant collective licensing agreements,
no reproduction of any part may take place without
the written permission of Cambridge University Press.

First published 1998

Printed in Australia by Ligare Pty Ltd

Typeset in Baskerville 10/12 pt

A catalogue record for this book is available from the British Library

National Library of Australia cataloguing in publication data

Contesting the Australian way: states, markets and civil society.

Bibliography.
Includes index.
ISBN 0 521 63306 0.
ISBN 0 521 63390 7 (pbk.).

1. Australia – Social policy – 1990– . 2. Australia – Economic
policy – 1990– . 3. Australia – Politics and government – 1990 .
4. Australia – Social conditions – 1990– .
I. Smyth, Paul, 1947– . II. Cass, Bettina.

361.994

Library of Congress Cataloguing in Publication data

Contesting the Australian way: states, markets, and civil society/
edited by Smyth and Bettina Cass.
p.   cm.
Includes bibliographical references and index.
ISBN 0-521-63306-0 (alk. paper).
ISBN 0-521-63390-7 (pbk.: alk. paper)
1. Australia – Economic policy. 2. Australia – Social policy.
3. Australia – Politics and government – 1945– . 4. Keynesian
economics. I. Smyth, Paul. II. Cass, Bettina.
HC605.C5437   1998
338'.994–dc21   98–8122
                                                                                         CIP

ISBN 0 521 63306 0 hardback
ISBN 0 521 63390 7 paperback

This book had its genesis in a workshop sponsored by
the Academy of the Social Sciences in Australia

Contents

List of Figures and Tables v
Contributors vi

Introduction 1

PART I Overviews: States, Markets and Private Life

1 States, Markets and the Global Dimension: An Overview of Certain Issues in Political Economy
   HUGH EMY 17
2 The Social Policy Context
   BETTINA CASS 38

PART II Historical Perspectives: Australian Settlements?

3 The Australian Settlement and Australian Political Thought
   GRAHAM MADDOX 57
4 The Australian Way
   JILL ROE 69
5 Remaking the Australian Way: The Keynesian Compromise
   PAUL SMYTH 81
6 Unmaking the Australian Keynesian Way
   TIM BATTIN 94

CONTENTS

PART III Public Institutions, Civil Society and Social Movements

7 Public Sector Reform and the Australian Way
   LIONEL ORCHARD — 111
8 Government and Civil Society: Restructuring Community Services
   DEBORAH BRENNAN — 124
9 Social Movements, Democracy and Conflicts over Institutional Reform
   JOCELYN PIXLEY — 138

PART IV Transformations of Economy and State

10 Economic Restructuring in Australia: Policy Settlements, Models of Economic Development and Economic Rationalism
   STEPHEN BELL — 157
11 Economic Rationalism: Social Philosophy Masquerading as Economic Science
   J. W. NEVILE — 169
12 The Accord and Industrial Relations: Lessons for Political Strategy
   ROY GREEN — 180

PART V The New (In)compatibilities: The Welfare State and Competitive Markets

13 Is Australia Particularly Unequal? Traditional and New Views
   PETER WHITEFORD — 197
14 A Competitive Future: The Industry Commission and the Welfare Sector
   JOHN ERNST — 215
15 *Working Nation* and Beyond as Market Bureaucracy: The Introduction of Competition Policy in Case-Management
   MICHAEL WEARING AND PAUL SMYTH — 228

References — 241
Index — 265

Figures

10.1	Income inequality in various countries	166
12.1	Australia's balance of trade, 1980–95	187
12.2	Components of Australia's export growth, 1979–93	189
13.1	The income accounting framework	207

Table

14.1	Industry Commission inquiries	218

Contributors

Dr Tim Battin
Dept of Politics, University of New England

Dr Stephen Bell
Dept of Political Science, University of Tasmania

Dr Deborah Brennan
Dept of Government, University of Sydney

Professor Bettina Cass
Dean of Arts, University of Sydney

Professor Hugh Emy
Dept of Politics, Monash University

Dr John Ernst
Dept of Urban and Social Policy, Victoria University of Technology

Dr Roy Green
Dept of Economics, University of Newcastle

Professor Graham Maddox
Dean of Arts, University of New England

Emeritus Professor John Nevile
School of Economics, University of NSW

Dr Lionel Orchard
Dept of Social Sciences, Flinders University

Dr Jocelyn Pixley
School of Sociology, University of NSW

Professor Jill Roe
School of History, Philosophy and Politics, Macquarie University

Dr Paul Smyth
Dept of Social Work and Social Policy, University of Queensland

Dr Michael Wearing
School of Social Work, University of NSW

Dr Peter Whiteford
Strategic Development Commission, Department of Social Security

Introduction

In the year 2001 Australia will become a republic. It is not a prospect which has ignited the public imagination so far. This may be because Australia has long enjoyed virtual independence and its becoming a republic may, incorrectly, be seen publicly as little more than a change of head of state. It may have to do with the decreased salience of the nation-state in an internationalising economy during the 1980s and 1990s. But it may also be the result of a nation ill at ease with itself. On the big questions of public policy concerning the broad directions of economic and welfare policies, and on racial and ethnic relations, there is more confusion than unanimity, and little sense of a shared national project. This book reflects on this dis-ease, this confusion, in an attempt to review what has been worthwhile in the values and institutions which have shaped our way of life hitherto; and on what might be Australia's policy directions in the twenty-first century. In doing so, we have been struck by the manner in which in recent times Australia's past policy strengths have been little recognised. A lingering cultural cringe still habitually expects imported rather than home-grown solutions. More recently, the novelties of globalisation have been emphasised to the extent that distinctive features of national policy are regarded as irrelevant. By contrast, we find much to value in the approach to public policy which Australians have developed during the twentieth century. While we also find this Australian Way to be in crisis, we suggest it offers things worth fighting for, things which would give substance to the celebrations in 2001.

Of course, the kind of policy malaise which is the object of our attention is not peculiar to Australia. Since the 1970s, all comparable countries have been faced with similar public policy dilemmas. Ramesh Mishra (1990) observed that their responses have tended to move in one of two directions: social corporatism and neoliberalism. From 1983 to 1996 Australia was governed by the Australian Labor Party which attempted to remake labour traditions along social corporatist lines. This experiment – which attracted the attention of labour movements elsewhere, notably in the United Kingdom – was characterised by considerable innovation in the area of social policy, but failed to develop a social corporatist alternative in economic policy. Its successor, the Coalition government of the Liberal and National Parties, has embraced the neoliberal approach in both social and economic policy. The latter has been in office too short a time for much to be said of its efforts in this book, but our experience of both these regimes has not only sharpened our sense of what has been distinctive about the Australian Way; it also contributes to that wider international discussion concerning the possibilities of social intervention in the kind of economic context which has developed since the 1970s.

Our notion of an Australian Way reframes radically the analysis of these issues in our national context, and some account of how our idea developed may be helpful before offering a more formal exposition. At the end of 1995, the Academy of the Social Sciences in Australia convened a workshop to consider the likely future trends of public policy. At that time, there was a sense that Labor's social corporatism was running out of steam. Upon its election to government in 1983, the Labor Party had established an Accord involving primarily the political and industrial wings of the labour movement. The thrust of the Accord was to facilitate jobs growth through expansionary macro-economic and active industry policies while securing wage restraint through an expanded social wage. By 1995, the interventionary thrust in economic policy had been largely supplanted by neoliberalism (or, as it is called in Australia, economic rationalism); inequality was rising and high unemployment had returned. The need for new policy directions was apparent. The central theme of the workshop was whether the social corporatist approach could be reinvented in some new social charter, or whether Australia was more likely to take the neoliberal path towards what was being called a contract state.

As workshop participants pursued these themes there was a growing sense that the familiar frameworks of analysis were insufficient. There was optimism that the stranglehold of economic rationalism on economic policy debate was loosening, that Labor's Accord was not the only way of thinking about alternatives, and that a space was opening for recasting the role of government in a more positive light. The sense of the need for new starting-points was particularly exciting because it was refracted through a range of disciplinary perspectives. In particular, Jill Roe's challenge to assert the value of the Australian Way created a sense that the past achievements of Australian public policy had far more to offer than was usually allowed. The workshop then created an agenda which has led us collectively to produce this book. This is not just a collection of workshop proceedings. It is the result of several years of effort to clarify and consolidate our original sense of the need to reframe Australian public policy debate.

The three key policy themes which we have identified relate to social welfare, employment, and the reform of public administration. Labor's approach to social welfare reform under the Accord was our first pointer towards the idea of an Australian Way. As Chapters 2 and 13 by Cass and Whiteford show, equality has always been a high value – relatively speaking – in Australian social policy. What has been distinctive, of course, is the way this has been pursued. At the beginning of the twentieth century, Australia established a residual – but very redistributive – welfare system, which, in tandem with a centralised wage system, provided the policy means of pursuing this goal through to the 1970s. At home and overseas, this approach was frequently ranked a welfare failure, and in the 1970s there were attempts to move beyond this welfare residualism to a more universal approach. Amid the welfare state crises of the 1980s, the Accord became the occasion for a retreat from this trend to universalism to the old Australian pattern of welfare targeting. Criticised at first, these reforms had by the early 1990s come to be widely recognised as a positive innovation. As Cass argues, reforms to the welfare system, as encapsulated in the social wage in terms of trends to gender equity accomplished a renovation of an Australian social policy tradition, with redistributive outcomes which mitigated the inequalities generated by unemployment and deregulation of the labour market. These outcomes were less unequal than in comparable Anglo-American countries. In the context of economic restructuring, unsuspected virtues were discovered in the formerly disparaged Australian approach and it was widely claimed that the 'wage-earners' welfare state' had been refurbished.

Nevertheless, it was thought that too much was being asked of the welfare system in the Labor Party's model of social corporatism. Deep cracks had emerged in the apparent consensus. Social policies had not been, and could not be, sufficiently redistributive to offset the rising levels of market-induced inequality. The economic rationalist approach adopted in economic policy had prevented positive interventions to deal with the unemployment undermining the social purposes of the Accord. These sharp reminders of the limits to welfare when economic policy is unregulated raised profound questions about the interrelationship between social and economic policy, and these became central to our deliberations.

In this context, it was evident that a growing reaction to economic rationalism had developed in the first half of the decade among various policy communities. As Emy depicts in Chapter 1, this was regarded as salutary, in the light of the evidence of the comparative economic success of managed over free-market economies, as well as their superiority in terms of social outcomes. At the same time, this shift had not become strongly rooted in terms of actual policy practice: economic rationalism remained dominant under Labor. What did seem clear, however, was that some renovation along the lines suggested in these writings was necessary if we were to get beyond the limits of a welfare response to the social questions of the day. Emy highlighted the contemporary reactions against the market model within the United Kingdom and the United States and alerted us to the dangers to our environmental, social and political systems which would heighten if there was not a determined effort to re-establish public authorities capable of governing market behaviour in keeping with new shared notions of public goods.

It was Emy's analysis of the need for markets to be publicly managed which brought us to what we think is truly novel and important about our thesis of an Australian Way. As we show below, the idea of managing markets had been marginalised in Australia by the hegemony of economic rationalist ideas. Fundamental flaws in these ideas were exposed by our contributors: they rested more on a set of libertarian social values than on economics as such; and their once triumphant case against Keynesian management had been effectively challenged. Not only had a case for economic management emerged in contemporary economic theory, but it also became apparent that the former centrality of such ideas in past Australian public policy had been obscured. In contrast, a dominant historiography, popularised in the theme of the breakdown of an 'Australian Settlement' (to be discussed below), had had the effect of condemning attempts to intervene positively in markets as self-defeating exercises in 'protection' that would allegedly reduce the sum of economic welfare. In refuting this interpretation, our contributors showed the centrality of the Keynesian approach to full employment in our past pattern of public policy. It was based on the idea of a superior economic outcome through state management; it effected a 'middle-way' compromise between contesting political traditions; and it absolutely underpinned the welfare and wage elements of the postwar welfare state.

Our third key focus was not so much the content of public policy as its administration. As Orchard recounts in Chapter 7, the Australian public service has been in a constant state of reform since the 1970s. Our particular concern was with the turn developing in this process towards what has been called a contract state. The impetus provided by National Competition Policy opened the prospect of a wholesale competitive tendering out of public service provision. Our analysis highlighted an overall tendency of the Labor years to view forms of public administration as ideologically neutral and a failure to see embedded in a model such as the contract state a set of libertarian assumptions about the role of government which were at odds with Labor's social democratic objectives. Australians, Maddox reminds us in Chapter 3, have historically placed a high premium on democracy, and in developing the appropriate public institutions have seen themselves as having a 'talent for bureaucracy'. Although some have argued persuasively that the 'new contractualism' might be a means of democratising our public institutions, our fear was that its purposes would be shaped rather by the economic rationalist thrust for small government.

If these policies for equality and full employment, together with substantial public agencies for the exercise of democracy, were core elements of the Australian Way, our conclusion from the workshop was that this pattern was at the point of a historic crisis. We set out to produce a book which would not only show this crisis, but which would explore the possibilities for a period of ideological and institutional innovation sufficient to meet the challenge of reinventing an Australian Way. Events since the election of the coalition government in 1996 appear to have intensified this account of a crisis. In terms of welfare, there has been an increased erosion of the idea of a right to welfare, epitomised in the work-for-the-dole program; an end to centralised wage fixation; an even greater emphasis on leaving employment outcomes to the market; and a growing trend to the wholesale contracting-out of government services. These policy directions have been associated with the very breakdowns in social cohesion – especially in ethnic and race relations – diagnosed by our authors. In this context, we believe that our analysis of a crisis in Australian public institutions can only grow in relevance, and that it is imperative that we begin to revalue and reinvent those key elements of full employment and equality which have been at the foundation of the Australian Way.

The Integration of Social and Economic Objectives: An Australian Settlement

Tackling the themes of equality, full employment and the Australian Way is of course an ambitious exercise, and this book in no way intends to be comprehensive. A strength of our analysis, we believe, is its interdisciplinary approach. While academic specialisation has its strengths, it can also foster fragmented thinking: this can be particularly debilitating when attempting to unravel the interrelationship of social and economic objectives in the overall public policy pattern. This book, then, is unashamedly an interdisciplinary exercise. What unites the contributors is not a common disciplinary background, but a willingness to bring their particular skills to bear on a common concern with finding ways of understanding and reintegrating economic and social policy objectives.

Reflection on the relationship between these objectives has developed in phases in Australia. When the economic reform program of the 1980s commenced, the social policy dimensions were considered to be secondary or marginal. At this time, public policy analysis laboured under a differentiated approach to social and economic policy created in the 1950s and 1960s (Smyth 1994). The two spheres were considered independently; where a relationship was perceived, it was in terms of how much social spending the economy could afford. With the fiscal restraints accompanying Australia's reform package, social policy was, in effect, placed on hold until the economy recovered (Saunders 1994). By the early 1990s, however, it had become apparent that the changes being undertaken in economic policy were such that, even assuming economic success, a very different society was likely to result. More than any other, Michael Pusey's book *Economic Rationalism in Canberra* (1991) alerted us to the contradictions which had developed between past Australian understandings of the nation-building role of governments and the implicit neoliberalism of the so called economic rationalism shaping the direction of economic reform. Pusey argued that developed societies are obligatorily co-ordinated through the two structures of state and economy. Various forms of social degradation are the cost of excessive burdens of co-ordination being placed on either structure, and economic rationalism, he believed, was placing an excessive burden on the market economy. The challenge put by Pusey was to find a new balance between economy and the state (Pusey 1991: 1–23). A polarised struggle between the economic rationalists and their critics ensued (Carroll and Manne 1992; Vintilla *et al.* 1992; Rees *et al.* 1993; James *et al.* 1993; King and Lloyd 1993).

The beginning of a new phase beyond this polarisation was signalled by Hugh Emy in *Remaking Australia*. His analysis looked beyond economic rationalism, exploring ways in which our political traditions and institutions might be reworked in order to 'bring the state back in'. Common to the myriad of individual policy challenges, he argued, was a 'conceptual thread linking all the major political issues, namely how to redefine the balance of the state and market'. In these terms, he wrote, the 'overwhelming challenge' was to 'determine what new amalgam of values, institutions and policies [will] replace the components of the Australian Settlement which finally disintegrated in the 1980s' (Emy 1993: 11). When Emy invoked the term *Australian Settlement*, he was borrowing a term coined by Paul Kelly in *The End of Certainty*. There Kelly had popularised a widely held analysis that located the old amalgam of values and institutions in a set of 'ideas which Australia had embraced nearly a century before and which had shaped the condition of the people' (1992: 1). The 'Settlement', a consensus of liberal and labourist ideologies, according to Kelly had rested on five pillars: White Australia, Industry Protection, Wage Arbitration, State Paternalism, and Imperial Benevolence. The core was protection, which encompassed the major political traditions until it finally unwound in the 1980s under what Kelly saw as the imperative of the deregulation and integration of the national economy with the forces of economic globalisation. The book was greeted enthusiastically by commentators – Beilharz, for example, described it as a 'magisterial survey' of the 'big picture' and 'long duration' shaping contemporary public policy – and the search for a new balance between market and state became readily understood in terms of the quest for a 'new Australian Settlement' (1994: 7–9).

The deep recession of the early 1990s punctured enthusiasm for economic liberalism in many quarters. It ushered in a new pluralism in Australian political economy, the high-water mark of which was the deliberations surrounding the National Strategies Conference, convened by the then prime minister, Paul Keating, in 1994. In Chapter 1, Emy surveys a literature in which the search for a new Settlement developed around the project of reasserting a role for social or collective intervention to balance the shift to market co-ordination that had occurred in the 1980s. The reintegration of economic and welfare policy within a shared, social vision was the master theme, together with a growing emphasis on the managed market as the alternative to the free market as the mode of economic reform.

From the Australian Settlement to the Australian Way

A major argument of this book is that the concept of an Australian Settlement offers an unsatisfactory historical framework for rethinking the roles of states, markets and civil society in Australia today. Certainly, the concept has been useful in encouraging us to think about social and economic policies in an integrated way; and it rightly highlights the fact that in any historical policy configuration there will be key policy decisions, such as the new protection, which are indeed foundational. It is 'characteristic of democracies', as Maddox writes, that 'they should produce a growing cloth of accepted policy' and that 'old battles are not continually re-fought'. Nevertheless the contributors to this book argue that the 'Settlement' interpretation has led to an extremely truncated view of the cultural and political and institutional diversity which has shaped the nation. We propose an alternative reading which is equally distinctive, more historically accurate, and far more positive about our past policy achievements as well as our capacity for the kinds of adaptation thought necessary by Cass and Emy. In our interpretation, what is at stake today is not the Australian Settlement, but what Jill Roe has termed the Australian Way.

In Chapters 3, 4 and 9, Maddox, Roe and Pixley offer detailed critiques of the idea of a Settlement. Here we emphasise its pedigree in the consensus view of our political past associated with Keith Hancock and the 'realist' revisionaries of the 1950s. In this view, Deakinite liberalism embraced a labour movement *sans doctrines* at the dawn of the century, creating a utilitarian unanimity scarcely disturbed by 'ideas' until the 1980s. Maddox is rightly appalled by this monumental disparagement of our past, which 'submerges' a near-century of 'conflicts, controversies and ideological competitions'. If Maddox emphasises the way this falsifying consensus silences the generations of contradictory voices which created an Australian tradition of political thought, Roe has a somewhat different approach. Her chapter elaborates an important proposition which she introduced several years ago (Roe 1993): the account of a people without political traditions, save the 'static', 'anachronistic' Settlement, misunderstands profoundly the distinctive pragmatism of Australian political life. Counter-posing Brian Fitzpatrick's conflict view of our past to the consensus tradition, she proposed that a history of conflict over the roles of state and market has been resolved in a distinctively Australian Way. The Australian Way represents the middle ground in this conflict, a dynamic space shaped and reshaped by ideological contests across the century. Certainly there has been no victory for the political extremes; but, Roe proposes, this is no evidence of an absence of ideas, and their contest but a mark of the subtlety of the middle way which Australians have negotiated between the state and market: 'The Australian way is both narrow and elusive, but also elaborately tested and contested over time, and it retains the potential to open out...'

Pixley joins Maddox and Roe in viewing the Australian political legacy in terms of contest and compromise elaborated during the century. This is important because it allows us to reconnect in a dynamic way with the institutional reforms shaped and reshaped by the various egalitarian social movements which have fashioned who Australians are. Also, for Pixley, it reminds us that change and conflict are ubiquitous, precluding any search for a settlement that would imply consensus. Like Maddox, she prefers to emphasise the importance of open and cohesive democratic institutions rather than attempts to prescribe an inclusive vision or Australian values. Roe's concept of an Australian Way is not, of course, an attempt at such a prescription, but rather describes a way of exercising democracy. At the same time, the concept also includes reference to that policy legacy of past political contests and compromises referred to earlier. Here the Australian Way is thrown down as a challenge to the cultural cringe which has prevented us from recognising and valuing our past policy achievement. While the book focuses on domestic policy, it should be noted that there is also a history of international achievements. These include Australia's role in the United Nations' reordering of the international economy after World War II, as well as more recent contributions in the area of human rights. In this context, the thesis of an Australian Settlement has proven particularly barren. A policy history portrayed in terms of 'protection all round' as a prelude to globalisation is an invitation to dismiss the past as little more than an irrelevant catalogue of errors.

Key Policies and Institutions

This book cannot offer a review of all the public policies and institutions relevant to a revised account of the Australian Way in public policy. It does offer, however, perspectives on the two most crucial areas in the interrelationship of social and economic policy: inequality and unemployment. The Australian social welfare system is now rightly recognised both as distinctive and as having fair claims to effectiveness in eradicating poverty and reducing inequality. At a time when globalisation is creating pressures to reduce welfare in industrialised countries, it becomes especially important to be clear about what these institutions have achieved. An opinion has been promoted in recent times that the Australian welfare system has failed in its overt objectives; and similar arguments have helped pave the way for the demise of welfare in the United States. If it is the case that the Australian welfare system has failed in its objectives then, as Whiteford writes in Chapter 13, 'its demise may not be strongly regretted'. On the other hand, if it has succeeded, then the political choices become very different. Whiteford's chapter reviews the development of Australia's unique combination of a highly redistributive income support and tax system complementing its centralised wage system. He concludes that historically this policy combination made Australia one of the most equal of the industrialised countries, a position it retains despite increasing market-generated inequalities. Clearly there has been no welfare failure in Australia to cloud debate about our social policy futures.

There is no more important factor in determining levels of poverty and inequality than the degree of unemployment. On this count, a major purpose of this book is to bring together a body of new research which squarely shows that the challenge of contemporary public policy in Australia is shaped less by the breakdown of the policies of the Australian Settlement established at the beginning of the century than the collapse of the full employment policy regime established in the mid-1940s in the context of a re-regulated international economic order. If the Keynesian welfare state represented Australia's most far-reaching attempt to manage markets for social purposes, then its demise creates a very different perspective on the present to the post-protection scenario offered by the Australian Settlement. As Smyth argues in Chapter 5, the latter leads to the conclusion that the logic of the market must produce a superior economic outcome to past interventionary practice, and leaves a subsidiary role for government in terms of devising social compensation for the losers in a market-led globalisation. The Keynesian view hotly contests this account. The Keynesian settlement inscribed on our postwar public policy pattern the principle that a degree of collectivism would produce not only better social results, but economic results as well. It is this positive view of the economic role of government which, as Bell and Nevile indicate in Chapters 10 and 11, has been the casualty of economic rationalism, resulting in the rejection of the 'social contract to maintain full employment'.

Nothing could be more at odds with the legacy of the Australian Way than high unemployment. But high unemployment, as Nevile shows, is a necessary accompaniment of economic rationalism. This contradiction must prove the fault-line of Australian public policy for the foreseeable future, and this book suggests ways in which this fault-line is likely to open out. In the first place, economic policy is likely to be more politicised: as Nevile writes, economic rationalism will be seen less and less as a 'logical consequence of orthodox economics' and more the outcome of a particular set of social and political values. Contributing to a new politics of choice in economic policy will be the resurgence of post-Keynesian and institutional economic theory which, as Battin shows in Chapter 6, rejects the mainstream rationale for the abandonment of postwar Keynesianism. Battin and Green (Chapter 12) draw on these traditions to sketch out a policy program for full-employment today. The second line of debate over employment suggested here concerns the possibilities of a full-employment program, and of economic management more generally, in the context of a globalising economy. Nevile and Bell stress the constraints, while Battin, Green and Emy are more sanguine about the potential for national economic management. Such debates are for the future. Radical departures from the egalitarian welfare system, and the heightened use of the unemployed to absorb the shocks of market failure, must exacerbate social polarisation and conflict.

Public Administration, Civil Society and Social Movements

The book's analysis of the crisis in the Australian Way places special emphasis on the state of public administration. Indeed, in recent years debate about reinventing government has arguably taken over from economic rationalism as the site of keenest conflict over the future of Australian public policy. Our analysis of this conflict suggests that it is now poised in a similar fashion to the crisis in social and economic policy. Thus in Chapter 7 Orchard shows how, in the federal sphere, Labor undertook a reform program which attempted to wed social democratic objectives with the techniques of managerialism. His analysis reveals a similar 'masquerade' to that discussed by Nevile in relation to economic policy. Thus administrative reforms which were dressed as value-neutral techniques actually masked libertarian assumptions about the role of government which were hostile to social democracy. He concludes that the pursuit of the managerialist agenda by the Coalition government will diminish basic functions of government and expose this fundamental opposition.

Historically, we might re-emphasise, the middle way embodied social objectives fashioned as much by Deakinite liberalism as social democracy. The threat to the idea of such public ends, and the distinctive role of the public sector which they imply, is a concern of Chapter 8 in which Brennan explores the blurring of the boundaries between the government and non-government sectors in the welfare state. She also examines the way in which managerial reforms have been accompanied by gestures towards an inflated, but usually unspecified, role accorded to civil society. Brennan exposes contradictions between the rhetorical elaboration of the contributions expected of civil society and the administrative regimes of the competition model which must frustrate the realisation of those contributions. These conclusions are given substance by Chapter 14, in which Ernst analyses the impact of competitive tendering policies on the welfare sector; and Chapter 15, in which Wearing and Smyth examine the competing managerialist and social democratic agendas which shaped the White Paper on employment, *Working Nation*. In Chapter 9, Pixley moves beyond the various critiques of the market-oriented reforms to the public sector and looks to the future. Her focus is the implications for social movements and civil society or the public sphere of the idea of a developmental state which, as Emy indicates, has emerged as the principal alternative political economy to neoliberalism. She questions the priority accorded economic development, and stresses the potential for authoritarian or pseudo-collaborative forms of governance to substitute for a truly democratic governance.

Rethinking the Australian Way

This book comes at a critical time in the history of Australian public policy. The period of writing has covered the transition from Labor's experiment with social corporatism to the reassertion of economic rationalism under the Coalition. The Labor years were distinguished among Anglo-American countries by the commitment to a strong safety-net in terms of social policy, as a form of compensation for the pursuit – at least by the end of its period of government – of a neo-liberal economic policy. We argue that the lesson of this experiment is that welfare is not enough. The Coalition parties have subsequently implemented a policy regime broadly characterised by economic rationalism in both the economic and social policy spheres. Their period in office has done nothing to alter our conviction that a policy regime which places extreme emphasis on the unfettered market, while downgrading the social protection afforded by the welfare and wage system, can only exacerbate our social problems. In short, we need new directions. We have to go beyond these two alternatives, and it is for this reason we seek to recast the challenge in terms of reinventing the Australian Way.

What are the prospects? Roe sees the Australian Way as a middle way, and the term will be immediately recognised as a popular descriptor of the 'mixed-economy' compromises characteristic of postwar Western political economies. Less well recognised will be the climate of economic thought which gave birth to the idea of the mixed economy. At least in Australia, the Great Depression destroyed the theoretical hegemony of what we would call today neoclassical economics. So much so that, by the middle of the 1940s, the slogan 'We are all planners now' was the common currency of political debate. Within a very few years, of course, liberal-capitalist ideas and values had been reasserted, a synthesis with planning founded in Keynesian economics, and more radical ideas of state economic planning were no longer discussed. It is tempting to suggest parallels with today. The collapse of state-planned economies encouraged the notion of 'the end of history'. Economic rationalism soon encompassed all sides of politics, dissolving past arguments for the merits of positive government intervention and offering a market utopia. Now, we believe, is the time for a new realism in Australian political economy. The failures as well as the strengths of the Labor model, and the already-rehearsed shortcomings of the Coalition's direction, argue the need to reassess past policy strengths, strengths which we have identified principally in terms of policies for equality and full employment. The core requirement is to rethink the idea of a mixed economy. We must aim to secure our pursuit of social objectives through some new balance between the roles of the state and market in economic policy, as well as social policy, and we must do so through debate in a reinvigorated public sphere.

PART I

Overviews: States, Markets and Private Life

CHAPTER 1

States, Markets and the Global Dimension
An Overview of Certain Issues in Political Economy

Hugh Emy

The period from about 1990 to 1996 witnessed a noticeable shift in the field of political economy. We seemed to have moved on from the kind of impasse which threatened to polarise – and paralyse – debate and policy development at the beginning of the decade. One could detect a growing consensus on the major outlines of reform, although one question remained: how far was this merely an elite consensus, distrusted by the community at large and unsupported by the respective wings and constituencies of the major political parties? The federal election of 1996 and the subsequent policy direction of the new Coalition Liberal–National Party government also threaten to undermine that consensus. It is, of course, too early to anticipate what may transpire in Australian political economy in the last years of the century. The new government's free-market policy orientation, if maintained, may well rekindle the kind of polarisation experienced under the Labor government's economic rationalism. Given this possibility, it might be useful to review the ideas which shaped the 'elite consensus' which superseded that polarisation – consistent as they are with developments in political economy internationally. Arguably, such ideas provide better guidelines for Australian policy-makers than another round of economic rationalism.

By the mid-1990s, support for Australia's reversion to the protectionist policies associated with the Australian Settlement had receded, but there was lively debate over what kind of policies and values should prevail in the next ten years. From the outset, different responses to the strategy of internationalising the economy coloured the various positions taken in the political economy debate. The perspective which informs this chapter is that the changes created by and imposed through globalisation have established a reality with which Australia has to come to terms. There is a logic, an unremitting pressure behind the strategy of internationalising, that is hard to deny or resist. This has set a final test for policy-makers up to and including the present. Now, however, there is a growing case for second thoughts about the overall effects of globalisation – or the kind of techno-economic forces identified with global capitalism – upon societies, democracy and the environment. The operating assumption here, which some may not accept, is that one has to accept the case for internationalising, for relying more upon the market, for reinventing government, before one can talk about placing more explicit emphasis upon ecological or social values, or relying more upon the state to discipline and steer the market. Nevertheless, there is a growing case for doing just that, which is also part of changing responses to globalisation. The challenge is to find the policy conduit which will allow Australia to keep adapting to, and repositioning itself in the face of, continuing global change – which will also mean internationalising further – while placing more and more emphasis on the defence of social, political and ecological values.

The Elite Consensus

Ever since issuing its election manifesto *One Nation* in February 1992, the Labor government had been edging away, pragmatically, from the hardline free-market position which dominated its thinking between 1987 and 1991. Its social and cultural agenda came to the fore. It had also experimented with policies which, implicitly at least, allowed a more constructive role for government. Arguably, it had at least been trying to get back in touch with its social democratic principles. Meanwhile, the then Opposition too had sought to distance itself from the type of economic liberalism which mostly informed its election manifesto *Fightback!* So the two major parties seemed much closer in their ideas about what kind of society they wished to create. There seemed to be general, if sometimes grudging, recognition of the need to internationalise and create a more productive, open and competitive economy, with a stronger export base in manufactured and other value-added goods.

At the same time, there was a greater awareness of the need to build an economy that was socially and ecologically sustainable. This was most evident at the National Strategies Conference in 1994, which proposed that 'the basic vision for Australia . . . was of a country that is creative, productive, inclusive and sustainable'. Or, as Paul Keating put it: 'If the various aims of this Conference can be boiled down to one, it might be this: how do we balance economic imperatives with human ones – for security and peace of mind, for a decent environment, for cultural nourishment, and, particularly in this era of relentless change, for confidence, hope and belief?' (EPAC 1994: 8,13). The conference also noted a significant convergence of thinking among influential pressure groups:

> just as business groups . . . have broadened their focus to social and environmental concerns, so community and labour organisations . . . have increasingly broadened their strategic concerns to matters of internationalisation, micro-economic reform, infrastructure provision and the like. The agenda for the future has emerged as one increasingly held in common and, indeed, many of the necessary elements of strategy for that agenda are also increasingly agreed in ways that might have been unthinkable in Australia a decade ago. [EPAC 1994: 4]

This all implied that debate *had* moved on: markets were now a central fact of political and economic reality. The debate was about what kind of market, or about how much freedom a free market needs to work effectively. At issue was how to reconcile the policies required to create a globally competitive economy with Australia's own traditions of a fair go, worker protection and, one might add, a very weak version of the developmental state model more recently associated with East Asian states.

The conference noted three areas in which there had been some retreat from the hitherto dominant paradigm. First, there was a greater willingness, especially among business, to pay heed to strategic vision, which implied some degree of strategic or corporate planning. This marked a growing realisation that the previous strategy of leaving it to the market would not suffice. Second, this was in turn a partial step towards bringing government back in as a body whose responsibilities went beyond establishing a framework for the market, dealing only with limited cases of clear-cut market failure, providing a social safety-net and military security. As one report somewhat gingerly remarked, it was 'possible to say that the rumours of the death of the state are much exaggerated. Perhaps the state is not so much dead as undergoing a cultural change.' Third, there was a shift away from a primary focus on macro-economic concerns to 'structural strategies' in which social, environmental and human rights received more emphasis.

These three points suggested that, while free-market thinking remained the single most important influence on the reform agenda, and statism was still anathema, previous strict adherence to the notion of a minimum state had been relaxed – although not everywhere. At the federal level, social values received more weight, although the environment remained a growing source of contention. Especially in an era of continued high unemployment, radical uncertainty caused by rapid social and technological change, and changes in and to the global economy, it was likely that governments would have to play a more constructive role than earlier thought. The future role and scope of government, the balance between state and market, remained at the core of the awkward choices which have to be decided before a new Settlement, or compromise, could emerge.

It is not possible to consider here a wider Australian literature concerned with reconceptualising the relationship between economy and society which might be associated with these developments (Dow 1992; Marsh 1995; Smyth 1994). What needs to be emphasised is that, in all this rethinking of the role of the state, globalisation established a difficult bottom line. In this regard, there is no doubting the influence in Australian policy-making circles of some people who thought, and think, that the only realistic strategy for Australia is to go with the flow of globalisation, revamping society and social institutions in the cause of global competitiveness.[1] At the core of this position is a liberal (and modernist) theory of progress and development, now reinforced by the neoclassical regard for free markets as key vehicles of progress, and by a kind of technological utopianism, the hallmark of those whom Hugh Mackay terms 'compulsive futurists' (1993: 267).

Elsewhere, this latter way of thinking has come under increasing criticism from persons on both the left and the right of the political spectrum who are more conscious of the risks posed by globalisation (see, for example, Gray 1993; Hutton 1995; Lind 1995; Reich 1992). Although they agree that individual countries must adapt to the new global realities, they strongly suspect that further, relatively uncontrolled expansion of this new kind of global capitalism will accentuate existing inequalities and undermine social cohesion and stability, creating social conditions inimical to the survival of civilised democracies.[2] Some of this literature is discussed later. The next sections try to locate the thinking behind the elite consensus within a wider frame by suggesting two points. First, in other countries the tide has been indeed turning in favour of bringing governments back in, while rethinking their role and functions extensively; second, there is reason to look more critically at globalisation, because of its effects – direct and indirect – on social cohesion, political stability and democracy.

Bringing the State Back in? Changing Perceptions

In political science, the state has been a highly contested concept since the 1930s. In the 1950s, the American behaviouralists rejected the utility of the term for empirical research, but their rejection was itself overruled in the 1970s. By the early 1980s, the state had become a key concept once again in politics and sociology, generating a flood of studies. Coincidentally, the revival of neoclassical liberalism, both in economics and in some parts of political science, targeted the state as a major structural cause of the growing economic problems experienced by developed countries – especially the United States and the United Kingdom – after 1973. The 'special-interest state' or the 'nanny state' was said to be an obstacle to growth. The solution was to rely more on the market and individual energies, and to shrink the state in favour of private enterprise and the private sector.

This is a familiar story and cannot be reiterated here, but two developments ought to be noted. First, as the report of the National Strategies Conference noted, the death of the state has been much exaggerated. Despite the ongoing reassessment of the state, attempts at downsizing, experiments in privatisation and so on in OECD countries in general, and in the six largest economies in particular, general government spending as a percentage of gross domestic product increased between 1978 and 1995, although the increase in the United Kingdom was minimal.[3] At the same time the state is undergoing a major reconstruction or reinvention, as Part III indicates. By and large, the language of reinvention is neither minimalist nor statist but is typically concerned with describing a new role for government – the clever state, or the catalytic state.[4] All mark attempts to advance beyond old categories.

Second, one wonders whether the implications of these developments have been fully digested in Australia. European countries, the United States to an increasing extent, and the United Kingdom under New Labour are either reinventing government or finding ways in which a strong state can positively assist the development of a market economy under conditions of globalisation; in Australia, meanwhile, the notion of state versus market still seems to be prevalent.[5] In the four liberal democracies, the United Kingdom, the United States, Australia and New Zealand, there has been a stronger ideological hostility towards the state and in favour of the market than has generally appeared elsewhere. The idea of the minimum or nightwatchman state is culturally and historically specific to these countries. European countries have certainly retreated from statism or *dirigisme*, but they have retained a positive view of the state as a necessary agency of economic development and social integration – which has always been a central part of their political traditions. This makes it easier for them to move in the direction of 'collaborative capitalism' or the 'partnership state', whereby state and business try to act together to cope with globalisation.

Bringing the State Back in? Specific Positions

The proposition is that the intellectual tide is turning in favour of making governments more central players in systematic strategies aimed at maintaining the viability of both economy and society in the face of rapid and often destabilising forms of change, socio-cultural as well as techno-economic. Neither statist nor purist market positions are adequate; a new synthesis is required. This section provides a brief sample of the trend of debate which supports this proposition.

A fundamental point often made by political scientists, historical sociologists and social theorists is that free markets did not evolve naturally or spontaneously, the result of the onwards and upwards march of reason in human social evolution. Rather, markets and market behaviour emerged as part of lengthy and complex processes of pacification, territorialisation, centralisation, modernisation, civilising, and so on which accompanied the growth of nation-states in Europe, and the subsequent transformation of the European state system into a world system. These processes have been going on for the best part of a thousand years. They are still going on: globalisation is simply their latest stage. States and markets always developed together. From this perspective, recent attempts to declare markets and market forces to be prime movers in social and economic progress, or to claim that the current triumph of market societies over statist regimes represents some kind of historical endgame, are naive.

There is a huge literature in several disciplines drawing on different schools to support this point, far too large to rehearse here.[6] A book by Weiss and Hobson (1995) conveniently restates the core points in a way which bears directly on contemporary debates. From the early modern period, first economic development and later industrialisation occurred through the efforts of strong states,[7] not weak ones. The formation of strong, integrated, centralised states with a secure system of property rights was 'vital to the economic development of the European core countries'. Strong states were accompanied by strong societies. Weak and despotic states usually sought to undermine alternative sources of power in civil society. While states provided different factors or resources during the different stages and circumstances of economic development, their broad conclusion was that 'non-economic – especially political – institutions are vital to the constitution, maintenance and transformation of the modern market economy' (Weiss and Hobson 1995: 11, 2).

Such a bald summary does not do justice to the authors' impressive argument, backed up by six case studies. However, the contemporary policy implications are more relevant here than the historical details.

Neoliberalism tends to conceptualise the relations between state and society, or state and economy, in antagonistic terms or as a kind of zero-sum game: scope for one detracts from the other. But on the historical evidence, a state that is embedded in society and enjoys significant infrastructural power generates more social and economic energy than a weak or minimalist state. We should not dichotomise state–society relations: if one brings the state back in, one is not necessarily kicking society out.

Weiss and Hobson do *not* claim that the state is the crucial or decisive agent 'causing' economic development. They favour a multi-causal argument: the state is one necessary factor among a set of factors helping to catalyse economic development. This is especially the case in East Asia, where the state's role has been one of strategic oversight and guidance: It provided the 'central coordinating intelligence' steering economic development, while acting in close conjunction with private sector institutions. The authors suggest such a capacity is crucial to a modern economy, whether 'mature' or 'late industrialiser', because continuous industrial adjustment to global change has become the dominant reality. 'The modern economy demands a corrective agency with strategic, think-tank, coordinating functions to make extensive reorganisation possible. And in many countries where the technological and organizational shifts are under way, this is precisely the enabling role that the state has come to play, in combination with organized industry and industrial finance' (Weiss and Hobson 1995: 202).

Today, the more successful economies are those which have a high capacity for coordinating activities between private and public sectors, between banks and industry, and between savings and investment. The points made by Weiss and Hobson could be extensively elaborated by reference to extensive analyses of the East Asian developmental states (see Bell 1995; Johnson 1986; Wade 1990; White 1988); small European corporatist democracies (see Katzenstein 1985); the Scandinavian nations' 'social citizenship state' (see Scharpf 1987); and the German social market model (see Emy 1993; Hampden-Turner and Trompenaars 1993: 202; Razeen 1994). Here we can simply note certain factors prevailing among the mature member states of the European Union, without exception (though to varying degrees): strong regard for market outcomes, coupled with a positive regard for the state (and large public sectors); collaborative or corporatist policy styles coupled with systematic attempts to institutionalise partnership arrangements between public and private sectors; a preference for guided capitalism; and a strong sense that economic and social development must proceed together. Indeed, the latter point, together with an emphasis upon citizenship rights, has been built into the further development of the European Union via the Social Chapter of the Maastricht agreement and adherence by the member states to the European Human Rights Convention. On all such points much has been written (see Allum 1995; Hayward and Page 1995).

In the mid-1990s, as distinct from the mid-1980s, European neo-corporatism looks, on balance, to be performing rather better than UK or US capitalism. The real point is that, excepting the United Kingdom, the mature economies in the European Union have chosen to manage the market in the interests of social cohesion and political stability. There appears to be a rising sense in Europe in the 1990s that some form of neo-corporatism, coupled with the features noted above, and including social compensation for the effects of change, is the only way to cope with globalisation. The best way to preserve the core features of a viable market economy, or open markets generally, is to steer market forces in the direction desired by national governments, hopefully acting in concert through the European Union.

There is, of course, enormous variety within the East Asian and European models of political economy, but there are also suggestive overlaps. They both recognise that the spheres of state and market have to be adjusted continually in light of changing circumstances. They both favour some version of strategic planning, sectoral development policies, institutional bridge-building and forms of strategic industry policy. Typically, they recognise that the strength of the market is dependent upon social cohesion and solidarity. Overall, they imply that the kind of tentative steps beyond the Anglo-American approach which had emerged in Australia in the elite consensus of the early 1990s did not go quite far enough.

New Ideas in the United States and the United Kingdom

The United States has produced a series of striking books with similar messages (see Porter 1990; Reich 1992; Thurow 1993). Since the mid-1980s, it is proposed, a new kind of world trading economy has emerged, with very different methods of production and wealth-creation, while the balance of global economic power has shifted dramatically, away from the United States and towards Asia and Europe. Specific markets for value-added goods, especially for elaborately transformed manufactured goods, have become disproportionately important. Success in these is said to depend less on traditional forms of comparative advantage and much more on a different notion of competitive advantage which governments can help to develop. Americans, it is argued, must realise that capitalism is no longer a single or monolithic entity, if it ever was. These authors stress that other countries have adapted free-market capitalism to fit their own cultures and developmental circumstances, and what has emerged is an intense 'world competition between rival cultures of capitalism' (see Hampden-Turner and Trompenaars 1993; Thurow 1993). There is a strong sense that one major, underlying source of competitive advantage in the global economy is the nature of the culture itself.

The most recent book by Fukuyama (1995) illustrates the way the wind is blowing. Fukuyama does not resile from his main proposition that democratic capitalism is the only viable model now available to the world's advanced countries. He also thinks that neoclassical economics is 80 per cent correct, but it has one major flaw: its model of human nature overvalues the significance of human beings as rational, utility-maximising creatures. More generally, it fails to appreciate the cultural foundations of economic life. It fails to see that the viability of both democracy and capitalism depends on a society's accumulated stock of *social capital*. This concept refers especially to the habit of sociability and the climate of trust which exists among and between the members of a given society; producing the capacity to work together cooperatively. Social capital, and especially the phenomenon of trust, is itself a crucial resource endowment which economists often overlook. 'Law, contract and economic rationality provide a necessary but not sufficient basis for both the stability and prosperity of postindustrial societies; they must . . . be leavened with reciprocity, moral obligation, duty toward community, and trust, which are based in habit rather than rational calculation' (Fukuyama 1995: 11).

Capitalism and liberal democracy are neither free-standing nor self-sustaining. The viability of both – indeed, the viability of social-contract societies – depend on other cultural resources, or social capital, which predate the emergence of both. The viability of modern democratic capitalism depends on the social capital created by, and inherited from, a more traditional form of society (see Fukuyama 1995: 350–7). Capitalism, as an engine of 'creative destruction' (Schumpter) always erodes the traditions and social institutions which helped it develop. Now, in the United States, the development of rights-based liberalism, allied to individualism and libertarianism, is further eroding habits of sociability and all forms of community. Evidence for this proposition is wide and varied: the rise of violent crime and civil litigation; the breakdown in family structure; and the decline of a wide range of intermediate social structures like neighbourhoods, churches, unions, clubs and charities. Americans are much less likely to join local associations than before, less likely to engage voluntarily in the group activities which previously contributed so much to the vitality of both civil society and local, pluralist democracy (Fukuyama 1995: 309–10).[8]

The conclusion follows that, under the impact of techno-economic and cultural changes catalysed by globalisation, the social capital on which US democratic capitalism for long depended is running down rapidly; its replenishment has lagged badly in recent decades. The loss of trust is undermining both the civic culture on which democracy depends, and organisational efficiency throughout the economy. It makes it more difficult for the United States to emulate the kind of business practices which work successfully in Japan or Germany. In the United States, liberal individualism and the emphasis on self-interest has gone too far. The United States needs to recover some of its indigenous communitarian traditions. The erosion of trust strikes at the whole structure of a civilised society because it undermines the norms of tolerance, respect, accommodation and reciprocity on which democratic capitalism depends. There is a further risk: if people cannot cohere voluntarily for common purposes, 'they will need an intrusive state to provide the organisation they cannot provide themselves' (Fukuyama 1995: 357–8). The neoliberal agenda can bring about a result diametrically opposite to what it intended. The main priority now in the United States is to replenish the stock of social capital on which democracy and capitalism depend: an efficient society is also a civilised society with high levels of trust and cooperation.

Yet this may not be easy. Michael Lind (1995) is another conservative intellectual who offers a much grimmer account of the plight of the United States. He thinks it must replace the present unholy alliance between neoclassical liberalism and left-wing multiculturalism with a more 'straightforward' nationalism, which he terms *liberal nationalism*. Very briefly, his argument runs as follows. Since the mid-1960s, the United States has been preoccupied with the politics of race and ethnic identity, with trying to reconcile its racial divisions with liberal values and overcome the more blatant racial inequalities. This has been an overwhelming problem, because there are now five separate racial categories in the United States. Elaborate programs of affirmative action and preferential categories have been introduced everywhere. But this focus has distracted Americans from the rising significance of class divisions and class power. Since the late 1960s, there has also been a concealed revolution by the rich (Chapter 5): a new oligarchy, a mostly white overclass, has arisen, which has consolidated its power behind the outwardly liberal manifestations of multicultural America. The overclass has played up 'culture war' in order to conceal the new realities of class war. It has used identity politics to divide and rule. Meanwhile, and especially since the 1980s, it has striven systematically and with great success to minimise its own tax burden and transfer it to the poor and middle-income earners. Between 1973 and 1992, while the richest 10 per cent of American families experienced an 18 per cent increase in real income, the real income of the poorest 10 per cent sank by 11 per cent. Taxes, including the Social Security payroll tax, have increased steadily for middle America since 1981, while the rich have benefited extensively from the tax cuts introduced by Reagan and Bush. The tax system is now highly regressive, and income inequality is greater than at any time since the 1930s (Lind 1995: 181, 190–5; see also Danziger and Gottschalk 1993).

The overclass has also identified strongly with efforts by business to drive down labour costs through, in particular, assaults on trade unions and support for a mass immigration policy. The driving influence here has been the impact of globalisation on business. The systematic assault on wages, welfare and job security which went on through the 1980s is all part of the response by business, and the material interests allied with business, to maintain profitability in the face of increasingly difficult conditions. The neoclassical program of smaller government, lower taxes, deregulation and so on has helped justify and legitimate policies which business and the overclass see as vital to maintaining their own wealth and power.

The overclass has also encouraged extensive moves towards privatising public services, for example: replacing national highway systems with private toll roads; replacing police forces with private security forces (the latter already outnumber the former in the United States); undermining resources for public schools and redirecting them to private schools. With the extensive creation of gated or walled communities by the rich, the latter refuse to pay taxes for public municipal services arguing that, on top of the fees they pay to maintain their own private communities, this amounts to 'double taxation' (Lind 1995: 212–15). The result is a new feudalism, which 'reverses the trend of the past 1000 years towards the assumption by the government of basic public amenities like policing, public roads, transport networks and public schools. These things are once again becoming private luxuries, accessible only to the affluent few' (Lind 1995: 211).

Lind fears not the Balkanisation but the Brazilianisation of the United States, not fragmentation along racial lines but fissioning along class lines.

> Brazilianization is symbolized by the increasing withdrawal of the White American overclass into its own barricaded nation-within-a-nation, a world of private neighbourhoods, private schools, private police, private health care, and even private roads, walled off from the spreading squalor beyond . . . Protected like medieval barons by their private police forces, the affluent classes could transact worldwide business or seek diversion at their computer workstations, while only a few miles away the poor lived and died in conditions of Third World squalor. [Lind 1995: 14, 213]

The outcome of the anti-statist program, if seriously pursued, would be 'an archipelago of privileged whites in an ocean of white, black and brown poverty . . . something like a high-tech Holy Roman Empire on American soil'.

Within his call for liberal nationalism, Lind also advocates constructing a variant of social market capitalism, with 'a strong, genuinely democratic government that intervenes in the economy to protect and raise the living standards of the wage-earning majority' (1995: 347,15, 196–7). He calls for 'government activism to promote a high degree of substantive social and economic equality', an end to regressive taxation, and a form of capitalism friendly to workers and the middle classes, rather than the overclass alone. This will require a sharp break with the neoclassical view of markets and free trade. Indeed, 'it is difficult to avoid concluding that civilised social market capitalism and unrestricted global free trade are inherently incompatible' (quoted in Lind 1995: 203), an illuminating remark from a former colleague of William F. Buckley and Irving Kristol, whose implications will be discussed further in the next section.

In the United Kingdom, John Gray – himself identified with the New Right agenda ten years before – has emerged as the champion of the Old Right, anticipating Fukuyama's message. The New Right, he says, is over-rational, ahistorical and economistic, seeking to reduce all human conduct to a calculus of exchange. It has ignored the 'cultural matrix' which supports the market, refusing to acknowledge that 'market institutions fail insofar as they are not underpinned by trust, integrity and the other virtues of fair dealing'. Markets are 'legal artefacts, sustained by cultural traditions and sheltered by governments' (Gray 1993: vii–viii). Tory social engineering is destroying the life-support systems on which free markets depend. Thatcherism failed to produce a stronger economy or sustained growth, while devastating local communities and regions, flouting norms of fairness and decency hitherto deeply ingrained in British culture. 'A strong and flourishing market economy cannot be built on a divided and demoralised society in which crime is endemic, and family life neglected and fractured . . . Market fundamentalism has resulted in a sleazy and rundown economy, lacking in skills and beset by short-termism' (Gray 1994).

The market is historical, not natural; culturally conditioned, not free-standing. Like all human institutions, it is imperfect: it will work only if its inherent limitations are fully acknowledged and addressed by governments. Gray, too, favours a form of social market capitalism. He argues for 'an enabling welfare state' to provide better protection for individual autonomy, a broader conception of public goods, and greater emphasis on ecological values. He and supporters of 'civic conservatism' (Willets 1994) wish to elevate the aims of traditional conservatism over the naked pursuit of self-interest: support for families, for an extensive civic culture, and for policies to prevent the social chasm between rich and poor widening further.

There are real affinities between Gray and the Left in Britain. Will Hutton (1995) provides a savage critique of the social and economic consequences of Thatcherism, especially the emergence of what he terms the 30:30:40 society and the marked increase in inequalities.[9] He and others document the growth of a more highly centralised executive state in Britain and the widening gap between the 'constitutional fictions' maintained by the doctrine of responsible government and political realities, a gap which has serious consequences for democracy (Hutton 1995: Chs 2, 11; Jenkins 1996). Hutton's position is similar to Lind's: the driving force behind the program of deregulation in Britain is the rentier capitalist class, entrenched within the institutions which support the Tory party, who wish to maximise their freedom to exploit the wealth-creating opportunities offered by globalisation with little or no regard for the consequences upon society overall, from which they can readily insulate themselves. The response, for Hutton and the Progressive Left, is to stress the need to reassert social and democratic control over markets and market forces. This involves either a social market model or market socialism, with the majority opting for the former. To quote the editor of one substantial collection:

> There is ... acceptance throughout the book of the role of markets in allocation and production, but an insistence that they are social institutions, subject to social regulation and the demands of the social interest. The notion of a 'free market' is a contradiction in terms. Markets and market economies are political, in the broadest sense. They are shaped by political rules and collective institutions. [Miliband 1994: 9]

Modern capitalism needs a social infrastructure of collective goods that free markets cannot generate. The Left's aim is to make markets work in the interests of all the people, and to ensure that market outcomes are compatible with democratic values: to elevate 'the free association of citizens' over 'the free association of the producers' (Miliband 1994: 10–11, 142–3). The means envisaged draw selectively on the style of 'communitarian capitalism' and the strategies for acquiring competitive advantage followed by the European neo-corporatists, and by Japan, coupled with strong pursuit of the full-employment objective and policies of regional development and political decentralisation to give effect to the idea of rebuilding local communities (Hirst 1994). Although there are differences in emphasis, these ideas are central to New Labour under Tony Blair. Blair's position is that the only way the United Kingdom can reverse trends to social disintegration and greater inequality, cope with technological change and adapt to the global economy, is to accept the case for strong markets but stress that their viability depends on a strong (that is, fair and fully integrated) society. This can only be done by consciously pursuing 'communitarian capitalism' in the context of neo-corporatist strategies for power-sharing. Blair's program closely resembles the German, or European, mainstream preference for some version of social market capitalism.

What this literature shows, overall, is growing support for three related points. First, the contemporary Anglo-American version of *laissez-faire* capitalism is less suitable for ensuring competitive success in the global economy than other forms of capitalism (Borrus *et al.* 1992; Eisenger 1990; Weiss and Hobson 1995). Second, too great a faith in deregulated free markets has produced outcomes which are destroying the social and cultural foundations – the social capital – on which market capitalism depends. Third, the overall process of governance remains the responsibility of the state. The greater the evidence of social breakdown, the greater the threat to a stable public order, the more important this responsibility becomes. Market and rational choice theory sidesteps problems of order, justice and legitimacy. It overlooks the point that the viability of democratic capitalism depends also on ethical values and behaviour which often conflict with pure market theory (see Self 1993; also Stretton and Orchard 1994). The challenge for politics is to reconcile the two.

This literature suggests that the emerging problems of order, in liberal democracies especially, cannot be solved by market theory, because its compass is too narrow and because it is too committed to the self-sufficiency of its own premises and terms. So there is not only a case for bringing the state back in to deal with the social problems free markets have created, and to safeguard the kind of values associated with citizenship and democracy: there is also a case for reviving the independent, conceptual status of the state, because the state remains the residual guarantor of order and cohesion, justice and community, in highly differentiated societies undergoing rapid, even revolutionary, change.

The Possible Consequences of Globalisation

In Australia, the gap between those who support the main game and those who place more emphasis on social and ecological values is wider than appears. Whether one favours moving from a free to a social market depends on how seriously one views the evidence of a widening gap between rich and poor – especially in the United States and the United Kingdom – in the breakdown of public order, and the emerging threat to the stability of democratic capitalism. Those who support the mainstream policy agenda acknowledge the existence of social problems but do not, apparently, see them as critical. Implicitly, they tend to discount warnings that the erosion of social capital and trust places democracy at risk. Their position is that Australia must first secure its position in the global economy, then deal with other problems from the proceeds of growth. Their critics say that poverty and inequality are already sufficiently entrenched and, on the evidence to date, the proceeds are likely to flow disproportionately to the better-off. Meanwhile, the level of anxiety and insecurity amongst Australians is already disturbingly high (Mackay 1993). The level of disenchantment with politics and politicians is also high, though higher elsewhere.[10] The environment is also under threat. Such persons might agree with Hobsbawm: 'we have reached a point of historic crisis' (1994: 584). So the real choice is between those who want to push on with the main game, and those who say that to do so puts the democratic public order at risk.

For Hobsbawm and the Progressive Left in Britain, the choice for liberal democracies is whether to follow policies that are consistent with the laws of motion of global capitalism, or to defend society against a world economic and financial system which is out of control. In his view 'the fate of humanity in the new millennium [will] depend on the restoration of public authorities' (Hobsbawm 1994: 578). This is very different from the outlook of the major party elites in Australia, who look forward to securing a greater share of global wealth by constructing efficient markets at home and helping to expand global free trade. Which view is more accurate? The question is impossible to answer in a limited space, but it is an issue which bears directly on the debate over state and market. If one agrees with Hobsbawm, or Hutton, or Lind, that global capitalism will produce regimes very different to those desired by liberal free-traders, that the more international markets are left to run themselves the greater the problems for society and democracy, then the case for trying to regain control of markets strengthens.

Globalisation is a multifaceted phenomenon and difficult to summarise (see Waters 1992: 5; Camilleri and Falk 1992). One can certainly argue that a force which erodes the powers of sovereign states, territorial monopolists, to do what they will with their own, and which strengthens the fabric of international law, is no bad thing. And that the progressive incorporation of more and more countries within a global free-trading system, if this is possible, offers a better future than any general relapse into protectionism or neo-mercantilism. Whether it *is* possible, or whether the competitive pressure unleashed by the dynamics of globalisation will drive states into defensive trading blocs, is a moot point.

Generally, the authors mentioned here fear that, beneath all the hype and enthusiasm that surrounds globalisation, especially as a cultural phenomenon, one aspect has been overshadowed: the degree to which the drive for global free trade in and through deregulated markets, including financial markets, reflects the agenda of global firms and their supporting interests, who see enormous opportunities for wealth in breaking free from the rules and standards previously maintained by states. Deregulation is, among other things, the logical, structural response of globally organised firms to the kind of trading environment, and the opportunities for profit, which began to emerge in the 1960s and then, with increasing speed, in the 1980s. It is a response to the growth of multinational and transnational corporations, to the expansion of the international trading system, to the technological and product revolutions of the late 1970s, and to the development of transnational production systems and the decentred global firm. The combined effects of these changes have driven firms with global reach to maximise their freedom to compete by emancipating themselves from the traditional nation-state, which seemed more and more an obstacle to their attempts to reposition themselves globally. Global firms, previously of national origin, now find their interests diverging from and overriding those of the host state. Business logic in the global economy forces a global firm to calculate its strategy and policy towards its native country in exactly the same way as towards any other. The largest firms are, in effect, quasi-states which negotiate with 'real states' over competitive advantage from a position of near parity (see Stopford and Strange 1991). The quasi-states obey market imperatives to cut costs and expand profits: they bear little or no responsibility for their impact on the peoples or environment of their, often temporary, host society.[11]

Hobsbawm and others argue for a realist, rather than a naive, account of the political economy of globalisation. It is not another giant leap forward for humankind. Rather, a complicated set of changes have radically transformed the nature of business and the power of capital *vis-à-vis* the state. The ideological assault on the state, the attempt to replace states with markets, reflects the real power of capital as it seeks to dissolve the terms of the compromise struck between capital and labour between roughly 1870 and 1970 in the name of economic freedom – its own. Consequently, one should think twice about how far one wants to roll back the state, because it will probably be replaced by quasi- or business-states concerned only with their viability in the global economy, the interests of their stakeholders, and largely unaccountable to host societies for their actions.

With this fear goes another: the emergence of a new category of persons whose creative and technical skills are highly valued in the new systems of production, who are well paid and enjoy high mobility, and who are therefore well placed to enjoy the personal benefits of globalisation while insulating themselves from its social costs. This category is variously made up of the symbolic analysts of Reich (1992), well-paid professionals in the service industries, including finance and computers, plus higher executives and managers from the corporate sector; these people see increasing benefits for themselves in opting out of the public provision of services, especially as these decline in quality, preferring to purchase their own. Their self-interest leads them to favour a smaller state, fewer restrictions on how or where they spend their money, and lower taxes. The emergence of something like a cybereconomy may give them – as well as 'virtual corporations', which have no territorial headquarters – the ability to avoid taxes altogether. Their material situation contrasts markedly with that of the underclass, which, without education or the necessary skills, is increasingly marginalised by technological advances in production. In so far as this growing and wealthy category can withdraw into its own havens and gated communities, minimising taxes, this represents a significant threat to a state's revenue base and extractive capacity. Overall, the trend here, which follows on from Lind's account of the new feudalism in the United States, threatens the infrastructural capacity which is seen by Weiss and Hobson as a very necessary feature of the clever state and a viable economy in the modern world.

Globalisation brings riches to a sizeable minority of the population, in both developed and developing economies, who favour deregulated markets and weak states as the road to wealth, and who can protect and insulate themselves from the adverse social effects of globalisation. As the latter require more money and attention, weak states find it more difficult to raise the money and are further handicapped by the strength of the call for small government, low taxes and non-intervention in the marketplace. This ideology is disseminated to great effect by opinion-makers in the media and the corporate sector, supported by the new clerisy of neoclassical liberals in state bureaucracies, international agencies and some university departments of economics. The latter may hope and believe that by emphasising 'production values' or wealth creation – or simply the freedom to make money – all will benefit from the trickle-down effect, but this has clearly not happened in the United States or the United Kingdom. Lind's overclass in the United States and the entrenched rentier capitalist class in the United

Kingdom have gained disproportionately in wealth during the 1980s and 1990s and are the strongest opponents of any attempts by either a Democratic President or New Labour to qualify or reverse policies on which their own wealth and power are based. Globalisation has created a new constellation of material interests that strenuously opposes any attempt by liberal democratic states to develop the kind of program now required to arrest their slide into incipient anarchy.

Some who think globalisation is the shape of the future, such as Reich (1992), Strange (1995) and McRae (1995), warn of its darker side while implying that little can be done about it.[12] More alarming is the appearance of arguments which welcome or encourage dualisation, the trend to a two-tier society. Ian Angell begins from the circumstances described by Reich, Drucker (1986) and Strange, to portray a future which will be *really* competitive (1995: 10–12). The number of states will increase greatly as city-states and company states emerge and nation-states fragment:

> Not only will state be pitted against state, but area ... against area, town against town, even suburb against suburb. It will be inevitable that nation-states will fragment: rich areas will dump the poor areas. Such shakeout trends can be interpreted as *downsizing* ... To protect their wealth, rich areas will also undertake a *rightsizing* strategy, ensuring a high proportion of ... knowledge workers to (wealth depleting) service workers ... These rich areas will reject the liberal attitudes of the present century, as the expanding underclass they are spawning, and the untrained migrants they welcomed previously, are seen increasingly as economic liabilities ...
>
> As far as global enterprises are concerned liberal democracy is an artefact of the Machine Age, an ideology from a time when the masses were needed – but it will soon mutate into an irrelevancy.

Conceivably, the underlying purpose of this article is satirical. Lord Rees-Mogg (1995), however, was not being satirical when he looked forward to the imminent collapse of the 'monolithic ... nation-state' because it would no longer be able to raise the taxes to pay for its basic functions. The outcome of the revolution in electronic communications would take most taxable transactions, especially those of the wealthy, into cyberspace. 'That is a country with no taxes, the greatest tax haven of them all, Bermuda in the sky with diamonds.' The emergence of a global cyber-economy is already well in sight (May 1995). Rees-Mogg hails its emergence enthusiastically:

> the most successful country of all will have no geographical location. The ... so-called cognitive elite will deal with each other on the networks of cyberspace, outside the existing jurisdictions. By 2025, cyber country will have at least 250 million citizens; some of them will be as rich as Bill Gates, worth

over $10 billion each; the cyber-poor may be those with an income of less than $200,000 a year, but there will be no cyber-welfare, no cyber-taxes and no cyber-government. Cyber-country ... could be the greatest economic phenomenon of the next 30 years.

If such scenarios are realistic, if this is what lies at the end of financial deregulation and more-or-less ungoverned technological change, then it is fair to ask what kind of 'society' will then exist? If one begins to think that the forces and interests driving globalisation are likely to bring about even greater inequalities of wealth and power, more hierarchical and less accountable methods of rule, then one may well agree with Hobsbawm or Hutton that trying to re-establish political control of these forces is imperative: that states which can maintain civilised and legitimate public orders are preferable to some variant of high-tech neo-feudalism.

Conclusion

Elsewhere, a shift of emphasis is occurring in the field of political economy. On both Left and Right, there is growing interest in the proposition that viable market economies require strong states rather than weak ones. The balance between state and market is historically variable. The nature of competitive advantage in the global economy, especially for manufactures, requires governments to play a selective interventionist role, and coordinating strategic intelligence which extends beyond the concept of the minimum state. In the United States and among New Labour in the United Kingdom, there is growing interest in the forms of 'communitarian capitalism' and institutionalised partnership arrangements between the public and private sectors found in Europe and East Asia. In both, there is growing recognition that leaving it to the market is not a sufficient strategy, that deliberate efforts are required to overcome tendencies to short-termism and secure the long-term viability of the production system, especially in the context of globalisation. Societies also need more protection against the impact of the latter. Social stability and democratic political development do not necessarily occur in tandem with market-driven economic development. Market capitalism is a socially destructive force. Globalisation, with its very rapid rate of social and technological change, places additional stresses on people and institutions. Therefore, one has to give special and separate emphasis to preserving the social capital on which democratic capitalism ultimately depends.

The elite consensus which was apparent at the National Strategies Conference in 1994 appeared to register these shifts in thinking about

Australia's political economy. There is no evidence, however, that policy-makers under Labor, especially the bureaucratic elite, took seriously suggestions for long-term strategic planning and collaborative arrangements between public and private sectors. They remained opposed to a more explicit strategic industry policy or sectoral development policies. With the Coalition's election victory, the apparent advance of the conservative parties towards the middle ground in the early 1990s was reversed, and policy became pervaded by faith in the sufficiency of market solutions and competition policy. The possibilities of a new synthesis between social and economic values, which would also give real substance to the objective of sustainable development, have diminished and it seems quite likely that political economy debate will revert into the kind of ideological sparring that prevailed in the early 1990s. At the same time, this chapter has argued, the rest of the world has in fact moved on and in ways which suggest that a mere reworking of economic rationalism will prove politically, socially and economically unsustainable. Such policies will once again create countervailing political forces requiring a new consensus or compromise.

Notes

1 See, for example, the views expressed by several participants in 'Forum for the Future' (EPAC 1994: 431–50).
2 See especially the argument by Hobsbawm (1994), Part 3: 'The Landslide'. Also Miliband (1994).
3 In 1978–95, general government spending as a percentage of GDP in Europe increased from 43.7 to 50.2. Individual countries as follows: UK, from 41.4 to 41.6 per cent; US, 30–33.4 per cent; Japan, 30–37.4 per cent; Germany, 47.3–49.1 per cent; France, 44.6–53.9 per cent; Italy, 43.7–50.2 per cent. Taxes and other governments receipts also rose similarly, in Europe from 39.7 to 45 per cent of GDP; in the US from 30.2 to 31.6 per cent. OECD statistics reported in *The Times*, 24 August 1995.
4 Lind (1992): 'A catalytic state is one that seeks its goals less by relying on its own resources than by acting as a dominant element in coalitions of other states, transnational institutions, and private sector groups, while retaining its distinct identity and its own goals. As a catalyst, this kind of state is one that seeks to be *indispensable* to the success or direction of particular strategic coalitions while remaining substantially *independent* from the other elements of the coalition' whoever they are (original emphasis).
5 Or, as in Victoria, government is being reinvented in such a way as to increase the scope and autonomy of the business sector. Arguably, in Victoria the government has equated the public interest with providing developmental opportunities for selected business groups who are increasingly shielded from the processes of public accountability. See, for example, Alford and O'Neill (1994).
6 To mention only names: Michael Mann, Anthony Giddens, Charles Tilly, Ferdinand Braudel, Karl Polanyi, Norbert Elias, Eric Jones, Theda Skocpol, plus many period schools, Weberians, Marxists, world systems theorists, etc.

7 Defined as one wielding significant infrastructural power, comprising penetrative power: able to reach into, instruct and communicate effectively with the population; extractive power: can extract resources of whatever kind from society; negotiated power: able to act in a cooperative and mutually influential manner with other major power sources in society; able to coordinate their activities.
8 This draws on a recent article by Putnam (1995).
9 Hutton (1995: 105–10). 30 per cent of the population are the disadvantaged, primarily those without jobs or economically inactive; another 30 per cent are marginalised and insecure, mainly part-time or short-term workers; 40 per cent are the privileged whose market power has increased since 1979. See also ch. 7, 'Why Inequality Doesn't Work'. A 1994 Report from the Department of Social Security revealed that, since 1979, the richest 10 per cent of Britains had become 60 per cent better off. Incomes of the poorest 10 per cent had fallen by 17 per cent in real terms. The number of people living below the European poverty line (half the average income) rose from 5 million to 13.9 million, a quarter of the population in 1991–92.
10 The opening sentence in Miliband (1994) is 'Politics in the advanced capitalist world has rarely been held in lower esteem'. See also Mulgan (1994).
11 For more detail, see Hobsbawm (1994: ch. 9); Hutton (1995 *passim*, esp. chs 3, 10); Sklair (1991).
12 Reich (1992, esp. ch. 17); Strange (1995). According to McRae, 'Quite large parts of the US economy will leave the industrial world and revert to something akin to the standards of the developing world' (1995: 215–16; see also pp. 186–95, 204–5).

CHAPTER 2

The Social Policy Context

Bettina Cass

Contested Concepts of Australian Social Policy

In considering the social policy context in which debates about the Australian Way have arisen, this chapter asks a number of questions.

What are the possibilities of incorporating a greater measure of social justice into the distribution of income and resources in Australia? Given that policy developments since the early 1980s have shown that market wages and the social wage are inextricably linked, how have Australian policy debates framed the issues of justice in these two forms of resource distribution? In the industrial relations debate, deregulated, enterprise-based bargaining and individual contracts are rapidly replacing the centralised wage-fixation system, where collective representation by trade unions was the expected mode of negotiation; how might this be linked to issues of redistribution by means of taxes and benefits? An increasingly internationalising economy allows economic liberals to argue that labour market, employment and unemployment trends and wage distributions are less and less accessible to effective domestic state regulation and determined by global, competitive market imperatives, driven by the relatively free movement of capital (Mishra, 1995); in this context, what is the future of full employment, and how is it linked to the preceding questions? The final matter recognises the gender dimensions of these debates and asks: how have sex inequalities been historically embedded in Australian social policy, and how might these inequalities be counteracted and redressed in any restructuring of Australian distributive institutions?

In order to place the peculiarly Australian configuration of market, state, and civil society within a comparative framework, I turn to contemporary analyses of Western welfare states. It has become customary to accept the categorisation by Esping-Andersen (1990) of the Australian welfare state as a 'liberal welfare regime', along with other Anglo-American countries, to denote the relative reluctance of governments to intervene in market arrangements, particularly labour-market arrangements, and to provide comprehensive systems of social protection. The European literature on welfare regimes focuses on the relationships between work and welfare; it analyses the extent to which various welfare systems, in their economic, social, ideological and cultural interconnections, have enabled labour to be decommodified, that is, have enabled individuals to survive, more or less adequately, outside the commodified relations of paid employment. These accounts have emphasised the concept of *decommodification*, analysing various forms of social security and the extent to which their rules and procedures of entitlement, coverage and generosity redistribute income to population groups who are excluded from market participation by unemployment, old age, disability or illness (Esping-Andersen 1990; Kolberg 1992). Such analyses explore the several forms of the relationship between work and welfare in liberal democracies and social democracies, identifying the political practices and discourses of political parties and key social movements which have a keen interest and stake in welfare outcomes and financing (labour movements, agrarian parties, social democratic or conservative parties, institutionalised religious parties, etc). According to these analyses, welfare regimes with equalising and socially cohesive objectives are based on the principle of welfare rights; welfare regimes that maintain or exacerbate market inequalities and reduce social integration do so by constructing a much narrower and more precarious categorisation of 'welfare need' (Mitchell *et al.* 1994a; Saunders 1994).

In analysing relations between market and state in Australia, Castles and Mitchell (1992b) and Whiteford (1994) focus not on the principle of decommodification but on the principle of 'redistribution', on the extent to which tax-benefit systems redistribute sufficient income which is effective in reducing the inequality of market incomes which would otherwise prevail. The concept of *welfare need* in these analyses tends to lose its opprobrium, since the redistributive objective of means-tested welfare systems is placed at the centre of the analysis, and, if the quantum redistributed is sufficient, is seen as a form of justice and redress. While the concept of *decommodification* draws attention to the relative effectiveness of tax-benefit systems in mitigating 'the disciplinary whip of the market', the concept of *redistribution* draws attention to the effectiveness of tax-benefit systems in reducing the inequalities which market-driven systems of income distribution would otherwise generate.

Esping-Andersen, in *Three Worlds of Welfare Capitalism* (1990), categorises Australia as a residual liberal welfare regime because of its historical dependence on means-tested social assistance, needs-based conferral of entitlements, construction of a dualism between work and welfare, and grudging emphasis on decommodification. In accounts which place redistribution at the centre of the analysis, Australia is categorised as a redistributive regime, because of the relative efficiency and effectiveness of its means-tested social assistance system in ameliorating (at least to some extent) the inequalities which market incomes alone would construct (Castles and Mitchell 1992b). This redistributive function is seen as especially important in ameliorating the increase in market income inequality caused by unemployment and labour-market deregulation since the early 1980s (Harding and Mitchell 1992; Whiteford 1994).

It must be emphasised that, in much of the mainstream literature, *welfare* is given a restricted interpretation, referring largely to redistribution through the tax-benefit system. It is not explored in the contexts of public policies that affect employment, education and training, and wages policy, which comprise the primary sources of income distribution. Welfare is conceived narrowly as social transfers made necessary by full or partial exclusion from the labour force; in the process, the dichotomies between work and welfare characteristic of neoliberal thought and public policy are not challenged. Welfare may be conceptualised inclusively to cover all forms of 'social protection', following the work of Polanyi (1944) to include the range of state interventions which aim to protect individuals from unimpeded market processes and their outcomes. In this case, the analyses also examine investment policies, employment and labour-market policies whose concern is the sustainable creation of high levels of employment and the reduction of unemployment. Markets themselves are politically constructed and therefore the product of many forms of policy regulation (or the relative absence of regulation); moreover, the processes of social protection involve not only social security systems and revenue-raising tax processes, but also policies concerned with employment, unemployment, wage determination, housing, transport, health and education.

Another related critique is made in the feminist literature on welfare regimes. It argues that the privileging of market–state relations renders invisible the informal, non-market provision of caring services carried out predominantly by women within family, households and communities (Lewis 1992; Fraser and Gordon 1994; Edwards and Magarey 1995). Jane Lewis (1992) argues persuasively that the various ways in which different social policy systems treat the market work and the non-market family-based caring work of women are associated with the strength and pervasiveness of the 'male breadwinner model' in labour-market conditions, employment patterns and cultural expectations. In the male breadwinner model, a man is the only, or the primary, breadwinner in a couple family; a married woman or mother is either fully supported as a home-based non-market carer, or partially supported as a secondary earner. All modern welfare regimes have subscribed to this model to some degree, but they vary in the extent to which it prevails in its pure form in actual social and economic arrangements (in all social classes and ethnic or cultural population sectors), and the extent to which it is institutionalised as one of the bases of social protection. Ignoring this fundamental issue in both welfare state analysis and in debates about the Australian Way renders invisible the intimate, welfare-generating relationships which are an essential partner in forging interconnections between the market, the state, and civil society.

Contested Bases of Social Protection

The Australian system of social protection was based historically on five fundamentals of social policy. From the consolidation of the welfare state in the mid-1940s until the mid-1970s in some cases, and in others until the mid-1980s, these fundamentals determined market-based allocations of resources. They can be described as follows.

- From the first decade of the twentieth century until the latter part of the 1980s a centralised wage-fixation system set minimum wage rates and through the awards system established a floor of minimum wages and conditions. It worked by means of negotiation and mediated contestation, in which employees were expected to be collectively represented by trade unions.
- From the end of the World War II until the mid-1970s, historically low levels of unemployment (considered in the light of earlier decades) were made possible by Australia's system of industry protection behind high tariff walls, by high growth rates as an essential outcome of Keynesian public investment policies, by the industrial dominance of the First World, and by the relatively low participation of adult women in the labour force (Aspromorgous and Smith 1995).
- A categorical and flat-rate system of social security, tested against income and (sometimes) assets, redistributed essential resources to low-income individuals and their families when they were excluded from the labour market through old age, unemployment, sickness or disability, or the obligation to care for vulnerable and dependent family members (predominantly children).
- Very high rates of private home ownership in the period from World War II (considered both historically and in comparative terms)

provided the major form of asset and savings for working and middle-class households through the life-course, and substantially reduced the experience of poverty for the aged.
- The entrenchment of the male breadwinner model in all aspects of public policy, social and political culture, including employment policies, wage fixation and social security. All the planks of Australia's system of social protection in the period after World War II were predicated on this model, particularly in wage fixation (from 1907 until 1972–75), the taxation system, the social security system, and the paucity of provision of maternity and parental leave and childcare (Baldock 1988; Shaver 1988; Brennan 1994). However, the changes in women's labour-force participation since the mid-1970s have made significant inroads into the social validity of the model, and have had far-reaching effects on social policy changes. An analysis of this question applied to changes in income support and employment and family policy shows severe cracks in the male breadwinner model as a result of women's increased labour-force participation in the formal market economy and their struggle to combine the responsibilities and pleasures of employment and intimate life as mothers and partners. Nevertheless, at the level of social and cultural norms in gender relations and in many public policies, except some key aspects of social security, Australian arrangements could best be described as a 'modified male breadwinner model', characterised by deep ambivalence (Cass 1995a).

It has become commonplace to describe the relative demise of these five fundamentals of social protection in tones of nostalgic mourning for a lost world of innocence, as if the distribution of resources which then prevailed had no attendant patterns of advantage and disadvantage and the 1980s and 1990s saw only loss and erosion of principles of equality. This is a misguided and dangerous premise on which to base contemporary debates. Even in the period of full employment before 1975, those individuals and families expected to be protected by the family wage, by the social security system, and by the male breadwinner model of social protection were the very groups most likely to be in poverty. These groups included large low-income families, sole-parent families, the aged, families with an unemployed, sick or disabled breadwinner, indigenous families, and individuals and families excluded from home ownership because of labour market disadvantage or because they were headed by women (Commission of Inquiry into Poverty 1975). Women-headed families were most likely to be severely disadvantaged, as the direct result of a discriminatory labour market, discriminatory wages, and a social security system predicated on the male breadwinner model.

Since the collapse of full employment in the mid-1970s, Australia, like most industrial countries, has been shaken by many factors: four bouts of declining economic growth; rising unemployment, particularly long-term unemployment; labour-market deregulation framed within the discourse of flexibility in a globalising economy; advancing or threatened commodification of health, human services and basic amenities, compared with earlier postwar developments; and threats to the equalising trajectory of social policies, with concomitant threats to social cohesion (Purdy 1994). Neoliberal critiques have gained ground and postwar systems of social protection have been partly or completely dismantled, particularly in the United Kingdom, the United States and New Zealand (Mishra 1990; Mitchell 1992), and in Australia with the burgeoning of neoliberal policies over the last several years. Like these countries, Australia saw an increase in both market-income inequality and disposable-income inequality (post-tax and post-transfer income), but this increase was considerably less than in other Anglo-American countries. It was mitigated by the wage protection for low-wage earners embedded in the centralised awards and industrial relations system and the gender equity regulations in the centralised wages system which reduced the gap between male and female wages; and by the more effectively redistributive tax-benefit system. Nevertheless, since the latter part of the 1980s, market trends and deregulatory economic policies which increased inequality ran counter to the more equitable social policy trends (Whiteford 1995).

Transformation of Work since the Mid-1970s

Contested debates about the future shape of interactions between market, state and civil society in Australia must be understood in the context of a significantly transformed labour market. Following the period of employment recovery from the 1981–83 recession, a recovery which lasted in Australia until 1989, the recession of the early 1990s saw employment growth in the OECD countries come to a standstill. By 1996 the average rate of unemployment had risen to 10.4 per cent in the European countries and 8.7 per cent in Australia (OECD 1996). The OECD notes that these labour-market trends are structural in origin and have exacerbated the problems of high and persisting levels of unemployment, underemployment, long-term unemployment, poverty and marginalisation.

There has been a significant decline in employment in manufacturing in the advanced economies of the West – a decline evident in each recession since the mid-1970s. Despite the strong growth of manufacturing output in Australia and the G7 nations between 1970 and 1990, the share of manufacturing in gross domestic product has fallen sharply, reflecting in large part the accelerating growth in services (Australian Bureau of Industry Economics 1995; Green 1996b). This has occurred primarily at the expense of labour-intensive, low-productivity manufacturing in the old industrial countries, including Australia, rather than manufacturing as a whole. The fall in the overall importance of manufacturing in the economies and labour force of most of the advanced countries of the OECD area (excluding only Japan and Greece) has been accompanied by an increase in the share of gross domestic product accounted for by the service industries (finance, insurance and business services; community, social and personal services) which are increasingly organised into part-time and casual employment previously not an intrinsic part of the organisation of the mainstream manufacturing industries (OECD 1994b). In some countries, such changes have resulted in the emergence of a two-tier labour market, comprising a core of secure, well-paid workers and a growing periphery of insecure, part-time workers who are most at risk of recurrent bouts of unemployment. This trend has been identified by Hutton (1994) in the United Kingdom, while the OECD *Jobs Study* (1994b) sees the growth of low-paid, low-quality jobs in the United States as akin to the higher levels of overt unemployment evident in Europe, Australia and New Zealand.

In some countries there has been an increase in temporary employment, which is broadly defined as employment circumscribed by contracts of very limited duration. In Australia this is termed casual employment: it does not offer annual leave or sick-leave and usually attracts a loading as compensation for the lack of employment entitlements. This loading (of the order of 20 per cent) has been evaluated as insufficient compensation either for the forgone value of employment benefits, or for the greater precariousness of the labour duration contract (Simpson *et al.* 1995). In the period 1984–94, the proportion of temporary employees as a percentage of all employees increased in Australia, France, the Netherlands and Spain: in Australia from about 16 per cent in 1984 to almost 24 per cent in 1994 (OECD 1996a).

To summarise these labour market changes in Australia and in similar countries:

- The importance of manufacturing in the overall economic and industrial structure, in particular the older forms of low-productivity, labour-intensive manufacturing, has decreased, and an increased share has been taken by the service industries in the generation of gross domestic product and the industrial structure, with concomitant changes in the national and international organisation of manufacturing as well as the service industries.

- Labour markets are increasingly characterised by part-time and casual employment and irregular self-employment characteristic of the organisation of the service industries; there has been a reduction in full-year, full-time employment in manufacturing and construction, which was seen as the norm under the male breadwinner model in most of the countries of the OECD during about thirty-five years following the end of World War II (Blackwell 1992; McLaughlin 1991).
- The labour-force participation of married women and women with children has increased as a result of women's increased participation in secondary, vocational and higher education, and the growth of part-time employment in the service industries; and influenced also by transformations in patterns of relationships and family formation, increased rates of separation and divorce and formation of sole-parent families; with the consequently much stronger expression of women's aspirations for full economic participation (Cass 1995).
- Rates of unemployment and the incidence of long-term unemployment have been high compared with rates prevailing in the thirty-five years following the end of World War II. As long-term unemployment has become entrenched, it is recognised, at least by some commentators, that strong rates of economic growth and high levels of investment in effective and equity-based labour market programs are required to lower the rates of long-term unemployment, even in periods of economic recovery (OECD 1992, 1993).
- From the early 1980s in the OECD area, growth in real wages moderated and wage shares in national income fell back to or even below their 1970 levels. In the Anglo-American countries there were falls in the real wages of low-paid workers, and the wage differentials between low-skilled and high-skilled workers widened, with increased inequality in the dispersion of wages. In the continental European countries, on the other hand, wage differentials were either broadly unchanged, or increased only slightly (OECD, 1994b). The OECD *Jobs Study* speaks of unemployment taking two forms: either overt unemployment, or low-paid, low-quality jobs. Widespread unemployment in Europe, Canada, Australia and other Anglo-American countries is matched by an increase in the proportion of poor-quality jobs in the United States, accompanied by unemployment.
- Since the mid-1970s, a much greater proportion of people of working age have relied on income support, not only because of the contingencies of illness and disability and infrequent periods of short-term unemployment, as had previously been the case, but in much greater numbers because of exclusion from full-time, secure,

labour force participation, as a result of unemployment, underemployment and the joblessness associated with family-caring responsibilities (Saunders 1994).

What are the political debates which have been generated in Australia in response to such transformations of employment security and social protection?

Debates about the Transformations of Work and Social Protection

It is simplistic to posit a dichotomy between Labor and Liberal–National Party governments' respective policy responses to these major issues. In some respects these governments' public policies have shown continuities, particularly in relation to deregulation of labour markets, industrial relations and financial systems, and reduction in social expenditures; but there are also significant differences. The economic and social policies of the Hawke and Keating Labor governments (1983–96) were developed predominantly within the context of the Prices and Incomes Accord with the trade unions, introducing for the first time in Australia a co-ordinated attempt to integrate wages, taxation and social security policies. By 1988, however, the initial policy priority of employment growth had been sacrificed to the control of inflation and foreign debt through the reduction of social investment and the imposition of very high interest rates. In the ensuing deep recession of 1990–93, a 'battle of the plans' emerged: the Labor government produced *One Nation* (Keating 1992) followed by the *White Paper on Employment and Growth: Working Nation* (Commonwealth of Australia 1994b), while the Liberal–National Parties produced *Fightback!* and *Jobsback* (Liberal and National Parties 1991). These plans proposed alternative futures through substantially different configurations of market and state: on the one hand, an extension of Labor corporatism, augmented by significantly increased investment in employment and training programs; and on the other hand, a redirection of Australian public policies towards a more privatised, deregulated, market-driven agenda similar to the neoliberal policies of the United Kingdom, the United States and New Zealand. Most importantly, the role and influence of the trade unions were to be removed totally from public policy development. It is the latter trajectory which has gained dominance since the election in early 1996 of the Coalition government under John Howard: industrial relations have been overhauled, social security has become more residual and precarious, and there has been radical disinvestment in employment, education and training.

The economic and political debates responding to the transformation of work and social protection in the late 1990s focus on four central questions.

- Should macro-economic policies support public investment in strong economic and employment growth? Public investment in employment, education and training could be sufficient to increase employment and reduce unemployment in a substantial and sustainable way and reinstate the principle of full employment. Instead, it is designed as an intermittent and partial response to recession, rapidly reduced or withdrawn at the outset of economic recovery, or used as a suitable object of expenditure cuts in an agenda of budgetary contraction (McClelland 1994; Gill 1995; Aspromorgous and Smith 1995).
- Should unemployment be traded off against lower wages on the proposition that better employment outcomes can be achieved if the protection of wages and conditions for employees is reduced and the incidence of low-paid jobs increased (Whiteford 1995a)? Do the social costs of this 'diabolical trade-off' outweigh any gains to be made from reduced unemployment? Robert Reich noted that, while the United States has a better employment performance than most European countries, it nevertheless has the most unequal distribution of income of any developed country (quoted in Whiteford 1995a). The OECD *Jobs Study* notes that the United States has a much higher incidence of low pay than most other OECD countries. More than one-quarter of all full-time workers in the United States earn less than two-thirds of median earnings, compared with one-fifth of full-time workers in the United Kingdom and one-tenth in Australia. The debate in Australia is poised around a similar diabolical trade-off: should a floor of centralised wage regulation through national industrial relations legislation, the Australian Industrial Relations Commission and the awards system be reinstated in order to provide a strong safety-net of a living wage and protective standards for all employees, particularly the least industrially powerful in a context of enterprise bargaining (Evatt Foundation 1995; Australian Catholic Social Welfare Commission 1995)? This is countered by official advocacy for more thorough deregulation of the wages system through the entrenchment of enterprise bargaining and the increased spread of individually bargained employment contracts, which are the objectives of the Coalition government's *Work Place Relations and Other Legislation Amendment Act 1996*. The terms and implications of this act are well explained by MacDermott (1997).

- What should be the future role of social security in providing an adequate basic income in a substantially changed, increasingly deregulated labour market? The traditional expectation of the distribution of paid and unpaid work (a previous model of full-year, full-time employment for male workers through a full 'working lifetime', accompanied by interrupted, casual and part-time employment for women with children) no longer holds (Perry 1994). This is manifested as a debate about the advantages and disadvantages of tighter targeting of social security, making income support considerably more conditional and the surveillance of recipients more stringent; even reducing the value of income-support payments in line with reduction in wages for the lowest-paid employees. This debate takes place in a climate where budget deficit reduction is given primacy in the policy debate, as if the question could be settled as an issue of redistribution within a zero-sum revenue game, without reference to other interrelated public policy issues: the expansion of revenue by the reduction of unemployment and the broadening and strengthening of the tax base (Whiteford 1994).
- What attention should be paid to the gendered nature of income inequality and the greater risk of poverty experienced by women and their dependent children? This results from women's lower rate of participation in secure, full-time, uninterrupted employment, their unequal access to equal remuneration for work of equal value, and their greater reliance on income support as a result of the continuing devolution of caring responsibilities to women (Edwards and Magarey 1995).

Trends in the Distribution of Incomes

How have high rates of unemployment and reductions in the real value of wages for the lowest-paid affected the distribution of income? A mounting body of research indicates that since the early 1980s inequality in private incomes increased in Australia whether income is measured before or after tax (EPAC 1995). Analysts have found increasing inequality of market incomes, mitigated, but only to some extent, by a more progressive tax-benefit system (Saunders 1994; NATSEM 1994). Comparative OECD data indicate that market wage inequality for men and women increased during the 1980s in most of the OECD countries studied, including the United States, Canada, the United Kingdom, Japan, Austria, the Netherlands, Sweden and Australia (Whiteford 1995a). However, it is worth noting that the Australian market wage distribution over the period 1975–1991 remained considerably more equal than in the United States, Canada and the United Kingdom, and in the early 1990s Australia had a much smaller proportion of low-paid workers in the full-time labour force compared with these countries. Further, the ratio of female to male wage rates was significantly more equal in Australia than in most other OECD countries, particularly the United States and the United Kingdom. All of these factors tending to reduce market-driven inequalities are attributed to Australia's centralised wage-fixing institutions, which were still largely in place in the 1980s and which compressed wage differentials.

The increase in wage inequality is attributed to increased dispersion of earnings from market activity resulting from higher rates of unemployment, mainly affecting workers in low-skilled jobs and putting downward pressure on wages; technological changes in the workplace with the demand for a more highly educated and skilled workforce which has increased the earnings differential between highly skilled workers and those considered less skilled, whose employment has become more precarious (EPAC 1995). Saunders (1995) and Nevile (1995) posit that explanations must look to the impact of globalisation on world commodity markets, financial markets and labour markets.

How did social policy mitigate increased market inequality in Australia during the 1980s? The most important measures stemmed from the greater efficiency and effectiveness of the benefits system in redistributing increased levels of income to low-income families following the social security reforms of 1987–90 (Harding and Mitchell 1992; Whiteford 1994); the slight increase in the equity of the tax system produced by base-broadening (Harding 1995); and the effects of redistributive measures like health-care and housing policy (Landt *et al.* 1995). In addition, the increased participation of women in the labour force reduced the inequality of family incomes, assisted substantially by significantly increased public investment in child-care (Mitchell and Dowrick 1994).

This research identifies a deep contradiction between market processes and economic policies which have tended to increase inequality (with the exception of women's increased employment), and the more equalising impact of social policy. While the Australian system of social security, tax, health and community services was strengthened in its redistributive role, this could not mitigate sufficiently the increased inequality in the distribution of market incomes.

Policy Debates about the Australian Way

This section outlines four interconnected public policy arenas which research and debate have identified as central to the reconfiguration of relations between state, markets and civil society in the context of a transformed labour market and recognition of the ineffectiveness of radical deregulation in delivering just outcomes. These arenas are: reasserting the primacy of full employment as the necessary base for equitable and socially integrative policies; restructuring income support to meet better the needs emerging in a changing labour market; ensuring that industrial relations policies provide wage protection and the conditions necessary to live a fully human and sociable life; and ensuring that policies facilitate, rather than reverse, aspirations for gender equality.

Restoring Full Employment

Some Australian commentators are articulating the long-rejected policy priority of full employment, the linchpin of postwar Australian Keynesian policy, both of the Left and the Right, but abandoned either intentionally or by default since the mid-1970s. The implementation of full employment would require setting firm targets for sustained employment growth, reduction in unemployment, and measures to improve and maintain the employment chances of long-term unemployed people, set as political imperatives (Aspromorgous and Smith 1995; Chapman 1994; Commonwealth of Australia 1994b; Commission for the Future of Work 1996a). The research identifies three interconnected strategies: long-term employment generation based on strong investment in infrastructure and regional development (Australian Urban and Regional Development Review 1995; Task Force on Regional Development 1993); sustained investment in education, employment and training programs to ensure the equitable distribution of job opportunities in the context of employment growth; and ensuring that new jobs are characterised by high skill levels and secure employment arrangements, driven by a commitment to reduce the proportion of people who are locked into peripheral, precarious casual employment (Committee on Employment Opportunities 1993; Commonwealth of Australia 1994b; Freeland 1995; Speerings *et al.* 1996). Labour-market programs which are effective and equitable cannot be provided as a cheap option, or as short-term initiatives which will be subject to reduced investment or abandonment as a sacrifice to budgetary contraction (OECD 1993).

Such commentators argue that good government requires a long-term budgetary commitment to reducing long-term unemployment and to making the public and private investments essential for macroeconomic employment growth. This will involve fiscal policy which demands as much attention to the raising of sufficient revenue through the tax system as it does to promoting efficient and equitable expenditure; a national savings strategy, with better regulations for the investment of superannuation, particularly in infrastructure and in job-generating industries; housing, urban and regional development policies; and industry and trade policies (Aspromorgous 1995). Reform of labour-market policy must be placed in a comprehensive perspective of this nature in order to maintain a high level of aggregate demand for jobs (Gill 1995). In the world of political reality, however, a very significant reduction of investment in employment, education and training programs was announced in the federal Budget in 1996 ($1.8 billion over four years); this will have the effect of increasing both the rate and the duration of unemployment, with consequent increase in inequality and decrease in social cohesion.

A Participation Income

Turning now to income support policy, one of the democratic visions proposed in Europe to counter the policies of economic liberalism is to revitalise the social rights of citizenship through the idea of *citizens' income*. This takes various forms according to its various advocates, but is reasonably characterised as a universal transfer payment or minimum income guarantee made to all citizens, not on the basis of current or previous income, workforce history or willingness to undertake paid work, or demonstration of incapacity for employment, but only on the criterion of citizenship (Van Parijs 1992; Purdy 1994). In a departure from this approach, Tony Atkinson (1993) conceptualises his proposal for a guaranteed minimum income for the United Kingdom as *participation income*. Taking this idea as a point of departure and considering its applicability to Australia's income-tested and categorical social security system, *participation* may be defined as involvement in a range of social and economic spheres: participation in paid work, both full- and part-time; being unemployed and looking for work; participation in education or training; *and* involvement in unpaid, non-market caring work in family, household, extended kin network; and participation in a range of community projects. The debate in Australia is well analysed by Perry (1995).

The conditions for receipt of this payment would be based not only on relationship to paid work, but a wider definition of *social contribution and participation*. The crux of the debate in Australia centres on ensuring adequate income for people whose social citizenship would otherwise be denied by their poverty and labour-market marginality or by their responsibility to care for dependent children, relatives or close friends. The objective is to ensure that combinations of market income and income support provide adequate social protection and the basis for participatory citizenship. It is the principle of *adequacy* which demands urgent attention: adequacy of total income derived from combinations of market earnings and transfer payments in a much more integrated way than is now the case.

The objectives of a participation income would be to recognise and support adequately periods of the lifecycle when labour-force participation is made impossible by market failure (unemployment), illness and disability and old age; recognise and support non-market forms of caring work carried out in family, household and community; support the transitions into market work from education, unemployment and caring work, and the transitions out of full-time market work; support combinations of market work and caring work likely to be undertaken not only by parents but also by people with the responsibility to care for elderly and disabled relatives and partners; support full-time education and training and the combinations of education and training with market work increasingly likely to be undertaken through the lifecycle; provide a social wage floor in a deregulated and casual labour market, particularly for part-time and casual workers.

Under current labour market and industrial relations conditions, it is likely to be even more essential that the income-support system be made stronger, more adequate and more seamless, particularly given the increased prevalence of precarious labour. The Coalition government, however, has emphasised enforcement of a stricter activity test for unemployed people and increased penalties for infringement; this is evidence of a move even further away from the concept of generic and secure income support for people of working age. Rather, income support is to become more conditional and precarious, particularly for young unemployed people. As a consequence of Budget changes, the most disadvantaged unemployed young people will find income support is more tightly income-tested. Moreover, they are also highly likely to be screened out of eligibility to participate in labour-market programs because they are judged unable to benefit. This harsh rationing of opportunity is a denial of citizenship both through market work and through social security. Under these conditions, a seamless participation income is, on the one hand, even more desirable; on the other hand, it is even more elusive.

Industrial Relations Safeguards

Strong industrial relations legislation which protects the retention of collectively bargained wage determination and the role of trade unions is increasingly seen as necessary to provide an adequate safety-net of both wages and conditions to support enterprise bargains (MacDermott 1997). Other factors are essential to ensure good living standards where family and human needs are recognised: the strengthening rather than the eroding of leave arrangements, including annual and sick leave, leave for family purposes, maternity and parental leave; the movement to shorter rather than longer working hours; safeguarding of the gender equity principle of equal remuneration for work of equal value; safeguarding of the right to collective representation through trade unions. The objective of such policies is primarily to guard against the 'diabolical trade-off', where an increase in the incidence of low-paid jobs is pursued under the guise of a solution to high levels of unemployment, rather than being seen in its true light, as a form of precarious, poor-quality employment and the source of 'in-work' poverty.

Promoting Gender Equality

Intersecting labour-market transformations and changes in gender relationships have comprised a significant but partial challenge to the male breadwinner model. There has been growing advocacy for, and neo-conservative reaction against, the realisation that the majority of women (and some men) enter the labour market bearing the primary responsibility to care for dependent or vulnerable family members, bringing the issue to the top of the political agenda. The labour market has been traditionally based on the male breadwinner or single-person model, where atomised individuals are seen as the archetypal employee. On the one hand is advocacy that industrial relations policies recognise these intersecting responsibilities for both women and men, and that policy efforts be made to reduce the hours of employment, working against the thrust of the intensification of work in competitive workplaces and labour market. On the other hand is a counter-advocacy that is well-entrenched in Coalition government discourse and policy reform. According to this view, social policies (tax-benefit policy and radical disinvestment in public child-care) should encourage women to leave employment and return to full-time, unpaid, household-based, caring work. This is presented as part of the 'natural gender order', and legitimised as 'providing choice'. Underlying the politicised scenario of choice is the Workplace Relations Act; with its objectives of maximising individualised employment contracts and deregulating the conditions of part-time employment, while diluting pay equity safeguards for women, it is likely to undermine both the conditions of, and the rewards for, women's employment.

The advocates for reducing both class-based and gender inequality argue that widespread policy changes are required: consistent public investment in employment growth, education and training; sustained investment in services for children, the aged and people with disabilities; a redistributive tax and social security system which provides an adequate basic income and recognises the work of care but does not make it difficult for women to take up paid work; policies on social security and industrial relations which support the non-market work of care and recognise the family responsibilities of all employees, women and men; legislative safeguards which continue to regulate the wages system, to protect and raise the earnings of the least powerful employees, and to close the gap between male and female earnings (Edwards and Magarey 1995). There is little evidence that such policies are central to what has been described as the core business of government in the latter part of the 1990s (National Commission of Audit 1996).

Reconstructing the Interconnections of Civil Society, Market and State

The choices facing Australian democracy are poised between a new model based on distributive justice, developed from Australian conditions; and a neoliberal model, influenced by the United States, New Zealand and the United Kingdom in the 1980s and first half of the 1990s. In those countries labour market and wage deregulation, the reduction of wage protections for the least powerful employees, and increasingly residual income support systems have resulted in greater levels of income inequality than in Australia over the same period. The major question is this: to what extent does the Australian polity and civil society consider that one of the key responsibilities of good government is to establish and guarantee full employment, and to address the related issues of education and training with sufficient public investment? A social policy that focuses only on redistribution through the tax-benefit system runs the great risk of addressing only one part of the equation: to what extent can even the most effectively redistributive welfare system turn back the tide of increasing inequalities in the distribution of employment opportunities and market incomes? The Australian evidence during the 1980s and into the early 1990s indicates the contradictions of embedding equity principles only in social policy, while entrenching deregulatory and increasingly libertarian principles in economic policy.

In what ways will the social institutions of Australia's civil society respond to the unequalising trajectories of deregulated markets and increased levels of unemployment and precarious employment? There is little doubt that the reduction of inequality and the fostering of social cohesion must rest on policies which approach economic as well as social policy as social investment rather than social expenditure, and that necessarily requires a long-term view of fairness embedded in economic, social and civic life. In what ways will future contested debates about a new Australian Way deal with such fundamental matters?

PART II

Historical Perspectives: Australian Settlements?

CHAPTER 3

The Australian Settlement and Australian Political Thought

Graham Maddox

Conventional wisdom holds that Australia has no tradition of political thought. We cannot point to great landmarks of political literature like those visible in other terrain. We have no Hobbes, Locke, Montesquieu, Madison or John Rawls. Neither have we experienced the revolutionary sentiment that produced contractarians or federalists. The conclusion must be, it is said, that such political thought as we have is borrowed. To some extent, this must be true. Our own founders reflected on the thoughts of the world's great thinkers, adding to the work of US federalists and British constitutionalists the comparative observations, for example, of James Bryce (Irving 1994). We sometimes think in imported Western categories, like conservatism, liberalism and socialism, but this is scarcely surprising, given both that our political culture and our institutions are largely built on imported foundations, and that these concepts are, to an extent, universal.

Australian Political Thought

Too much can be made of our lack of the 'greats'. Not many communities can boast energetic outpourings of political works once you pass outside the periods of democratic Athens, the English or French civil wars, or the transatlantic Enlightenment. In any case, the more that comes to light on the work and life of the 'originals', the more we can see how much they borrowed not only from their great predecessors, but also from their lesser-known contemporaries. We may one day decide that Australia is, after all, rich in these lesser thinkers, whose work nevertheless provides the sound building blocks of subsequent authors. Certainly, J. D. Lang, W. G. Spence, W. M. Hughes, W. A. Holman, Deakin and Barton, Griffith and Higgins, Childe and Hancock had interesting observations to make about our polity.[1] Moreover, our historians, especially those of the speculative kind like Russel Ward and Manning Clark, and some social commentators like Donald Horne and Hugh Stretton, have offered much for the political theorist to dwell upon. A former diffidence about our political tradition has left many stones unturned, and no doubt much of great interest awaits discovery in the form of pamphlets and other ephemera (Hume 1994); remember that much of the important revolutionary literature – for example, that embracing the seminal libertarianism and egalitarianism of the English Levellers – was of this kind.

Australian history cannot boast too many levelling or revolutionary situations. In part this is because our entire community is the product of a levelling experiment, and here we risk the entrapment of single-factor explanations, of which the Australian Settlement is perhaps the most crude, for a burgeoning society nevertheless rich in its own brief traditions. Single-factor explanations are suggestive, even provocative, but they threaten with the same dangers as 'consensus politics' – that important alternative factors may be suppressed or devalued. We return to some such explanations in a moment.

Diffidence about our political heritage tends to downplay our most remarkable feature: the advanced nature of our democracy at the time of Federation. The signs of that precocity are well known: early votes for women, pay for parliamentary members, the secret ballot, compulsory voting, the early political organisation of the labour movement – producing the world's first labour governments. All these place the Australian colonies alongside their US colonial predecessors and their New Zealand neighbour as democratic 'laboratories' (*contra* Davidson 1997: 10–11 *et passim*). The principles of Australian democracy may have been born in the English electoral reform movement and Chartism, but they had to be put into practice here, and that was impossible without political thought.

We could, like some important American commentators, invest the strength of our political pragmatism or empiricism with great significance, making a virtue of having no theory, or, as some would say, of eschewing ideological politics (Boorstin 1953; Adams 1958). In this regard, the observations of a French visitor, Albert Métin, have a lot to answer for; he was puzzled by the lack of theory among working people he interviewed, believing that they could see no further than the next pay-rise (Métin 1977). All this neglects the fervour with which the working population, meeting in mechanics' institutes, schools of arts and private study circles, discussed the work of Karl Marx, Henry George, Edward Bellamy, the Bible – again, imported literature, but having its peculiar fit with Australian circumstances. The fruit of such discussion was far removed from the individualism of classical liberalism, and, indeed, the reverse of American republican self-sufficiency. As Russel Ward (1978) proposed, the Australian bush engendered a collectivism to challenge liberal ideas at their source.

The Australian Settlement

Single-factor explanations which seek to embrace the Australian political character, therefore, are likely to be misleading. Although composite in the set of policies it is said to embrace, the Australian Settlement is just such an explanation and, it is here argued, excludes a rich vein of Australian political thought. It is in some sense the culmination of a long line of characterisations which project Australia as a liberal society (meaning, among other things, that it cannot be conservative or socialist). We can accept, with Rosecrance, the Hartzian view that without a long-established landed aristocracy Australia lacked the deep-dyed conservatism of Europe (Rosecrance 1964: 275–318). Nevertheless, a new range of political aspirations produces its own spectrum. All proposals for political activity revolve around schemes for change or the determination to protect present configurations (Duverger 1964: 412–21). It will not take long for those with a vested interest in land-ownership or other forms of wealth-creation to marshal their defences of those systems. These we may legitimately call conservative, even if they lack the old patterns of conservative collectivist responsibility (Hartz 1955).

A Benthamite Community?

Much is rightly made of the European foundations of Australia as having been set in the age of the Enlightenment. It is nevertheless constricting to narrow the context to a single factor within European or transatlantic Enlightenment political thought. The notion that Australia could be conceived of as a Benthamite community, for example, gives great weight to the somewhat eccentric views of one thinker, however latterly influential, amongst many apologists for liberalism (Collins 1985: 147–69).[2] Having characterised Benthamism as consisting of three chief elements – utilitarianism, legalism and positivism – Hugh Collins concludes that developing Australian society was shaped by just such a mixture of elements. Although his discussion is full of insight, Collins's summation of characteristics as Benthamism is problematical. It privileges a liberal reading of Australian history and, although acknowledging challenges to the formulation from both conservative and socialist viewpoints, blunts those challenges for their failure to respond with their own epigrammatic formulation. More explicitly, since Bentham's approach to politics and philosophy was based on disaggregation down to the indivisible unit, this conception implicitly casts Australian society in an individualist mould (Mill 1962: 4–51; cf. Bentham 1973: 66–71).

Collins cites with approval Sir Keith Hancock's view that the Chartist legislative program had been fully implemented in the Australian colonies by the 1860s (Collins 1985: 150–1).[3] One of the main influences upon Chartist ideology and organisation was evangelical religion, which sits uncomfortably with Bentham's sceptical approach (cf. Piggin 1996: 8–14). Collins insists upon the utilitarian influence on Australia's formative years; his approach overlaps with those who adopt the Deakinite settlement of national policy direction, since for him utilitarianism underpinned Alfred Deakin's political program: 'land legislation; protection; free, compulsory and secular education; payment of members of Parliament; factory acts; early closing; anti-sweating legislation' (in La Nauze 1965 vol. 1: 107). Once more, however, both evangelical and trade union influences are evident in Deakin's compromise, along with his own liberalism.

The scientism of Bentham's hedonistic calculus, the supposedly practical application of utilitarianism to legislative programs, is scarcely evident in Australian constitutional systems. Collins is surely right to focus on the pragmatic adoption of federalism in Australia, but utilitarian aspects of the Australian federal Constitution fade to insignificance before the alluring model of the US Constitution, so apparently successful in fostering a great nation across a territory of continental proportions. Collins's thesis would be strengthened by acknowledging the lack of influence of the labour movement upon the shape of the Constitution, but a broader formulation of Australian political culture suffers from any label which marginalises the significance of the movement producing the first labour governments in the world.

So also with the 'positivism' of Australian politics. Obviously a certain empiricism reigns among political activists as they search for policies which will enlist the most voters to their cause. Yet here again the discerning eye differentiates the ideological bases from which the search for converging, popular policies commences. Collins notes the positivism of much social commentary, as typified by the tendencies of social science within the universities; a positivism which has been imposed upon the subject matter by the observers themselves. Again labour ideology, not to say socialism, is the casualty in Collins's account. Collins is undoubtedly right to emphasise the dominance of legal interpretations over political issues in Australia, but the connection of either legalism or electoral positivism in Australia with Benthamism is less than convincing.

Cultural Liberalism

Proceeding rather from economic doctrines, one of the more sophisticated recent analyses of Australia's liberal heritage, *Cultural Liberalism in Australia* by Gregory Melleuish (1995), adds much to our cultural discourse. Dr Melleuish locates the foundations of Australia's modern culture at the parting ways of colonial liberal thought, free trade and protectionism; but he loads these vessels with a greater significance than they have hitherto borne. Free trade approximates to a classical individualism in which each person's energetic application to a vocation, together with a vigorous entrepreneurialism, builds up an open and vibrant national community. Unlike many another classical liberal, Melleuish is careful to situate his free-trade version within a social and religious context so as to make free trade 'a doctrine of co-operation which, because it was invariably underpinned by Christian morality, was the antithesis of Social Darwinism and amoral individual selfishness' (1995: 29). Its foundation 'was a belief in the power of nature to heal social wounds and to create a world of harmony and co-operation'.

Protectionism, on the other hand, was enervating and inhibiting to national development. Melleuish refers (with approval) to B. R. Wise's comprehensive attack on protectionism not merely as an economic mechanism but as a *cultural* ideal: it helps factions against the majority; it saps the courage of manufacturers; 'Originality, ambition and enterprise are destroyed and the fibre of national life threatened. Protection threatens the self-reliance of individuals and consequently the good of society at large.'[4] Curiously, protectionism also stemmed from a religious understanding akin to the Calvinist community's, where it was everybody's business to see to the moral and spiritual welfare of everybody else in the flock. In either case – free trade or protection – the problems arise when the original religious understandings, and the committed faith which sustains them, fall away under the pressures of secularism.

Melleuish sees an approximation between protectionism and state socialism, although the distance between such a creed and any liberal origins would need some explanation. It is simply looseness to identify a form of liberalism with state socialism, since these two political attitudes proceed from quite different foundations. However compromised by protectionist ideology, liberalism insists upon the primacy of the individual person, whereas socialism, in seeing the individual consisting largely in inextricable relationships, gives primacy to the product of those connections – the community or the collective. No amount of cultural contortion can prise protectionism from its liberal foundations; it is an economic creed which explores methods for the development of industry on behalf of entrepreneurs. To connect it with legislation or executive state action does not make it socialist or collectivist; and, as averred by the chief critic whom Melleuish cites, protectionism itself is a method of co-operation. On the other hand, no amount of market-based economic intercourse will make free trade any less individualist and competitive – and in competition there are *losers* as well as winners.

Melleuish would be rescued from this dilemma by reference to the inner crisis within liberalism over the balance between the individual and the society which occurred in Britain in the early years of this century, and which continues wherever liberalism is professed to this day (Arblaster 1984: 284–95). Competitive individuals are not, and scarcely can be, the foundation of communities. All the cherished liberal devices to make it so – like the hedonistic calculus, the invisible hand, or the political contract – do not satisfactorily explain communities. They emerge through tradition and habit, and explanations which dwell on family feeling and interconnection, however remote and Aristotelian they may sound, have greater validity. Communities do not consist in markets alone, nor in entrepreneurship, competition and ambition, vital though these may be. They are cemented as much by interconnected voluntary associations – many of them charitable – by unpaid workers like home-makers, and by vocationally oriented professionals who do not seek success through increasing salaries and continuous promotion, but who devote their human creativity to teaching, nursing, and serving in a range of activities devoted more to the welfare of others than to the advancement of self. They are also shored up by tribes of honest, unambitious, non-entrepreneurial working people who perform a multitude of necessary functions for meagre returns.

As John Stuart Mill argued, English liberalism, as distinct from Continental varieties, was classical and individualistic – devoted to negative freedom, or freedom from interference, rather than an emerging collectivist freedom. Each individual should enjoy all the conditions to produce the fullest development of personal capacities which alone could provide the good life.[5] It was equally clear, as eminent liberals like T. H. Green or L. T. Hobhouse might quickly discern, that society did not produce the conditions whereby the bulk of humankind could *ever* develop their innate capacities, and state regulation was essential to provide even a modicum of leisure time, a living wage, a basic education. Even the best efforts of an interventionist state could scarcely provide the minimal conditions for the development of human capacity among the majority of the population. In Britain the crises in liberalism, created by the recognition that *laissez-faire* individualism did not produce communities, and that collectivist intervention of some kind was necessary to improve the lot of most people, led to an ideological split mirrored in the near demise of the Liberal Party itself (Freeden 1970:

549). Those liberals with a genuine concern for *all* their fellow individuals had little alternative but to team up with the socialists. Those who stuck with the obdurate belief in a sovereignty of the individual which should resist almost all outside interventions found themselves inexorably caught in a defensive web of old ideas; they may have lacked the old conservatives' sense of the unity and organicism of society, but they became conservatives nevertheless, so forever compromising the nature of conservatism. Under the pressure of internal crisis, most liberals therefore became collectivists of some kind, whether by absorption into a semi-socialist Labour Party or by association with the conservative inheritance from an older world.

To attribute socialism in Australia to a crisis-ridden liberal protectionism is to devalue the genuinely collectivist foundations of the Australian creed, and indeed of the organised labour movement itself. Yet this is exactly one of the damaging results of compressing Australian identities and traditions into a single Settlement, whether Deakinite or other. Hancock suggestively proposed that all sides of politics had agreed upon 'settled' policies, yet his insight has been given a significance it did not claim, as though it denoted something peculiarly Australian and, in context, something especially pragmatic and non-ideological (Hancock 1936; Miller 1959: 68–9). It is the competition for new directions in policy, not reflections on the acceptance of past actions, which adds vitality to the dialectic of an adversarial system. It is all too easy in hindsight to neglect the conflicts, and to discount the losing competitors, which made up the stuff of past, 'settled' policies. It is a genuine characteristic of democracy that old wounds are not perpetually reopened, or that old battles are not continually refought. When all this is said, however, our history does indeed reflect some monumental controversies, and the concentration upon 'settled' policies does much to falsify our understanding of the past, and to deny us an appreciation of the fact that even losing causes – the 'unsettled' policies – have nevertheless contributed to the substance of what we are today.

The 'End of Certainty'

Now 'settled' policies have been inflated into the Australian Settlement, and all the conflicts and controversies and ideological competitions of the past submerged under a near-century of 'certainty'. Perhaps Paul Kelly (1992) was merely savouring the popularity of the 'end of . . .' fashions (the 'end of ideology'; the 'end of history') when he announced *The End of Certainty*. His major point, however, unintentionally demonstrates that a single, one-sided reading of the past can produce an illusion of certainty, while any glimpse into the future can, or should, create uncertainty as we contemplate the range of choices before us. Certainty would quickly dissolve, however, were we able to wind back the clock and place ourselves at any point in the past of the twentieth century – to look forward from *that* standpoint would remind us of the uncertainties which have beset us at every turn. How could anyone speak of certainties in the face of – to name the most obvious – the complexities (and explosive conflicts) of the conscription fight in World War I, the unknowable threats of the Great Depression, the menace of Japanese invasion, the ideological conflicts of the Cold War, the moratorium campaigns during the Vietnam War or, indeed, the revolutionary implications of the Dismissal?

Paul Kelly proposes that the Australian Settlement which produced all this certainty can be gathered under five heads: White Australia, Industry Protection, Wage Arbitration, State Paternalism, and Imperial Benevolence.

Although the first three of these are accepted terms, they are situated in a loaded context wherein the last two cast a lurid glow from the dying embers of imperialism over the whole – now thoroughly tainted – Settlement. There are two basic things wrong with this Settlement. First, we have suggested, it gives a misleading impression of a monolithic past; second, in a quaint reversal of nostalgic sentiment, it sets up a version of our heritage which, couched in these terms, is clearly repellent, in order to set the scene for a vibrant, forward-looking, internationally open and internally multicultural present inaugurated by the new Labor Party of Hawke and Keating – although Kelly is willing to make some generous concessions to Whitlam and Hayden (1992: 19). White Australia is set up as 'the foundation idea of the Australian Settlement' – 'a *unique* basis for the nation and the indispensable condition for all other policies' (Kelly 1992: 2, emphasis added). White Australia is, of course, a most unfortunate name for a repulsive policy, and nobody could argue away this sickening stain on our past. The name is doubly unhappy because it seeks to label Australia as a *uniquely* racist country. The confronting fact is that the whole European world at the time was infected with racism. Unfashionable to say now, but Australian versions were mild compared with, say, the United States in the sordid aftermath of the Civil War, or South Africa, or even imperialist Britain – to say nothing of the racist horrors simmering in the cauldron of a recently unified Germany; look almost anywhere, and racism was a factor in European society.

The second pillar of the Settlement, Protection, 'became fused into a self-reinforcing emotional bond' with White Australia (Kelly 1992: 4). It was espoused by Deakin, whose 'conversion owed more to political convenience than to economic understanding, never his forté'. Kelly's protectionism lacks the dimensions of Melleuish's, especially the religious background. It was no more than a factionalising economic device, flawed from the start, since 'one industry's protection became another industry's cost through higher prices'. Kelly offers no mitigating counter-arguments, like regional development, avoiding the dislocation of particular workforces, or indeed creating self-reliance in certain strategic industries; to him the Hawke salvation 'offers a wonderful symmetry: that Australia will enter its second century as a nation in 2001 liberated from the protectionist shackles which stifled its first century'.

Arbitration, the third halter on a choking nation, emerges as a subspecies of protection, 'an effort to insulate wages from the international market'. Kelly acknowledges arbitration to be an attempt to create industrial and social peace after the class conflict of the 1890s. The social benefits, and the intention to seek justice in a living wage, are recognised, but cannot, for Kelly, counterbalance 'irresistible' pressures from the international economy (1992: 5–7, 9).

State Paternalism, conveniently (but insufficiently) defined as 'individual happiness through government intervention', marks the fourth element of the Settlement. Kelly attributes the growth of a paternalist state to our colonial origins as a prison, which, still holding the first warder's baton, was able to contort democratic elements to its own purposes and 'create a fusion between the interests of the individual and the state'. One could, of course, characterise the development of Australian democracy in several different ways, but I suggest, with due respect, that labelling the Australian state paternalist is itself patronising – certainly to generations of Australians who worked hard to build a democracy 'as comprehensive as anywhere in the world', only to see it devalued as 'the advance of state power' (Kelly 1992: 10). These words are easy to say; but who is the state? We live in a world of states of various kinds – some authoritarian, some indeed paternalist. The democratic state may be characterised as an authoritative association – among a plurality of associations – whose power is available for the use of 'the people' for their own protection and, where appropriate (that is to say, as sorted out among a multitude of conflicting forces and interests) for their improvement. The process may indeed be conducive to happiness, but the happiness surely proceeds from personal or social considerations that the state (the democratic association) may or may not be able to enhance. A little thought would convince that, on Kelly's terms, a democratic state would always be paternalist. His argument is not a case against the state, but against democracy.

Yet he persists in this vein to the fifth pillar of Settlement, Imperial Benevolence. We are not told precisely whether benevolence is paternalist or not, but it is unfortunate to turn a benign term into a malignant one, as though by association with other morally defective elements of the Settlement. 'The Royal Navy was the guarantor of White Australia.' Forget about German imperialism in the Pacific or the exiguous size of the population in continental Australia (Moses 1991). To cap off a misleading view of our past, 'Australia was a constitutional entity with a spiritual void at its core' (Kelly 1992: 11). Only Gallipoli – a weak and defeatist 'legend' – came in to fill the breach. So paternalism and benevolence were spiritless. This ignores the Catholic, Anglican and Dissenting communities who actually found a welcome spiritual home on this continent, and the spiritual heritage of the indigenous population. It forgets that the original prison-ships of 1788 brought in their company a chaplain of the Methodist missionary society. Religion might have taken unusual turns in Australia; did not bush unionism come to Australia 'like a religion'? Is not the Anzac myth a genuine (and benign) instance of civil religion (Moses 1994)? Whatever else, there was no spiritual void. There is a void, however, in unidimensional economic interpretations of history, and in the counterfeit mythology of economic rationalism.[6]

All could acknowledge that the Hawke and Keating governments addressed serious economic problems and that, indeed, they managed to maintain some commitment to traditional Labor policies in family welfare and sexual and racial equality. One could not make too much of traditional concerns when determined to equate tradition with a stifling Settlement of outmoded ideas. To suggest, as Kelly appears to do, that Australia's spiritual void may be filled by the declaration of a republic is absurd (1992: 11–12). Kelly associates Australian republicanism with self-assertion and nationalism, presumably because it implies breaking any remaining ties with the United Kingdom – a problematic assumption, given that republicanism (invented in Rome and elaborated in Britain, the United States and France) is more alien to Australian nationality than the foundational institutions imported from the beginning of European settlement. It is convenient for economic rationalists to adopt republicanism since, at least in its US version – the one most likely to affect Australia's future development should republicanism be adopted – it is strongly linked to individual rights and individual enterprise, to the detriment of coherent government action. There is little doubt but that US-style republicanism, while eroding the capacity of governments to implement policy, would also engender a climate of individual self-reliance as proclaimed by the successful, but with its consequent alienation of most ordinary people from the political system. One cannot predict the future, but there is a possibility that republicanism will fray the collectivist strands of our tradition.

His unfortunate deprecation of our past leads Paul Kelly into certain contradictions. John Curtin, true Labor hero, for example, languishes in the gulf over which Kelly leaps when bounding from the fixing of the Australian Settlement into the thick of a Hawke-led reconstruction. Curtin is overwhelmed by the momentum of a Settlement which, in Kelly's hands, brooks no rivals. An avowed socialist, Curtin is scarcely permitted to be one because being so would not fit the liberal, Deakinite pattern. Yet Kelly, in some exultation over Hawke's rhetorical win against Keating on the question of leadership greatness, cites Hawke's acknowledgement of Curtin as wartime saviour and founder of postwar reconstruction, a man 'light-years ahead of his contemporaries in understanding the nature of economic challenge' (1992: 624). Apparently Curtin could not have been part of the economically backward Settlement after all.

Our past has several strands, some falling quite outside the tidily packaged Settlement. The many sordid aspects of our history must be recognised and faced, but they should be viewed through the wider lens of international trends and perspectives, since our acknowledgement of an outside world did not actually begin in 1983. What the Settlement tends to do is to undermine the tradition of democracy which advanced so rapidly in this country as to make it, in some eyes at least, an instructor to other would-be democracies.

Democracy is not fashioned out of a spiritual void. It represents the highest aspirations of the political person, whose hopes are ultimately bred of a higher, spiritual hope. It is no accident that some of our seminal democrats sought to build a 'paradise of dissent' (Pike 1967), or that some of the features of the welfare state were proposed by people under other-worldly instruction to try to do some good for their fellows (Piggin 1996: 88–91; Bollen 1972; Duncan 1991; O'Connor *et al.* 1992). Even our first republicans drew upon wells of spiritual value sunk by Dissenting preachers (Lang 1850).

Australian Democracy: An Open Future

All of this may sound out of place in a country comfortably entrenched in its secular culture. What we in Australia have forgotten is that secularism was itself a prescription of Dissenting spiritualism – a necessary condition of the freedom of religion, and consequently of other freedoms (Carter 1993). Modern democracy irrefutably grew out of the transatlantic Puritan movement, with strong assistance from

Catholic conciliarism (Maddox 1996). Sparks of the Puritan fire alighted on these shores from the first entry of Europeans. Some of them illumined individual consciences. Others were fanned into collectivist confrontation. On whichever tinder they fell, here were pinpoints of the light of freedom.

Interpretations of our past – our 'political thought' – draw stimulus from suggestive formulations which seek to embrace the whole character of our history. However pessimistic some of them may be, they provoke lines of response and inquiry which only confirm that there is much raw material left to be explored before we conclude on the value of Australian political thought. Certainly the scope of our inherited political thought cannot be encompassed by policy settlements, nor indeed by exclusively liberal formulations.

Notes

1 Others have their lists of the influential. See e.g. Melleuish (1995: 50–2), where he includes Christopher Brennan, Marjorie Barnard, Charles Badham, Francis Anderson, Elton Mayo and James McAuley.
2 Lindsay (1943) thought utilitarianism was the 'silly' theory as an explanation of democracy.
3 Hancock construes Australia in Benthamite fashion: 'Numbers *are* the state' (1961: 54, original emphasis).
4 See also the important review of Melleuish by Sawer (1996: 83): 'Wise figures in [Melleuish's] story as a philosopher of free trade but never as a philosopher and architect of compulsory arbitration and union preference. This belief in state interference at home and free trade abroad was characteristic of British new liberalism and was present in New South Wales.'
5 The classical liberal argument, preferring liberty to equality, was strongly represented in Australia during World War II. See e.g. Anderson (1945); Partridge (1945); Passmore (1945).
6 In remarking on 'the transformation of America from a creditor to a debtor power in the Reagan era', Kelly (1992: 13) scarcely acknowledges the role of an ideological commitment to the new economics in that transition. On Australia, cf. Battin (1997).

CHAPTER 4

The Australian Way

Jill Roe

The Australian Way as a Dynamic Historical Concept

Each year, in conjunction with its annual general meeting, the Academy of the Social Sciences in Australia sponsors a symposium on a topical subject. In 1992 the subject was 'Market–State Relations in the 1990s', and the leading speaker was the distinguished Australian economist, the late Professor Fred Gruen. In response to what seemed Professor Gruen's rather too pessimistic projections, I first addressed the notion of an Australian Way as a critique of the excesses of the market. As an economist, Professor Gruen wondered if we were about to return to a nightwatchman version of the state, and looked in vain for signs of a fresh approach to the vital question of what might be the most productive future relations between market and state in Australia; in contrast, a historian might take heart from recent research in the field of Australian intellectual history, notably the suppressed Keynesian 'legacy of choice' and the lost tradition of cultural liberalism, and from new more humane approaches to the past, especially the surge in biography. As Manning Clark once remarked, Australian history is the Bible of the Australian people. Although it contains many stories and, unlike the Bible, can never have a concluding book of revelations, it certainly does evidence an emerging and too often underestimated Australian Way – first obscured in the positivist 1950s, it seems – especially in social policy. The resulting paper subsequently appeared as 'Social Policy and the Cultural Cringe' (Roe 1993).

For some to hear that a certain practice is distinctive to Australia is enough for them to think there must be something wrong with it. However, it is now widely accepted that it is no bad thing to be different, as we still are in some crucial respects. For example, in the 1996 election campaign it was pointed out that in Australia people in full-time work were still guaranteed a living wage, unlike the United States or the United Kingdom. Indeed, there may even be a comparative advantage in difference, as indicated by responses to an alarmist report in late 1995 on Sydney as 'a middle-class sweatshop' for transnational corporations in Asia (*Sydney Morning Herald*, 18 November). Among other advantages of Sydney as regional headquarters over, say, Hong Kong and Singapore, mention was made by firms of medical benefits; and what counted for one corporation, American Express, was 'multiculturalism and the quality of the labour force'. Meanwhile, the old adage what's good for the goose is good for the gander has again been demonstrated. The phrase *Australian Way* is now most frequently seen by airline travellers as the title of inflight magazines. Older readers will recall it as a slogan of the publicly owned Trans Australian Airlines (founded 1945, now Qantas Domestic): 'TAA, the Australian way'. On American planes, the inflight magazine is called *The American Way*.[1]

It is often easier to discern what is distinctive about the Australian approach from a distance. Airline usage notwithstanding, my sense of an Australian Way was sharpened considerably by having observed the making and early stages of implementation of the Republican election policy entitled *Contract with America* – or on America – in 1994–95. Something on the new American harshness is in order here. The situation was summarised by the president of the National Organisation of Women, Patricia Ireland, at the 'We won't go back' women's rally in Washington in April 1995 to oppose the Republican agenda: 'The Republicans ... voted to dismantle the system of support which has been in place since 1935' – that is, to dismantle the New Deal. In particular, major social assistance programs (known in America as welfare, as distinct from social insurance programs, known as social security) were under attack, notably the Rooseveltian Aid to Families with Dependent Children program. Its projected replacement, the so-called Personal Responsibility Bill, contained such excesses as denying aid altogether to solo mothers under twenty years of age, an innovation opposed especially by the Catholic Church, on the grounds that abortion would increase if benefits were denied. (That clause was subsequently struck out in the Senate.) The more socially respectable social insurance provisions were under siege too, and the struggle to lift minimum wage rates continues (Roe 1997).[2]

The Republican counter-revolution in social policy – if not its bizarre preference for indoor relief, orphanages, and the like – has since made its way through the system. Punitive legislation signed by President Clinton in August 1996 is expected to cut federal welfare spending by $US55 billion over the next six years. As predicted, the aid to families program is no more, and with the end of guaranteed federal cash assistance to the poor, an estimated four million 'welfare mothers' will be looking for work. The word is, if they don't find it, 'they'll manage'. One gains the impression that in the United States, people no longer matter much, especially poor people, and above all poor women. (Some journalists referred to the Republican *Contract with America* as a 'contract on women'.) An Australian is almost bound to think social assistance and the Australian Way is better, as indeed Australians often have in times past.[3]

The Australian Way is a dynamic historical concept, unlike the legalistic notion of an Australian Settlement. That is, it expresses something which has grown out of the Australian experience, and presumably will continue to do so. Its origins lie in the risky world of the nineteenth century, where the colonial state had a big role to play; and the foundations were laid by an emergent Commonwealth at the beginning of the twentieth century. It was an optimistic period: 'State Experiment' (lately described as 'labour experiment') was the order of the day, and the inclusive ethics of citizenship and social democracy were in the ascendant (see Reeves [1902] 1969; Macintyre 1989; Roe 1994).

The durability of those early foundations has been remarkable. Even now, wages and working conditions are still to some extent protected by state tribunals whose lineage extends back to the first Conciliation and Arbitration Court, established in the state of New South Wales in 1901 by Bernhard Ringrose Wise (discussed further below). Likewise, the non-contributory social security system dates back to the first old-age pensions in New South Wales and Victoria in 1900–01; a reward it was said, in New South Wales at least, to worn-out workers who had contributed so much to national development (Kewley 1969: 20).

Notable also is the speed with which the new nation-state (1901) followed suit, with a national Conciliation and Arbitration Court by 1904 to deal with interstate disputes, nation-wide age and invalid pensions by 1909, and the universalist maternity allowance of 1912. Thanks to new powers gained in the 1940s and subsequent extensions, the Commonwealth of Australia now delivers a myriad of supports to needy citizens on principles laid down before World War I; additions and adjustments are the normal mode of reponse to new needs, for example the gender-blind sole-parenting benefit and the income cap on family allowances of the late 1970s. (There was a significant growth in the scope of the social wage thereafter, encompassing health insurance and worker superannuation, but only the latter is a totally new concept, creating as it did a second tier in social security arrangements.) It is worth adding that, in comparison with the United States, the liberal state in Australia has been fortunate in being able to control the size of its overall endeavour, due to secure borders and effective, if fluctuating and at times controversial, immigration controls (Brennan 1994a; Roe 1983: ch. 1).

More remarkable still, the Australian Way in social policy, once deemed mean and divisive, is now generally regarded as fair and effective. This is clear from both program-oriented research and opinion polls, and in the changed assessments of political scientists such as Francis Castles (1985), whose early work on Australia favoured European models. Evidently the collectivists and modernisers have been all too successful. Now the very foundations of the Australian Way are under assault, as privatising and profit-taking approaches, together with yearly cuts in public expenditure, take their toll on public utilities and services. Whether or not this amounts to an Australian counter-revolution it is too soon to say; but with the change of government in 1996, the situation seems ever more ominous.

The premise of this chapter is that, under the circumstances, it is more sensible and seemly to define and defend the Australian Way than to conjure up a new approach. Another look at the foundations is instructive. A sample of recent historical research in several areas follows: its tendency may surprise. Australian historians are taking ideas and agency seriously again; and as Chapter 3 showed, there is now an active interest in traditions of social thought in Australia, including religious thought – a subject previously not so much neglected as avoided, due to the blighting effects of sectarianism in Australian society until the 1960s.

Even now, well before the emergence of any new synthesis, fresh perspectives are already widely sought. An instructive, and on occasion eloquent, instance is *Transforming Labor: Labour Tradition and the Labor Decade in Australia* by Peter Beilharz (1994). Concerned by an apparent exhaustion of labour traditions during the Hawke–Keating ascendancy, Beilharz calls for a more respectful approach to the Australian experience, and deplores the denial of history apparent in the triumphal marketeer logic of Paul Kelly's *The End of Certainty*. Beilharz concludes:

> Kelly's larger historical vision soon lapses into special pleading regarding the allegedly fresh arrival in Australia of values such as competition and the pursuit of excellence which can only now slop over lowered tariff walls. This is finally a terrible insult to ordinary Australians of different classes and situations in life who spend their lives doing the best they know how. It presumes there are only two choices, that there is nothing left to be salvaged from a way of life many people still take to be salutary. It claims that this is now our chance to make history, but it shows only contempt for the history that has gone before. [Beilharz 1994: 10]

For Beilharz, the way forward is, of necessity, also the way back; the task of 'transforming labour' involves reconstituting the labour tradition. Interestingly, an attempt is made to accommodate Catholic social teaching; and in the end it is not so much labourism as 'the status of liberalism' which matters most (Beilharz 1994: 222).

More telling still is the strong defence of liberal nationalism in the Federation era to 1914 by Robert Birrell, *A Nation of Our Own*. Born of dissatisfaction with anti-idealist accounts, this timely 'revision of the revisionists' ends by placing its conclusions in the context of current social and economic dilemmas. But there is a long gap between Labor's emergence as the successor party to Deakinite liberalism in 1910 (and its failure to develop the legacy in the 1920s) and the 1990s, and the case for relevance is not strongly made. Perhaps it does not need to be. Certainly Birrell's systematic review of the characteristic achievements of the federal era is welcome. Meanwhile, his analysis of the 'tragic' White Australia policy is quite enough to be going on with.

The preoccupation of commentators based in Victoria, such as Beilharz and Birrell, with liberalism and its outcomes is understandable and appropriate. However, it is also somewhat limited in range. What follows suggests that the origins and dynamic of the Australian Way lie somewhere beyond these sociological summations and inquiries: they are to be found in certain ideological contexts, and in a range of ethical impulses. In the next section, an attempt is made to briefly characterise the Australian Way.

A Middle Way, a Narrow Way, a Fair and Flexible Way

In 'Social Policy and the Cultural Cringe', the Australian Way is described as a middle way, also a narrow way. The phrase *the middle way* refers to the mixed economy, and predates its coming by a small margin. It was first used in the late 1930s by British liberal conservative, the redoubtable Harold ('you've never had it so good') Macmillan, and became standard usage in Western Europe in the 1950s, following postwar reconstruction. In Australia, with its inheritance of Deakinite liberalism, the practice, if not the phrase, has had a resonance and vitality for much longer. One has only to think back to the public enterprises established by Labor governments in Queensland in the early twentieth century; and the phrase was immediately applicable in the 1940s, as acknowledged in Geoffrey Bolton's contribution to the recent five-volume *Oxford History of Australia* covering the period 1942–96, where it provides the sub-title. The Labor governments of the 1940s may not have reached the commanding heights of the mixed economy, but some of the public utilities privatised in the 1990s date from that decade, and it was then that the walls of the Australian version of the welfare state rose, on foundations laid at the beginning of the century (see Thane 1982: 345–6; Bolton 1996).

What of a 'narrow way'? As Paul Smyth (1994) reminded us in his penetrating study of the impact of Keynesian thought in Australia, there has seldom been much room for manoeuvre in the Australian polity, and even less by the 'realist' 1950s. A memorable example of narrowness from the era of the mixed economy is the Menzies government's two-airlines policy, when the arrival and departure times of flights on trunk routes by the publicly owned TAA and the privately owned Ansett were scheduled to within five minutes of each other. By such means was TAA allowed a market share. Another instance, this time from social policy history, is the apparently unending battle over the arcane, but really important, difference between non-contributory and contributory social service provision; the focus may change, but the issues have remained much the same. Innovation has been the fitful and partial exception, as in the tortuous construction and reconstruction of Medicare/Medibank as a compulsory and partly contributory national health insurance scheme, some thirty years after the medical profession rejected a UK-style national health sevice funded from general revenue (albeit for reasons not all objectionable, it has been shown by Gillespie) (Bolton 1996: 161; Gillespie 1992).

The notion of the narrow way indicates another and crucial dimension of the Australian Way, that is the participatory character of Australian democracy, with its distinctive electoral system of compulsory and preferential voting, established in the 1920s after decades of debate and experiment in the states. Albert Langer was jailed prior to the 1996 elections for advocating non-preferential voting, in potential the UK and US first-past-the-post system of voting, so this may seem merely topical; but it is relevant here in that the Australian electoral system is a rigorous system, demanding of both politicians and people, and the individual's vote can really count as it almost never can in the United Kingdom or the United States. While the system could be improved – for example the recording and counting of votes might be more efficient – the consequences of dismantling would be profound, especially for minorities and the poor, just as the abandonment of democracy would be in India. If people still matter in Australia, it is largely because a tight and sophisticated voting system has made it so (Stern 1993: 185).

The Australian way has sometimes been deemed outdated, somehow inappropriate to the modern world. Maybe. Society has certainly changed greatly since Federation, since the 1940s, even since the 1970s. It all depends on the fate of the mixed economy, which must find a way through the underlying clash between free trade and protection, recently resumed after a long period when protection prevailed in Australia (and elsewhere, New Zealand for example): that is, on maintaining the middle way. Regarding social policy, the real issue seems to be adaptability: as T. H. Kewley once observed, in effect the Australian social security system has evolved into something very like a guaranteed-minimum-income scheme. In any event, whatever the critics say, political scientists have found that a majority of Australians support the system, and state responsibility for health-care as well (Bean 1991: 81; Kewley 1969).

No doubt people tend to support the status quo. But over time a lot of effort has gone into maintaining and refining a system of entitlements which is at once universal in principle and selective in practice; and, at least in normal times, it seems to work fairly well. That is to say, it is effectively targeted (and policed); and, provided the tax system is progressive, it is fair, even redistributive. Nor are long-term generational inequities involved; and in comparative terms it is still quite cheap. As well, it is flexible. In principle, a 'categorical' system is an open system, and if in the 1940s more categories of need were (belatedly) recognised, so it can be done again.[4]

Another strength of the categorical approach is that it makes for a responsive system. That is to say, categorical recipients may respond as a group if mistreated, without stigma. Certainly they have done so in times past. Returned soldiers were the first, and most effective, group to do so during World War I; the unemployed protested strongly and to some effect in the 1930s, when the first old-age pensioner associations were formed by retired trade unionists; and pensioner protests in the 1940s provide some of the strongest evidence for the view that so far as social policy is concerned, the 1940s were at best 'Paradise deferred' (Garton 1996: 51; Scott and Saunders 1993; Duckett 1985; De Maria 1990, 1992). Another dimension is added when we remember that pension rights was a major claim of the first Aboriginal rights movement in the 1930s (*Abo Call*, 1938: 19). In general, there is much to be said for a system of citizen entitlements which is both targeted and – at least in principle – responsive. It should also be noted that the Australian Way – narrow, residualist, etc. – does command virtually unassailable moral ground. Not many are prepared to deny assistance to the truly needy or to lay themselves open to the charge that they think the poor should be left to die in the streets.

Mention of Aboriginal pension claims in the 1930s is a reminder of the other side of selectivity. The Australian Way is often said to be unduly bureaucratic and complex – some research suggests that Australian social workers really come into their own interpreting client entitlements. It has often been *too* tough, excluding rather than targeting; in short, too narrow. How to adapt the Australian Way further to Aboriginal needs is a question to which as yet no comprehensive answer is forthcoming. Maybe it cannot. Aboriginal Australia has for the most part still to enter the mixed economy and its social policy adjunct, and behaving as if it can may only exacerbate resentments and relative deprivations. For possible guidance in the direction of innovation and renewal by the coming generation of Australians, the next and final section looks back to the foundations of the Australian Way, focusing on five men and women who in various ways sought to broaden access to it.[5]

Five Founders

Sometimes the resonance of a phrase matters almost as much as its literal meaning. This is so when it comes to an understanding of the Australian way as 'a narrow way'. The image dates right back to the King James version of the Christian Bible, where it is to be found in the Gospel according to St Matthew, a verse in the Sermon on the Mount no less. In my South Australian-born maternal grandmother's Bible, which she received as a Christmas present in 1892 when she was sixteen years old – inscribed in copperplate 'Lillie Sharples a Xmas present from her Loving Mother, December 25th/[18]92' – the verse reads 'strait is the gate and narrow is the way, which leadeth unto life, and few there be that find it' (Matthew 7: 14). Incidentally, Prime Minister Chifley's oft-quoted 'light on the hill' line comes from the same source.[6]

It seems probable that, like the writer, few readers of this chapter could locate the phrase *the narrow way* without the help of a concordance or some more general work of reference. This possibility highlights another, historical point. Most of the people who laid the foundations of the Australian Way would have had no such difficulty. The Protestants among them would have had their own Bibles from a very early age. And while Australian Catholics did not start reading the Bible for themselves until the first popular Catholic translations in the 1950s, they too were taught social principles from the Bible via sermons and papal encyclicals (O'Farrell 1992). Jewish social teaching was also biblically derived, from the Old Testament. Only a tiny minority of Australians – and by the 1890s we should speak of Australians, since by then the native-born constituted a preponderance of the population – declared themselves at census time outside the Judaeo-Christian tradition (and they too laid claim to significant traditions of social thought and responsibility). Certainly the founding father of the Australian welfare state, Alfred Deakin, knew his Bible, and many other religious works, well.

Alfred Deakin

Alfred Deakin (1859–1919) led the liberal governments which introduced non-contributory age and invalid pensions in the early twentieth century. The liberalism of Alfred Deakin was, as Paul Kelly notes in the introductory historical chapter to *The End of Certainty*, 'creative and dynamic'. In Kelly's perspective (and index), *Australian settlement* and *Deakinite settlement* are interchangeable terms. How strange the word *settlement* would have sounded to Deakin. True enough that Deakin was a guilty man, having lost a good deal of his father's money in the great bank crashes in Melbourne of the 1890s. He had something to make up for. But he felt he had something to give, too.[7]

Deakin's world view is now remote; but it is not irretrievable. Al Gabay in *The Mystic Life of Alfred Deakin* records that, throughout his adult life, Alfred Deakin rose at 4 a.m. to pray and to study the latest religious works, on Buddhism and Theosophy and Swedenborg. A spiritualist in his youth, and typical post-Darwinian intellectual subsequently, he assumed that a new relgous synthesis was essential for progress, and actively sought to create one. An example, almost at random, comes from a book review for the *Australian Herald* (May 1896), entitled 'The function of religion', of Benjamin Kidd's influential work, *Social Evolution* (1893). The main thesis of *Social Evolution* is said to be 'To a large exent the history of the world is a history of its religions.' Alfred Deakin thoroughly agreed with the proposition that religion was the key to social evolution and 'the unity of humanity'.[8]

It was Deakin's tragedy that his mind went before he could embark on a synthesis of his vast reading and thinking. Whether that synthesis was ever possible we cannot say. He may have doubted it himself. However, as Gabay shows, he understood from various séances and monitions that he had in some sense been called to the political life, and that to him, a native son, had been allocated a historic role as a creator of the Commonwealth. In matters of social policy he was, as Australian social welfare historian Brian Dickey once remarked, the fine flower of Australian liberalism (1987: 93). An ardent protectionist, his idealistic liberalism was obviously of the home-made variety; and a good deal of it went into shaping more inclusive procedures, such as state pensions instead of charitable handouts.

Bernhard Ringrose Wise

Deakin's lesser-known contemporary Bernhard Ringrose Wise (1858–1916) is a contrasting case. Wise was a New South Welshman and convinced free-trader, apparently a secular man (if he had a religion it was probably free trade). Wise deserves to be better known, not only as the author of *Industrial Freedom* (1892) and *The Making of the Australian Commonwealth* (1913), but because he introduced Australia's first Industrial Arbitration Act, in New South Wales in 1901, previously mentioned. A native-born, Oxford-educated 'new' liberal whose thinking was shaped by T. H. Green and ethical state theory, Wise was well able to justify this distinctive and radical development. Under the act the trade union would stand on equal legal grounds with employers and – to quote – 'become an instrument of industrial peace which, with proper guiding intelligence, can be made effective of the highest social purpose' (see Ryan 1995: 81–2).

Wise had defended the strikers of 1890 on a similar basis. At that time, he opposed freedom of contract on the ground that 'there can be no freedom without equality', which the contract denied to workers; and he argued for the freedom to refuse work, for union preference and the common wage. This made him a pariah in his class, and although he rose to become deputy premier of New South Wales, he never found a secure place in colonial politics – too much of a toff, the others said. Nevertheless, a recent assessment is that he was a powerful influence for 'the better society'.[9]

Rose Scott

It is often recalled that in Wise's day social legislation was drafted on the dining-table of Rose Scott (1847–1925), at Woollahra, the Early (Shops) Closing Act of 1899 for example. Scott's closest student to date, Judith Allen, is not impressed by Bernhard Ringrose Wise, seeing in him a certain liberal authoritarianism, first manifest when he opposed votes for women and later raising the age of consent. Plainly there were limits to what a 'proper guiding intelligence' could accommodate. The point to bring out here is a different one, however. Rose Scott shared many causes with the radical liberals, even an interest in alternative religions; but, unlike Deakin and Wise, she was no federalist. She thought, and this is plausible, that Federation would do no good for the women and workers of New South Wales. For a long time after her death in 1925, Rose Scott herself was largely forgotten. The federal bargain marginalised women like her, but her feminism has lived on to inform and challenge the thinking of a later generation as to the proper, and protective, role of the state (Allen 1994; Roe 1983).

Catherine Helen Spence

The outstanding public intellectual from foundation days was probably South Australian Catherine Helen Spence (1825–1910). Unlike Scott, Spence was an enthusiastic federalist. She earned the distinction of being Australia's first woman political candidate when she stood for the Federal Convention in 1897. From the prize-winning biography by Susan Magarey (1985), we learn that Spence came late to feminism, in the 1890s, and when finally drawn to the cause, proudly announced,

'I am a New Woman and I know it.' Spence was proud, too, of the South Australian experiment in free colonisation, though by the 1880s she feared it had gone off track. By then, the causes dearest to Spence's heart were Unitarianism and 'effective voting'. She was a preacher in both causes, but her most public preoccupation was perfecting democracy, as she saw it, by proportional voting and the Hare–Clark system. Like Scott, she was largely forgotten after her death in 1910, except in South Australia; but she too was ahead of her time. Her significance here is that she saw structural weaknesses in the emerging Australian Way, later addressed – though only in Tasmania – in accordance with her particular prescriptions.

David Unaipon

Another South Australian of significance was feeling his way towards a more inclusive world in the 1900s. The mission-born Aboriginal intellectual David Unaipon (1872–1967), who now appears on the Australian fifty-dollar note, was by then preaching his version of Aboriginal advancement. His message was too gradualist for the 1930s radicals who mounted the Day of Mourning in Sydney in 1938, but his personal achievements and his faith in inclusiveness have since won respect and recognition; and it is clear that no one prescription will be enough to liberate Aboriginal Australia.[10]

Prospects

It may seem strange that what began as a quest for the social dynamic of the Australian Way has led to five distant biographies. Historians telling stories again perhaps? Not at all. Foundations are the work of founders, not abstract forces; and Australian historians increasingly look to biography and culture for answers to the big questions. With the five people portrayed, we have the archetypal liberal social policy-maker, a pioneer of industrial arbitration, a strong feminist voice, the country's most ardent democratic theorist, and a brilliant black man with a high-flown dream of harmony. In each case I have tried to indicate ways in which recent research has offered not some static celebration of past achievers, but a sense of creative lives and unfinished work. Ahead lies the prospect of an entirely new historical synthesis, particularly evident in the new interest in a range of ethical impulses, but also diverse preoccupations due to differences of class, gender and race. Altogether, I suggest, the biographies indicate something expansive and enriching about the construction of the Australian Way, especially compared with the static and anachronistic notion of a Settlement.

By way of conclusion, I reiterate the observation from 'Social Policy and the Cultural Cringe' that too often these days what passes for the story of the welfare state in Australia is related more to best international practice than to the aspirations and achievements of the Australian people, painfully qualified as these may be. This chapter has emphasised that the Australian Way has been a narrow way – too narrow in several respects – but never a closed way. It has been widened before and so it may be again.

Notes

1 'Clergy condemn Coalition IR policy', *Sydney Morning Herald*, and report, ABC 1 o'clock news, 22 February 1996; 'How Sydney became Asia's middle-class sweatshop', *Sydney Morning Herald* (Spectrum), 18 November 1995 and subsequent letters to the editor, 23 November 1995. The living wage has since been supplanted by the more limited American minimum-wage approach.
2 Detail and references are in Roe (1997).
3 Public Law 104–193, Personal Responsibility and Work Opportunity Act; 'State Welfare Demonstrations' Fact Sheet 1996.10.7 [www.os.dhhs.gov. etc] and 'Clinton and Welfare', *New York Review of Books*, 28 November 1996, p. 65. See Robert Birrell (1995: 257) for a late Federation example of opposition to American individualism.
4 On emerging generational inequities see e.g. Thomson and Tapper (1993: 20–3). The fear seems misplaced, since it rests on a proposition regarding the long-run operation of social insurance schemes: Mitchell (1991: ch. 9).
5 There can be little doubt that the so-called Hanson debate has exposed resentments in depressed regions and where the dismantling of protective structures has hurt most.
6 Matt. 5: 14, 'Ye are the light of the world. A city which is set on a hill cannot be hid'.
7 'Deakin, Alfred', *Australian Dictionary of Biography*, vol. 8 (R. Norris).
8 Benjamin Kidd (1858–1916); the review is signed 'D.A' but the copy in the Deakin Papers, National Library of Australia, MS 1540/5/667, is corrected in Deakin's hand.
9 Ryan, p. 84. Another interpretation of Wise as a free trade intellectual is given in Melheuish (1995: 30–1); see also Kingston (1988: 97, 273–4, 299).
10 'Unaipon, David', *Australian Dictionary of Biography*, vol. 12 (Philip Jones).

CHAPTER 5

Remaking the Australian Way
The Keynesian Compromise

Paul Smyth

In her account of the Australian Way of doing social policy in Chapter 4, Roe refers to it as a 'middle way', a term usually referring to that welfare state fusion of capitalism and socialism which characterised West European postwar political economies (see also Marshall 1972). It is the end of that fusion – whether cast in terms of the breakdown of 'the Keynesian welfare state', or, more latterly, 'the Fordist paradigm'[1] – which is typically taken as the historical context of the public policy crises facing such countries today (Miliband 1994; Amin 1994). Curiously, in Australia, the historical reference point has not been understood as the postwar middle way but as the turn-of-the-century Australian Settlement. This chapter argues that Australia is not the exception which this account proposes. The Australian Way was fundamentally reshaped in the 1940s within a Keynesian political economy, and it is the breakdown of this political economy which is the real frame of our current social and economic policy dilemmas.

The Australian Settlement

Paul Kelly's account of the Australian Settlement will be familiar from other chapters in this book. This chapter shares, and will not repeat, the critique of the very idea of 'a settlement' developed by Roe, Maddox and Pixley in Chapters 3, 4 and 9; it seeks to establish the Keynesian welfare state as a second, and arguably the most profound, reworking of the Australian Way in the twentieth century. It should be emphasised that Kelly's was not a work of history but a record of politics in the 1980s. If we seek support for the thesis in the wider research literature, Francis Castles's interpretation of Australian social policy in terms of a 'wage-earners' welfare state' presents itself as the prime candidate. Initiated with the book *The Working Class and Welfare* (1985), this interpretation emerged in a period of economic and political writing not given to broad historical characterisations of Australia's political economy, which may help explain its pervasive influence (Capling and Galligan 1992). Castles's book might be read as a contribution to that continuing puzzle of the Australian Way: a triumph to some, a failure to others (Roe 1976). Castles's book initiated the most sustained interpretation in terms of welfare failure. He saw in the minimum wage and residual income support systems legislated in the New Protection policies at the beginning of the century the historical key to Australia's failure to develop a more expansive welfare system in later years. Australia's early economic modernisation and evolution of democratic political processes had combined to present the Australian working class with an opportunity to achieve significant reform a generation earlier than their European counterparts. The resulting historic compromise with capital left a pattern of wage-earners' welfare which was basically undisturbed until the Whitlam years. This original interpretation has not passed without criticism within Australian social policy scholarship – and certain revisions by Castles himself[3] – but it has been accorded a central place in Australian writing on social policy, especially because of the connections made between welfare and economic policies.

In a subsequent work, *Australian Public Policy and Economic Vulnerability* (1989), Castles reoriented his account in the context of the economic restructuring of the 1980s, in a way which more directly paved the way for the idea of an Australian Settlement. With the undoing of tariff protection in the 1980s, he believed, Australia's traditional approach to welfare was now unsustainable. His new account placed greater emphasis on the historical role of the tariff in achieving a measure of closure of the economy to external economic shocks. Welfare via the wage system, he believed, had been dependent upon tariff protection as a viable program for social security. Buttressed by the control of the labour supply through the White Australia policy, this set of policies formed a coherent strategy which he termed 'domestic defence'. The lessons of the 1980s were plain. Tariff closure was not an option for a small economy seeking international competitiveness. As Kelly would write, Fortress Australia was finished. For economic reasons, integration into what Castles called the self-regulating market was essential. Australia, he thought, should adopt a domestic compensation strategy in the manner of certain small European corporatist states. These had managed to combine successfully an economy open to international competition with an elaborate package of social insurance and social wage measures, as well as labour-market programs designed to cushion the impact of economic fluctuations (Castles 1988: 38, 162).

Given the importance of Castles's work to the Australian Settlement thesis, two critical features of his argument for a welfare state beyond protection bear further scrutiny. First, it is apparent that Castles maintains a narrow understanding of the role of social policy in terms of redistribution. Second, his account displays an underdeveloped sense of the interdependence of welfare and economic policy beyond the wage and welfare nexus.

Castles argues that the only legitimate scope for social intervention in the economy lies in the realm of redistribution. Thus his preferred social amelioration model 'accepts the logic of the market up to and including the point of the distribution of incomes and wealth and seeks to modify it thereafter'. The role of successful social policy, he implies, is 'to tame capitalism by compensating the poor and weak for the inevitable dislocation caused by economic competition' (Castles 1988: 106, 108). This exclusive concern with redistribution appears to drive the analysis of the wider pattern of economic policy, and in particular excludes consideration of the social policy implications of the Keynesian revolution in economic policy. Thus he proposes that the Great Depression raised no question-marks over the basic thrust of economic policy. He writes: 'Certainly, the strategy of domestic defence came out of the depression unscathed, for tariff protection seemed to have worked at a macro-economic level by revivifying manufacturing industry and restoring employment levels, and employers were, at last, won over to the virtues of the arbitration system' (Castles 1988: 137).

Second, he simply asserts the irrelevance of postwar Keynesianism to the development of the welfare state. Thus he writes of the hold of the 'post-Federation historic compromise' in Australian public policy:

> For the generation of politicians who guided Australia into the postwar era, the fundamentals of that compromise were, moreover . . . part of the very fabric of the Australian political culture; a political culture which was as much a product of economic and political forces and their freezing through institutional encapsulation as it was now itself a force constraining the future directions of economic and political change. Throughout the long reign of Sir Robert Menzies . . . it was the older pattern of response, rather than the newer Keynesian welfarism, which was the dominant influence shaping public policy. [Castles 1988: 143]

Of course, Castles is in many ways merely representative of mainstream social policy research in identifying social policy with 'strategies of redistribution' and ignoring ways in which it has been central to postwar policies of economic management (Mishra 1984; Smyth 1994). However, the elision of the Keynesian period has major consequences for the present. If the foundation of Australian social policy in economics has in fact been tariff protection, and if this has become accepted as a demonstrable hindrance to economic growth rates, then the conclusion looms that it is time that Australians accept the logic of the market up to the point of distribution. Indeed, according to Castles, there has been nothing in our economic policy history to support social policy interventions beyond redistribution. This is reflected in his conclusion that: 'The succession of economic policy-makers who, since the fall of the Whitlam Government, have gone hopefully to the nation's economic cupboard, have found, like Old Mother Hubbard, that it was much emptier than they might have hoped or expected' (Castles 1988: 158).

Castles's work is not, of course, the exclusive source of the idea of an Australian Settlement. For example, the wage-earners' welfare state has more recently been joined in historical political economy by a rather unfortunate twin: the 'protective state' (Capling and Galligan 1992; Pons 1994). These accounts cannot be canvassed here. Needless to say, a protective state in the economic sphere complemented by a domestic defence strategy in the social sphere appear to provide an ample foundation for the Fortress Australia thesis. Little wonder that even an author with a clear sympathy for aspects of the social ideals of the Australian Settlement, such as Kelly, could find little in our public policy past to guide us into globalisation other than paternalistic counselling for our feelings of inferiority and insecurity, together with vague gestures towards the need for some social justice to temper the rigours of life in the international marketplace. For economic rationalists, of course, as Emy noted, the failures of protectionism 'provided the intellectual explosives to mine the tariff walls and overwhelm "the special interests" benefitting from the whole culture of protectionism' (1993: 16).

The Keynesian Compromise

Elsewhere I have explored in detail the postwar political and cultural developments in Australia which contributed to our Keynesian amnesia (Smyth 1994). To similar purpose, Matzner and Streeck write in relation to the practice of postwar economics, 'the constants in Keynesianism . . . represented central pillars of the real world and the life experience of a generation of economists and political decision-makers; as such, they were 'eliminated from the realm of the theoretically or practically remarkable' (1991: 2). For that generation, they continue, the world of the postwar Settlement after 1945 constituted 'a natural, rational, self-evident order'. With the passing of the postwar economic Golden Age, however, its characteristics have become indeed both theoretically and practically remarkable.

Given the concern of this book with rethinking the relationships between the state, the market and civil society, this section highlights the truly remarkable way in which the emergence of the Keynesian welfare state fundamentally recast these relationships in the 1940s. At stake is the central issue of the proper role of social policy: what things are best done collectively and what things are best left to individuals? As we have just seen, the Australian Settlement perspective delivers the general proposition that wealth-creation is best left to individual decision-making in the marketplace while the role of social policy is confined to 'protection' or 'compensation', that is, matters to do with distribution and redistribution. Above all, the significance of the Keynesian legacy rests on its claim that the sum of welfare can be increased if collective intervention is extended beyond redistribution into the sphere of wealth-creation.

Space permits only a gesture towards the significance of this shift in the 1940s. The Australian Settlement thesis counterposes today's 'uncertainty' with the 'protection' afforded by the Settlement. I argue that it would be better contrasted with the regime of social security which commenced at the end of the World War II. This term *social security* was the political talisman of that period in the way that New Protection was at the beginning of the century. To begin to understand the shift in Australia's social policy regime wrought by the Keynesian welfare state, we need only to look at the change in thinking which occurred during the deliberations of the Joint Parliamentary Committee on Social Security established early in the war years: according to Hasluck (1952), it moved from an emphasis on the planning of social security (as in social welfare) to the need for economic planning in order to achieve social security. In this way, Keynesianism emerged as the basis of postwar social security, and it is to the loss of the Keynesian framework that we must primarily attribute our current 'uncertainties'.

In this respect, it is notable that the beginnings of a recovery of Australia's Keynesian legacy has emerged among social policy researchers (for examples, see Watts 1987; Smyth 1994; Cass and Freeland 1994). Bettina Cass headed the federal government's review of social security in the late 1980s, which emphasised the need for active rather than passive welfare. This 'active society' framework was, of course, heavily dependent on the need for job creation, and in this context Cass's later work with Freeland (1994: 228) reminded us of the interdependence of full employment and social welfare in postwar social policy. Indeed, they argued, Keynesianism should be seen as a second 'historic compromise': 'The commitment to full employment and expansionary public investment policies ... represented a Keynesian development of the tradition of state intervention, effected in the name of equity and a "New Order".'

The return of high unemployment at the end of the 1980s, and the subsequent bout of employment policy analysis inspired by the federal government's White Paper, *Working Nation* (1994), also fuelled interest in the decades of full employment after World War II. Here the work of Langmore and Quiggin was exemplary. In *Work for All*, they emphasised that in economic policy terms this was 'a truly exceptional period of history'. The 1945 White Paper, *Full Employment in Australia*, they argued, 'was the defining document of economic policy for the thirty years between 1945 and 1975' (Langmore and Quiggin 1994: 57). The Keynesian period was marked by a historic acceptance of the idea that governments could and should act to maintain demand at full employment levels. Further, they said that this new government mandate rested on a Keynesian social contract which involved a commitment to a just distribution of productivity gains through the wage system and through the social wage. The centrality that Langmore and Quiggin ascribe to full employment in postwar economic policy, together with the proposition that it embodied a social contract, are enough to suggest the outlines of a second historic compromise in twentieth-century Australian public policy.

Any reinstatement of the Keynesian chapter in Australian social policy raises the question of continuities and discontinuities with the Australian Settlement. Continuities have already been noted in this book. In Chapter 4, for example, Roe suggests that the discontinuities suggested by the middle way, the compromise of capitalism and socialism forged in postwar Western Europe in the 1940s, were less pronounced in Australia because 'the practice if not the phrase' had had 'a resonance and vitality for much longer'. In Chapter 10, Bell also stresses continuity. Keynesian macro-economic policy was overlaid on existing micro-economic policies. Cass and Freeland (1994) too emphasise continuity; they see the second compromise as a reworking of, rather than a rupture with, the New Protection. I argue that these interpretations underestimate discontinuity. If Langmore and Quiggin are correct that full employment became the defining policy doctrine of the three decades following World War II, then the possibility emerges that the Keynesian welfare state did not extend the post-Federation parameters of public policy, but radically rearranged those parameters within a new pattern of public policy.

Even a cursory reading of economic history quickly persuades us of the magnitude of the shifts in policy practice which the new economic management inaugurated. Thus Dyster and Meredith introduce their discussion of policies in war and reconstruction with the assessment that they represented 'the swiftest changes in economic practice ... that Australia has seen in this century. Powers created in wartime secured full employment without inflation, and continued into peacetime in the hope that the dismal days of the Great Depression could be banished forever. It took the calamity of full-scale war to overcome the calamity that preceded it' (1991: 173–97).

The economic role of government was transformed, they write, as new uniform national income tax powers provided the opportunity for central economic management for the first time in our history. Equally momentous, in the light of the Great Depression and future employment policy, was the development of full central banking powers within the Commonwealth Bank, with a charter specifying full employment as an object of monetary and banking policy. A whole raft of federal policy measures – in areas such as economic infrastructure, industry and construction, education and labour markets, research and development, and housing – could be easily catalogued to show that the arrival of federal powers of economic management was accompanied by a period of major public policy innovation.

Simply to note the speed and quantity of new policy initiatives is perhaps insufficient to convey the sense in which Keynesianism signalled a radical transformation of Australian public policy. These initiatives have to be understood in the context of the revolutionary shifts in economic theory upon which they were premised. It should be observed here that the radical agenda of Keynesian theory has often been overlooked because of the subsequent harmonisation of Keynesianism with the neoclassical system in the mid-1950s (see Smyth 1994; Battin 1997). For our purpose, the sense in which Keynesianism represented a fundamental break with the past has been well explained by Whitwell (1995).

Whitwell emphasises that Keynesianism brought a new way of envisioning economic life, switching the emphasis from a micro-economic focus on cost and price to a macro-economic emphasis on output levels and a belief that overall demand could be managed at a level sufficient to maintain full employment. Keynes (as well as other economists in the period) encouraged a reconception of economic decision-making, in which a new emphasis was placed on the psychological, sociological and political factors influencing the expectations of individuals (see Smyth 1994). The integration of these factors into economic analysis not only indicated why real-world economies might fall short of full-employment equilibrium states, but also provided the rationale for a degree of 'socialisation' of economic decision-making if full employment was to be achieved.

It should be apparent that these propositions represented a radical departure from prior practice. The previous regime may have allowed scope for governments to be involved in distributing wealth and income for social purposes, but it insisted that the free market was the optimum vehicle for wealth-creation. Now, a second logic of economic organisation had been installed together with the market, in the recognition – to paraphrase D. B. Copland, the leading contemporary Australian economist – that the enterprise of private enterprise is not enough to achieve full employment without positive and continuing action by government.

The discontinuity represented by the Keynesian innovations becomes more obvious when we consider their implications for social policy. Social policy moved from a subordinate or dependent role on the market economy to one in which market and government became partners in production. Over and above individual profit-seeking, production might also have social purposes; hence the idea of a mixed economy. These implications were not lost on contemporaries. As H. C. Coombs wrote at the time: 'It was characteristic of the pre-war environment that the economic activity conducted was largely the result of decisions by individuals; goods and services were largely produced because individuals saw in them the opportunity for profit.' While there had been exceptions to this rule, he continued, in terms of education, public works and certain community services, these were 'frequently judged from the social point of view after the event, there was no machinery by which they were influenced by social factors beforehand' (Coombs 1944: 8–9). The measure of economic democracy in relation to volume and direction of investment legitimated under the rubric of the necessity for full employment represents the most striking public policy departure under Keynesianism.

If it is the emergence of the concept of the mixed economy which radically distinguishes the powers of the Keynesian welfare state from those of its predecessor, the argument for discontinuity does not rest only on the novelty of those new powers of economic management. The roles of the old instruments of social policy were redefined within the new regime. The income support system, for example, remained characteristically residual; but this was the flipside of the new emphasis on full employment in a properly managed economy as the royal road to social security. In relation to the old minimum wage, full employment promised the substance of a living wage. Moreover, Keynesian arguments enhanced the role of the wage system as an instrument of egalitarianism because they proposed that a more even spread of purchasing power was necessary to maintain demand. Langmore and Quiggin show further how wage policy was reworked within the new regime: if sustained high investment was not to be undone by inflation, then new social criteria were needed in terms of wages and prices; hence their reference to an implicit social contract.

So far in this section I have emphasised those elements in the economic theory and social policy of the period that most clearly distinguish the new regime from its predecessor. There is another, internationally focused literature more concerned with the postwar Golden Age which emphasises Australia's comparative failure to develop institutional strength in economic management (see Dow 1992; Bell 1997a). Whether Australian Keynesianism was strong or weak is an argument for another place. Either way, it should not diminish the case for discontinuity with what came before or after. Today's economic rationalism is not continuous with the postwar approach. We need only consider that proposals for full employment that we would regard as substantial and difficult to achieve in our own time (for examples, see Langmore and Quiggin 1994; Commission for the Future of Work 1996b; Nevile 1996; Dow 1996; Battin 1997; Manning *et al.* 1997) would require much less change than that which occurred in the 1940s.

The debate about the relative strength and weakness of Keynesianism in different countries is important for our purposes in so far as it highlights the importance of national political contexts. Writing of the emergence of Fordist regimes internationally, Lipietz, observes that the Keynesian economic policy dimension necessitated that 'armistices or compromises' were struck in the political domain (1994: 338–41). In Chapter 3, Maddox criticises the Australian Settlement's anaemic, consensual rendering of Australian political thought, and in Chapter 4 Roe protests at its static and anachronistic features. Indeed, it is somewhat incredible that any account of today's 'uncertainty' could ignore the unravelling of the politics of the Cold War which dominated the postwar period. In Australia, as in any comparable country, the Keynesian welfare state or middle way represented an armistice or compromise in the mid-century global contest of capitalism and socialism.

The political freeze of the Cold War was, of course, a feature of Australian politics from the 1950s, but the ideological lines were drawn in the 1940s in the contest over Keynesianism. The novel political demands of a Keynesian regime were not lost on contemporaries. Full employment, according to L. F. Giblin, would require 'the rebuilding of democracy from its foundations' (1943: 5). With the onset of peace, according to E. R. Walker, 'full employment and a more complete system of social services' had become policy imperatives for any political party (1947: 341), but there agreement ended. What was at stake was whether the so-called mixed economy would 'evolve radically in the direction of complete socialism, or would continue to offer a field for private investment'. The 1945 *White Paper on Full Employment* is best read as an attempt to chart a political settlement between free enterprise and socialism at a time when the viability of any middle road was unknown. Battin (1996) and Coombs (1984) rightly emphasise that it was the Labor Party which enjoyed the ideological initiative in the new policy settlement; through its fusion of traditional socialist ideals and Keynesianism, it shifted the policy environment to an acceptance of the imperatives mentioned by Walker.

In Chapter 6, Battin stresses that what Labor was attempting to achieve through the Keynesian initiatives embodied in the White Paper has to be understood in the light of its demonstrably larger ambitions to secure more direct economic controls and extend the nationalisation of industries (see also Smyth 1994). Battin presents these larger ambitions in terms of *social democracy*, which he believes underpinned Australian Keynesianism. I believe the contemporary usage, *democratic socialism*, is preferable because it signifies the more dynamic political environment suggested by Walker, in which the economic debate was framed in terms of free enterprise versus socialism, and the viability of a stable middle way had yet to be fashioned.

At the same time, it is also important to emphasise the positive contribution of Australian liberalism to the philosophical underpinnings of the Keynesian Settlement. Battin's historical analysis is concentrated on the 1940s when for most of the decade the role of non-Labor was largely negative. Bell (1993) also inclines towards a negative view of the role of the business community; he judges that it welcomed government assistance while rejecting interference in its prerogatives. These negative judgements underestimate the positive turn towards state economic planning among liberals in the late 1940s and early 1950s. If the ideological conversion to the mixed economy came more slowly among liberals, in the hands of politicians like Menzies and intellectuals like Copland and Eggleston it was none the less creative. Australian liberals evolved an increasingly positive, Deakinite reading of full employment: they endorsed the doctrine as a means of enabling individuals to participate in the life of the community while leaving co-operation with government economic plans up to the free choice of the individual (see Smyth 1994). Indeed, Australian liberalism was more at home with the limited, indirect measures of economic control contained in the 1945 White Paper – which ultimately provided the parameters of what Battin terms the watered-down Keynesianism of the 1950s and 1960s – than was Australian labour.

Australian labour, as Rawson (1958) has pointed out, moved further to the Left in the 1950s in the circumstances of the split in the Labor Party. This had the effect of marginalising those like Heinz Arndt (1956) and Lloyd Ross (1953) who were proposing to adapt or compromise traditional socialist ideals to the realities of the Keynesian mixed economy along the lines of the welfare state models emerging in New Fabianism in the United Kingdom and in Swedish social democracy. It was perhaps in keeping with its comparatively radical approach to economic democracy in the 1940s that Australian labour argued that real gains for the working class would come through advancing democratic controls over the economy, not through welfare measures, and that the more important objective was to secure the full-employment policy regime.

Thus Jim Cairns argued that the history of the Australian welfare state demonstrated the overriding significance of full employment for the working class. An examination of changes in workers' living standards over time showed, he wrote, that until World War II 'the great efforts that have gone into building the welfare state have not made much difference'. Only with the achievement of full employment had there been a significant shift in favour of workers. However, full employment remained a fragile gain under the terms of the Keynesian Settlement. Inflation was, according to Cairns, the 'Achilles' heel of the welfare state' especially in an economy exposed to large price fluctuations as a result of its heavy dependence on international trade. The defeat of inflation and the maintenance of full employment, he believed, ultimately required the socialisation of the volume and direction of investment (Cairns 1957: 356, 363–5).

If labour's commitment to Australia's Keynesian Settlement could only be described as provisional compared with the less ambiguous commitments of Australian liberalism, there is nonetheless no doubt that the Keynesian welfare state fundamentally recast the pattern of Australian public policy. 'We are all planners now', wrote J. G. Crawford, secretary of the Department of Trade in the late 1950s (1959: 45–7). The role of government could no longer be that of a passive keeper of the ring. Its role, he said, was to determine the nation's social objectives such as full employment – and devise a total plan or compromise to achieve them within the limits of a free society. The role did not entail detailed planning, he continued, but required government first to achieve a climate of opinion that the objectives were attainable; second, to act as a helmsman keeping the economy on course; and third, to provide the welfare services and economic infrastructure without which industrial objectives could not be achieved. Government and industry, he concluded, now had a complementary relationship. Crawford spoke with authority. Legitimated by the success of Keynesian management, his generation of economists had come to occupy the heights of the bureaucracy and were seen by contemporaries as 'statesmen in disguise'.

Conclusions

Recognition of the Keynesian welfare state as a second historic compromise in twentieth-century Australian public policy points up the breathtaking naivety of those who have identified our history of government economic intervention with protection as a prelude to the economic revival they anticipate from the liberation of market forces. The contrast should not be with trade protection but with the regime of Keynesian economic management installed precisely because of the perceived failure of the market to deliver sustained economic growth. The theoretical arguments for the market today differ little in substance from those discredited in the Keynesian revolution.

The implications of the Keynesian compromise go beyond economic arguments narrowly conceived. Positive, as opposed to passive, economic governance is as much a political as an economic achievement. It requires a political compromise, if not consensus, which can underpin a positive role for government, establish agreed social objectives, and ensure the support of economic actors. The foundation of the Keynesian welfare state reminds us of the extent to which today's economic libertarianism is disconnected from the positive notions of government and social co-operation embedded in both our major political traditions, liberalism and democratic socialism. Further, the Keynesian period offers a record of extraordinary governmental innovation and bureaucratic achievement in putting into effect a consensus on full employment which contrasts starkly with the negative images of government spawned by the post-protectionists and the new managerialism which their scenario has encouraged.

In terms of policy substance, the Keynesian compromise reminds us of the priority accorded economic stability and growth in the Australian Way in social policy. The post-protectionist argument for a free market with a package of welfare compensation could hardly be more removed from a bipartisan tradition enshrined in the 1945 *White Paper on Full Employment*. If Australian social policy was exceptional in comparative terms, it was precisely in terms of the priority accorded employment over welfare. The goal of full employment may well be defined differently today but an Australian post-Keynesian perspective points away from 'domestic compensation': not, of course, towards a revival of protection, but towards a social security grounded in new institutions of economic democracy.

Finally, to recognise in the Keynesian welfare state a second historic compromise in Australian public policy is to dispense with exaggerated notions of Australian exceptionalism encouraged by the post-protectionists. The Keynesian perspective shows that the second policy settlement reached in Australia was, by and large, typical of other historic compromises reached throughout the industrialised world at the close of World War II. Today the same countries face the same challenges of high unemployment and growing inequality. The significance of the Keynesian heritage in a globalising economy is a theme taken up in following chapters.

Notes

1 For some, Keynesianism was implicated in a larger phenomenon of Fordism. The latter refers to much more than a form of economic policy, or even the politics of economic policy. Fordism is, rather, an attempted characterisation of a whole epoch of economic, social and political development. It links the mass consumption associated with Keynesianism to the mass production facilitated by the production techniques associated with the name Henry Ford. These in turn are related to a certain societal paradigm within which the welfare state political compromises of the middle of the century played a key part (see Amin, 1994).

2 As a class-based analysis it has been said to fail in terms of capturing the multi-dimensionality of power relations (Cass and Freeland 1994; Pixley 1996). Others seek to balance Castles's stress on the policy initiative of the labour movement with a much more positive account of the role of the Deakinite liberals in creating the terms of the compromise (Birrell 1995). More seriously, the underlying premise of welfare failure informing the model has been rejected by others (Roe 1993; Cass and Freeland 1994). They emphasise the redistributive potential of the Australian welfare system, its openness and flexibility as a categorical system and its virtual moral unassailability. These factors, together with its cheapness, have increasingly been argued to be comparative assets at a time when the European insurance-based systems are being criticised as obstacles to economic flexibility. Indeed, Castles's most recent work reflects an acceptance of this type of critique (Castles 1994).

CHAPTER 6

Unmaking the Australian Keynesian Way

Tim Battin

In the late 1970s and the 1980s it was a commonplace preoccupation of the Right to decry Keynesianism as the cause of economic ill, while today the same protagonists have seemingly won an ideological struggle so comprehensively that they bother to pour cold water on Keynesian ideas only when the occasional need arises. In challenging some of the ideas of the 1980s and 1990s, the present chapter shares in a growing international dissent, expressed in the United Kingdom by Will Hutton in *The State We're In*, and in the United States by John Eatwell in *Global Unemployment*. Specifically, this chapter argues that the broad Keynesian policy direction followed during the postwar boom, to the extent it was actually followed, was the source of economic and social prosperity in the form of secure employment, and would have given Australians even greater prosperity had Keynesian policy been pursued along the lines set down by the immediate postwar reconstructionists in and around the Chifley government. The first section makes preliminary observations about the historical significance of the Keynesian revolution, highlighting the connection between the economic and the social. The second section proposes that Keynesianism came under attack for essentially political reasons, and that charges of inherent weakness in Keynesian economic policy have no reasonable foundation. The concern of the third section, then, is to advance an argument for Keynesian policy-making, and to propose that the Australian Way in economic policy-making bequeathed a valuable legacy. Underlying all three sections is a suggestion of why Keynesianism was undermined.

A Defence of Australian Keynesianism

The argument advanced here is that, in debating what mix of economic and social policies would be best for an advanced economy like

Australia, there is much to gain from looking at the reasons for the collapse of Australia's own version of Keynesianism in the 1970s. The concomitant retreat of social democracy in that period, and in the 1980s, betrays the *political* nature of the defeat of Keynesian thought, not its logical defeat. By this I mean that the explanations offered for the demise of the Keynesian mixed economy which point to the allegedly faulty economic foundations of Keynesianism vary between being mistaken on the one hand and deliberately misleading on the other. Among that which follows, therefore, is a mixture of a post-Keynesian and institutionalist defence of the mixed economy which was, until the 1970s and 1980s, a valued part of Australia's unique form of welfare.

None of this is to suggest that every feature of Australia's past forms of social protection are to be celebrated or that each and every one's passing is necessarily to be lamented. In Chapter 2, Cass reviews the features of this peculiarly Australian mix, and rightly argues that there were ineffectual aspects of Australia's social and economic policies in the so-called halcyon days of the 1950s and 1960s and that the philosophical assumptions apparently underlying some of these policies are not ones that most would, in any event, any longer accept. But, inasmuch as the policies of the postwar period failed to fulfil their promise, it might be argued that these were failures of compromising the political integrity of the Keynesian mixed economy – or so I would argue. As we will see, it was largely, though not wholly, the *compromised* nature of Keynesianism during the 1950s and 1960s which undermined it by the time the long boom came to an end in the mid-1970s. When the recession of 1974 began to bite, the erosion in Australia's economic institutional capacity made it more difficult than it otherwise would have been to deal with the rising unemployment of the time. Of course, the further assault on the mixed economy and social democracy in the 1980s and 1990s eroded institutions further, and has made the problem even more intractable – perhaps beyond solution.

The philosophical position adopted here, then, is neither Marxist nor neoliberal. The present (democratic socialist) analysis places itself apart from (Marxist-informed) claims that Australia never had thorough-going Keynesian institution-building and that the prerogatives of capital have never been transgressed; and places itself in opposition to particular kinds of liberal-orthodox arguments that Keynesianism was bound to fail as soon as it confronted its own contradictions and theoretical shortcomings. This analysis sees much to be gleaned from Australia's Keynesian experience. More specifically – and contrary to some Marxist claims – the immediate postwar reconstruction period stands as the crowning achievement of economic institution-building along Keynesian lines (see Battin 1993). True enough, in the 1945 to 1975 period Australia's record in building institutions appropriate to a vigorous mixed economy is not what all radicals, socialists, and social democrats would celebrate in unqualified terms; but, with equal certainty, it is fair to suggest that something of significant value must have disappeared if only because of the deploring, by a wide cross-section of society, of the shift in economic and social policies in the 1980s and 1990s.

One point to raise at this early stage is to observe the fundamentally different understandings of the relation between the economic and the social on the part of the Curtin and Chifley governments, on the one hand, and the Hawke and Keating governments, on the other. Particularly in the case of Chifley's government, social policy was envisaged as something which would complement full employment economic policy. It was in this sense that the two were seen as separate (though interrelated). The greater emphasis was never on social security simply because it was envisaged as something which would rarely be necessary. When Chifley used the metaphor 'palliatives' to describe social security measures, it was not to relegate social security policy to a lower status at all, but to recognise that such measures could only be effectual in a full-employment economy, and in this sense the social and the economic went hand in hand. As a keen student of the intellectual foundations of the welfare state, Chifley understood that the fiscal burden on the state would be brought to an absolute minimum in such an economy. As we will discover, this prescient recognition has been laid out for all to see in the 1980s and 1990s. The Hawke–Keating regime, by way of contrast, maintained a separation between the economic and social, but a distinction in no way similar to the distinction *and connection* that Chifley drew. The Hawke–Keating, or New Labor, understanding was built on an assumption that a free-market economy should be allowed maximum rein, and that social policy would be funded from a kind of largesse to be distributed *after* free-market economic processes had, more or less, run their course. To the governments of Curtin and Chifley, who understood economic policy as something which would serve *social* ends, such an idea was, quite simply, abhorrent.

The point in mentioning all of this is to reinstate an insight that has been overlooked: the Australian architects of full employment envisaged it not just as an economic policy, but as the foundation of social policy as well. It is no surprise, then, that social policy has been under increased attack since the collapse of full employment in the mid-1970s.

It is worth retracing the way in which the Keynesian consensus collapsed, to sketch briefly a theoretical perspective on how such a breakdown might be conceptualised, and by so doing, to combat some of the fallacies that abound concerning the supposed inefficacy of the Keynesianism of the postwar period.

The Political Attack on Keynesianism

Fundamental shifts like the transition from Keynesian to anti-Keynesian economic policy never have single causes (Battin 1997). Of course, one of the fashionable arguments in the recent past has been that international constraints are now of such an order that domestic policy-making of a Keynesian kind is no longer possible. I have not the scope to address such an argument here, but some readers will be pleased to know that this orthodoxy is now being challenged by international opinion (see Weiss 1997; Weiss and Hobson 1995; Weiss 1998; Hirst and Thompson 1996; Glyn 1995). None of this is to dismiss the traditional Left emphasis on the role of material interests. On the contrary, a contribution from the Left ought to have the role of powerful economic interests at the centre of an explanation of policy shifts; the point, however, is to explain how or why these interests are able to mobilise when they do (Bhaduri and Steindl 1985; Steindl 1989, 1993).

Certain individuals and, where relevant, the institutions they represent, are able to effect policy changes when a confluence of factors favours such change. The raw power of the interests themselves is not always enough to bring about change – or at least this is the case with the abandonment of the commitment to the Keynesian mixed economy. It is not enough to state that capital opposes full employment and consonant macro-economic policies. For one thing, when it is stated so baldly, it is not accurate. Full employment and the Keynesian means to achieve it were favoured by manufacturing sectors of capital in Australia, for instance. Finance capital, on the other hand, was another matter. As Bhaduri and Steindl (1985) have documented, the rise of monetarism followed the increase of power enjoyed by finance capital which began to occur in the mid-1960s. The profit-maximising potential for markets outside the then developed world, the surplus funds generated in OPEC countries, and the increased personal savings resulting in most OECD countries from the prosperity of the postwar boom all acted as preconditions. However, the fact that it took ten years or more for monetarism to take hold, and that it rapidly lost academic respectability, should suggest that some other factor (or factors) is relevant in explaining the significance of the movement from Keynesianism to monetarism, to neoliberalism.

In short, there also needed to be a change in ideas. And while it is accurate to observe that there were always those throughout the 1950s and 1960s who provided at least part of the intellectual framework to challenge the Keynesian mixed economy, it is still worth recalling that these were seen essentially as disaffected – until, that is, circumstances changed in the 1970s. While an economic framework which was ostensibly Keynesian delivered outcomes such as full employment and manageable inflation, the anti-Keynesians – although they represented powerful interests – had little chance of ideological success. Then as now, the representatives of interests advantaged by stagnant economic conditions and concomitant economic and social policies very seldom disinterestedly state what those interests are. For almost everyone, to admit to favouring unemployment rates of 9 or 10 per cent is simply out of the question. What must be added to a mobilisation of interests for a successful transformation of macro-economic policy is a change to the ways ideas are imparted, and, more importantly, to the ideas themselves. Where it was once respectable to believe, in the 1950s and most of the 1960s, that full employment was perfectly achievable, it then became commonplace to claim in the early 1970s that it was only possible under conditions of low inflation. Once increasing unemployment began to accompany the inflation of the middle and late 1970s, it became acceptable to argue, from the 1975 Hayden Budget on, for a causal connection between the two: inflation had to be reduced if there was to be any hope of restoring lower levels of unemployment. By the early 1980s, the expression of economic ideas had turned the optimism of the postwar reconstruction period completely on its head: it had, by that stage, become heretical to claim that full employment was possible at all – at least, by Keynesian means.

These claims and their counter-claims, of course, derive from the conflicting traditions within the economics discipline itself. It is worth considering in more detail how the Keynesian ideas which were once ascendant became widely regarded as defunct. A number of explanations present themselves. Not least among them is the proposal that Keynesian ideas, like any set of ideas, are accepted as satisfactorily underpinning policy formation as long as the consonant policies meet with enough success. As soon as this success falters, the philosophy buttressing the policies is likely to be questioned or, in exceptional circumstances, replaced. It is now a commonplace observation that Keynesianism came under most sustained attack after the stagflation of the mid-1970s, and that this attack began with the 1975 Hayden Budget.

There seems no point here in disputing the dating of the origins, but it is noteworthy, for the purposes of this analysis, that the change in ideas seemingly occurring in 1975 had as part of its background a fundamental misunderstanding of Keynesianism. The Budget speech by Hayden (1975) was typical of the times: 'We are no longer living in that simple Keynesian world in which some reduction in unemployment could, apparently, always be purchased at the cost of more inflation. Today, it is inflation itself which is the central policy problem. More inflation simply leads to more unemployment.'

A fundamental weakness in Keynesianism was not its theoretical position at all, but rather that many so-called Keynesians simply did not understand what constituted Keynesian economic theory. Hayden's understanding, for example, is replete with the notions associated with the Phillips curve interpolation, which, according to the theories of post-Keynesians and authentic Keynesians, is itself a gross misunderstanding of the relationship between unemployment and inflation.[1] It seems inescapable that the hegemony of neoclassical economic thought in Australia in the 1950s and 1960s is chiefly responsible for such large-scale misappropriation of Keynesian thought (Groenewegen and McFarlane 1990; Smyth 1994). This is the main focus for the next section, but first we come back to other explanatory factors proposed for the collapse of the Keynesian paradigm.

Hugh Stretton (1993) has made a valuable contribution to analysing the demise of Keynesian social democracy, especially in its Australian variant. He dismisses the notion that there has been a leaders' conspiracy. Yes, he says, the leadership of each major party has abandoned its respective traditions, but leaders do not conspire to achieve this outcome. It is their dramatic change of mind that needs to be explained. The reasons surveyed by Stretton are varied: there was some conservatising of the electorate by the very success of the mixed economy; alternative beliefs (both neoclassical and Marxist) about how the economy worked were far from discredited, although clearly not in the ascendancy; the costly Vietnam War is thought to have given rise to inflation; the power of economic departments within the bureaucracy (Pusey 1991) is believed by some to be pivotal; the OPEC oil-price shocks are thought to have placed enormous constraints on macro-economic management; the colonial cringe produced a determination that Australia had to replicate overseas policies; and, as already noted, there was the view that Australia had no choice because globalisation was coming. As Stretton has observed, there is something in most of these factors; but, even taken together, they cannot be seen as sufficient explanation of the breakdown.

Something as extensive as the abandonment of Keynesianism is best explained, I argue, by broadening the terms of reference to include the triad of interests, ideas, and institutions. The triangular model needs to be supplemented by a fourth factor of occasional shocks on the interaction between interests, ideas, and institutions already in place. This is a growing field of international scholarship, and the debate centres on the question of what relative emphasis is to be assigned to each of these agencies (see, for example, Hall 1989, 1992; Garrett 1993; Pontusson 1995; Hood 1994). Accepting the broad ambit of this model allows room for many or all of the determinants already mentioned to be considered as playing some part in the collapse of Keynesianism. One of its chief strengths is that it puts particular factors, such as the oil-price shocks of the 1970s, into their place. They are not insignificant, but their role should be seen as underscoring, rather than giving rise to, the changing interaction between ideas, economic interests (and their coalitions), and institutions.

The widespread nature of the collapse of full employment and spiralling inflation in the 1970s suggests that economic circumstances and economic interests are central to the picture. The fact that these conditions were not universal across the OECD, however, points also to the important role played by institutions in determining the economic performance of a country (Therborn 1986). But in asking how these institutions are built and in how powerful interests are resisted we come back to the role of ideas. If nothing else, ideas are central to how people conceive of their interests. Further, it would seem that not enough thought was given to this by the democratic Left from about the mid-1950s. More specifically, any failure of Keynesianism was a failure of many of its advocates to understand it thoroughly, and a failure to realise fully its political implications: a constant vigil against hostile ideas would be necessary to protect what Keynesianism stood for. Keynesianism did not fail because of inherent weaknesses in its theoretical and intellectual structure, and the remainder of this chapter is devoted to developing and defending this point.

Arguments for Keynesian policies

In the context of significant debate over the efficacy of current policies, the slightest hint of returning to Keynesian policy-making (even in its mild version) is enough to send contemporary orthodox economists and commentators into apoplexy. As the mainstay of their attack, they invariably invoke the past performance of Keynesianism. Leaving aside the observation that the economic performance of governments from 1945 to 1975 is vastly superior to those of the 1980s and 1990s, it is crucial to sort out what aspects of Australia's economic performance are to be correctly ascribed to Keynesianism and what ones are not. In some of the more reckless commentary, inflation is often ascribed to Keynesianism point-blank. (While it might be claimed by some critics of my position that one should not focus on the less reputable commentary of one's foes, such a focus is defended here on the grounds that it is precisely this kind of commentary which often holds greatest sway in the reproduction of ideas inimical to the Keynesian mixed economy.) A variant on this theme, witnessed in the debates surrounding *One Nation* (1992), and thence the Green and White Papers on unemployment (1993 and 1994), is that any return to government-led jobs growth is tantamount to 'throwing money at the problem' or 'making Mickey Mouse jobs'. Of course, when an attempt to find a solution to unemployment is represented in rhetorical terms such as these, the opponents of Keynesianism have already gained the upper hand. Similarly, a return to Keynesian policy is sometimes misrepresented as throwing money at unemployment, an action which will take us back to the days of inflation. As suggested above in reference to the 1975 Budget speech, this is a common misunderstanding, and perhaps it needs to be dealt with more seriously.

In Keynesian and particularly post-Keynesian theory, inflation comes about primarily because of the struggle over income share. In the absence of any constraint – institutional or otherwise – workers in trade unions will engage in activity to secure for themselves a share of the national income which they regard as fair. Keynes expounded on this, but his Polish contemporary (and an unsung genius of economic theory), Michal Kalecki, spent more time theorising on the institutional means to alleviate the tension. One of Kalecki's great contributions to the broad Keynesian–socialist tradition was to highlight the need for institutional control over the distribution of income. This was needed for two important reasons. First, control over the distribution of income afforded the government of the day the means to regulate demand much more effectively than is otherwise possible. Second, and directly following from this, inflation which arises both from cost-push *and* excessive demand pressures can be checked. Further elaborating each of these insights may serve to dispel some of the claims made against Keynesianism since the mid-1970s.

The importance of being able to regulate and manipulate demand goes beyond controlling inflation, and it cannot be overstated. Institutions such as the Conciliation and Arbitration Commission – and later the Industrial Relations Commission – gave Australian governments in the Keynesian era the means to control significantly the distribution of income. Some debate is possible over to what extent this facility was utilised (and what other means might have been used in addition), but there can be no doubt that, in Keynesian theory and practice, reduction of inequality of income was and is seen as crucial in controlling the level of economic activity. As a significant contributor to the Australian and comparative literature, Geoff Dow, has argued, other things being equal, the more equal the distribution of income in an economy, the greater the total level of economic activity (1996: 154). Conversely, a maldistribution of income makes it more difficult for a government or its central bank to gauge – much less manipulate – overall demand. Control over economic activity is crucial in determining policies that facilitate full employment. It allows government, for example, more accurately to anticipate the investment levels needed to enhance employment prospects. The belief that this was understood by the Chifley and, to a lesser extent, the Whitlam governments could be defended at length, but the more salient point to make at the moment is that, although the Prices and Incomes Accord was originally predicated on a more equitable distribution of income, its actual implementation eschewed and in some ways contradicted such initiatives. A cruel irony of Keynesian policy-making in Australia is that it was more blamed for Australia's economic ills the less it was practised. This is evident when it is realised that the Accord – the very kind of structure needed to allow for Keynesian management – was instituted precisely at the time that the Labor Party was abandoning any belief in such management.

So, when the inflation of the 1970s is attributed to Keynesian macroeconomics, there ought to be a sense of irony. The false ascription of inflation to the 'Keynesian' policies of the 1970s comes from at least two misunderstandings of institutional relationships: the first has to do with the bastard Keynesian muddle of the wages-unions-inflation nexus; the second has to do with the monetarist misconception of the link between government spending and inflation. Together, they each had a hand in falsely charging Keynesianism with errors not committed. We will presently see some empirical evidence for this, but first let us return briefly to a theoretical viewpoint.

The stance of Keynesian and post-Keynesian theory on inflation emphasises cost-push and political pressures. Inflation occurs, post-Keynesians argue, when there is a struggle over income share, and the institutional means of an incomes policy is needed. The bastard Keynesians misconstrued this as meaning that union wage-bargaining should be repressed as much as possible, while the monetarists emphasised a different form of inflation altogether. Monetarists, no longer as much in vogue as they were in the 1970s and 1980s, argue that the problem is the quantity of money in circulation. By their own extension of logic, they then go on to argue that it is *government* spending that is to be curtailed. One of the puzzles in the intellectual argument, then, is that the protagonists of each school are talking about different forms of inflation. This may not seem important until we realise that the confusion was often made, and acted upon, by those in influential positions in the 1970s, as is evidenced by the quotation from Hayden above, and in the 1980s and 1990s as well. The outlook adopted by Hayden and his advisers – and by almost every treasurer since – was dangerous and damaging because it conflated a number of contradictory beliefs, and misunderstood others. (Keynesians do not deny the reality of the inflationary effects of excessive demand; they simply hold that this is an issue only in times of boom or in extraordinary situations such as war.) The more general misunderstanding might only be a sad comment on Australian political history were it not that contemporary arguments against Keynesianism and consonant policies are no less confused. It highlights again why the power of ideas is significant in the collapse (or emergence) of a set of public policies.

On empirical grounds, neither the bastard Keynesian nor the monetarist positions can explain what actually occurred in the 1970s or the 1980s. The former position, to reiterate, holds that excessive wage demands are the chief source of inflation. (We have seen that, at the conceptual level, this can only be half-right, at best: a tug-of-war needs at least two antagonists.) At the empirical level, the Australian evidence of the 1970s and 1980s points to a brief period where there were real wage increases (1972–75); but this was typical of general patterns in the OECD, and was followed by a period of real wage decline (1975–79) which was almost unique to Australia. Taken as a whole, the 1970s was a period of below-average real wages growth in Australia (Dowrick 1991). The 1980s evidence sketches a similar picture. Taken as a whole, the 1980s represented a period of real (and nominal) wage decline (as well as a decline in wages share), and yet, leaving aside the former Yugoslavia, Australia had an inflation rate among the top six in the OECD. To the extent that inflation is caused by a grab for a greater share of income, someone other than, or in addition to, workers was grabbing it.

Of course, the post-Keynesians had always warned that institutional control over the distribution of income would be needed, not least because it provides a mechanism to alleviate the struggle over income. It also allows government to have a direct hand in striking a bargain in the relationship between the market wage and the social wage. This brings us to the other criticism of the Keynesian position: the monetarist attack.

In contrast to the bastard Keynesians, the monetarists emphasise government spending, not excessive wage demands, as the cause of inflation, and practising politicians have a mish-mash, or grab-bag, of causes. (According to monetarists, along with neoclassicals, excessive wage demands will lead to unemployment rather than inflation.) But here again, the empirical evidence does not support any of these claims. Australian governments have simply not been big spenders at any time since the late 1960s. Monetarism, as it was expressly stated in the early 1980s, has become quite discredited (even according to many of the orthodox), yet its logic lives on in other contemporary delusions. The current notion implicit in much economic commentary, for instance, of a non-accelerating inflation rate of unemployment, a floor rate of unemployment below which government cannot risk a more expansionary fiscal stance through a fear of inflation, attests some faith in at least some assertions of monetarist theory.

That the Australian economy does not currently face inflationary problems is obvious enough. However, its absence seems not to have quelled orthodox obsessions. Because of this, a contemporary Keynesian and progressive position must be entirely clear about the chief cause of inflation: the political struggle over shares of income. Accordingly, a contemporary Keynesian program would be based on establishing institutional control over the distribution of income, for the reasons already mentioned, and checking inflation, were economic policy to enable greater proportions of people to take up paid employment. Inflation is best checked by guaranteeing workers maintenance – and, where possible, growth – of real wages, and enhancement of the social wage. It is not checked by deflationary policies which work only after prolonged periods and only at the great cost of further unemployment. When there is institutional control over the distribution of income, cost-push pressures can be minimised, thereby reducing inflationary pressures. When institutional control over the distribution of income is abandoned, inflation can only be kept at a low level by using severely restrictive monetary policy. Yet it is precisely this institutional control which is being progressively abandoned in Australia.

Without much doubt, one of the major reasons the Labor Party lost the support of its own constituency in the 1996 election was that a large section of that constituency felt betrayed – most obviously by the Labor governments' inability to do anything about the growth of unemployment. In contrast to many of the public statements made by Labor figures suggesting that Labor's problem is one of a lack of communication (or, in less guarded parlance, that its traditional followers were too stupid to understand the imperatives of globalisation), it has to be said that Labor will not win back support from working people unless it demonstrates an ability to tackle unemployment and other blatant injustices. A number of scholars have devoted attention to this, and it is not the aim here to rehearse the detail of a full-employment project (see, however, Langmore and Quiggin 1994). What will be emphasised, however, is that Keynesian insights, far from being discredited, can be rescued.

None of this is to suggest that no serious mistakes were made by those who were avowed Keynesians in Australia's past. One error, for instance, was that Keynesianism became interpreted as fine-tuning, or simply managing demand, in an otherwise free-market economy. As suggested above, this was not the understanding of many of those who were influential during the reconstruction years, but it did become the received wisdom in the 1950s and 1960s. Macro-economic demand management does not constitute authentic Keynesianism. The Left Keynesians have a number of strings to their bow, one of which is the management of demand. From a micro-economic perspective, there is the crucial role of positive industry policy, a matter Green takes up in Chapter 12.

From some other perspectives, there has sometimes been a neglect or unwillingness to credit the Whitlam government with the attempt it made to convince the trade union movement of the importance of the social wage. Certainly, the social wage goes well beyond cash transfers and consumer spending, but it seems this may have been at least partly appreciated by the Whitlam government. There is, however, much power in the way perceptions are conveyed, and, as wrong as it may be, the perception has been conveyed that Keynesianism is tantamount to throwing money at unemployment and other social problems. Keynesian theory, by way of contrast, emphasises that demand is regulated, as we have seen, partly by an equitable distribution of income, and partly by government investment together with consumption expenditure. It is well documented that the level of Australia's public capital investment has been falling for two decades and is now alarmingly low (Dow 1996: 175).

To consider how the problem of falling investment may be overcome, we turn again to the work of Kalecki. His contribution in this matter was twofold. The first aspect was that he took seriously Keynes's declaration that there had to be a comprehensive socialisation of investment; independently, he came to much the same conclusion himself. The second was that this commitment should be institutionalised if we are to have *permanent* full employment. It would have to be institutionalised, Kalecki (1943) held, because the capitalist economy is inherently prone to boom and slump, and the government of the day would, in all probability, be tempted to neglect the measures needed to avert a slump. Kalecki was reluctant to prescribe what these institutions might be, but we are able to extrapolate a number of features which would be consonant with his vision. Ranging from the conservative to the radical, we can list features such as full-employment charters defended by central banks; earmarking of certain funds by government for investment purposes; allocation of funds by government-owned banks according to full-employment priorities; constitutional change giving central control over pricing and marketing; and, equal in their revolutionary nature, nationalisation of whole banking systems and the establishment of full employment investment boards that enjoy statutory authority. These are all characteristic of what would be needed in an institutionalised, full-employment economy.

If Australia's Keynesian past is to be criticised, let it be done with the knowledge that the more successful Keynesianism is to be, the more institutionalised a society's – or a polity's – commitment has to be. The Chifley government either seriously considered, pursued, or implemented every one of the features mentioned above. It is less well known that one of the more radical proposals to come before it, the establishment of a full-employment investment board, was included and seriously considered in the early drafts of the 1945 *White Paper on Full Employment* (Smyth 1994). One may engage in debates about why such an outcome did not occur, but the more relevant point, for the purposes of this discussion, is that liberal criticisms of Australia's Keynesian experience – whether made by avowed liberals and conservatives or by 'Labor liberals' – need to be seen in the context of the necessary changes that the socialist Keynesians were trying to achieve. The point is that many criticisms of Keynesianism made during the 1980s and 1990s have a temerity in not recognising the degree to which socialist Keynesians in the reconstruction years were thwarted in their aims. This is of paramount importance for an assessment of the economic performance of the Whitlam years and the reasons for the collapse of Keynesianism.

Conclusion

This chapter has canvassed a number of views on Australia's economic and social policy past, and, in particular, has focused on the misrepresentation of Australia's 'Keynesian' past. It has been falsely associated with the economic problems since the long recession of 1974 to the present; the more thoroughgoing attempts of the authentic Keynesians were either partly frustrated or defeated. It is true that new ways of finding solutions have to be discovered, but there is much value, too, in recovering those parts of Australia's economic and social policy that were carried out with skill. From this perspective, we will be in a position to see those aspects of economic and social policy that could be improved and, moreover, what theoretical stance will help policy-makers achieve such improvement. Without a sound theoretical basis, we can neither invent new solutions to old problems nor identify old-fashioned solutions still worth pursuing. Without a sound starting-point on the matter of socialisation of investment in the mid-1980s, for example, the debate over superannuation funds was almost no debate at all; because of the inaction of the then government, Australians may have squandered any hope to find an ideal source of funding for permanent full employment. The instance demonstrates once again the importance of the role of ideas, interests, and institutions in explaining widespread policy shifts. For what it is worth, the argument here has been that Keynesian and post-Keynesian theory offers us a deep matrix of suggestions about how economic and social problems are to be viewed, and that, far from being outdated, such a theoretical starting-point is relevant to tackling these problems in our own times.

Note

1 After A. W. Phillips published an influential article in 1958, there grew a received wisdom in the 1960s that there was a simple or virtuous relationship between inflation and unemployment, whereby the price of a little less unemployment was a little more inflation, and vice versa. This was a misappropriation of Phillips's findings, however. Phillips's study was based only on the UK and had relevance only in an economy where there was no possibility for institutional control over the distribution of income.

PART III

Public Institutions, Civil Society and Social Movements

CHAPTER 7

Public Sector Reform and the Australian Way
Lionel Orchard

Australian society and governing has always expressed a 'talent for bureaucracy' in A. F. Davies's famous phrase. This applies to the state development activities of the nineteenth century – what some have called an era of colonial socialism; to the Keynesian-inspired postwar reconstruction period; to the more tempered but no less significant public intervention of the Menzies era; and to the reforms of the Whitlam government. The public sector has always played a central and constructive role in Australian public policy. In the account by Paul Kelly (1992), a paternalistic state has been one important pillar of the Australian political settlement.

Since the mid-1970s, though, the public sector and bureaucracy in Australia have been under relentless examination and challenge. Governments of all political persuasions have set in train vigorous programs of bureaucratic and state reform, much of which has curtailed the role of the public sector in Australian society. The Hawke and Keating Labor governments (1983–96) undertook extensive reform in this area. Its first expression was a 'trilogy' of limits on taxation, deficit financing, and public spending and investment by the national government, introduced in 1984. Through the late 1980s and the first half of the 1990s, a whole series of changes to the organisation of the Australian bureaucracy were instituted under the umbrella of new managerialist approaches in public administration. Program budgeting, 'letting the managers manage', 'managing for results', emphasising outputs rather than inputs, centralising control over financial resources but decentralising the authority to deploy those resources, reducing hierarchy, rationalising the number of departments, and introducing commercial and corporate principles in some areas of government – these were the main dimensions of the changes (Boston and Uhr 1996; Schwartz 1994, and forthcoming).

In 1996 and 1997, the Howard Coalition government extended the application of private sector principles in the Australian public service, challenging the idea of permanent tenure and common pay-scales across the service. The Coalition government sought a more competitive public sector, with greater emphasis on contracting-out and benchmarking against best practice in the private sector (Reith 1996). Staffing cutbacks gathered pace as many people took up redundancy packages, a process which had started under Labor in the late 1980s (Steketee 1997a, b).

Some argue that the Labor government reforms represented 'a complete change in the geist of the Australian federal public service' (Schwartz, forthcoming). That change of geist, or ethos, has continued apace under Howard.

The Australian experience reflects the trends in many other Western democracies. The movement to reinvent government in the United States has sought a more streamlined, responsive and entrepreneurial bureaucracy, which 'steers rather than rows'. The proper role of government is to ensure that public goods and services are provided through a variety of market and local, communitarian means – steering the ship of state – rather than to do the provision – rowing – itself (Osborne and Gaebler 1992). The civil service reforms of the Thatcher government in the United Kingdom have involved internal managerialist reform, along with extensive privatisation and contracting with private business in areas of traditional public provision. Charters of responsibilities and expectations of government have been introduced (Self 1993). In New Zealand, the market model has been adopted more completely. Privatisation and contracting-out of government services to the private sector have been pursued with vigour (Boston *et al.* 1991).

The main purpose of this chapter is to give an account and assessment of the debates about the Australian public sector reforms, from the era of the Whitlam Labor government in the early 1970s to the Howard Coalition government. The weight and importance of the various ideas underpinning the reforms will be examined. The chapter also examines whether ongoing public sector reform on rationalist and managerialist principles is facing some policy and political limits, at least in Australia.

The Intellectual Catalysts for Change

There have been three main schools of thought on change in the Australian public sector and bureaucracy since the 1970s – social democracy, economic rationalism or public choice theory, and managerialism.

Social Democracy

The social democratic case for change in the role of public institutions in Australian society, at the national level at least, grew out of the ideas for social democratic reform of the 1960s and early 1970s and the experience of the Whitlam government in implementing them. Before the election of that government, there was considerable debate and ferment about the need for reform in Australian society, much of which stressed the role of the public sector in addressing problems in a range of new ways. The Whitlam government established new institutions to implement new ideas and programs in many areas – social, urban, education, health and legal, among others. At risk of oversimplification, the reforms of that period used the power of central government to deal with a range of social needs and problems, and to open and democratise existing approaches to policy and administration at all levels of government in Australia.

The problems experienced with the reforms of that time led many intellectuals associated with the effort to reflect on the causes of those problems and what should be done about them. Many highlighted the difficulties posed by traditional approaches to public administration and its inherently conservative character, themes reflected in the influential report of the Coombs Royal Commission into the Australian public service published in 1976. One of the key intellectuals associated with the Whitlam reforms, Peter Wilenski (1980), argued, against the Marxist Left, that while public institutions and government action were an important vehicle of Left reform, change was required. The bureaucracy needed to be 'responsive and sympathetic to the programs of social reform government' and have 'a bias towards the promotion of social democratic innovation'. Wilenski also argued that 'the value of equity as a guiding principle of administration might be raised to at least the same level as that of efficiency; humanity raised to the same level as economy'.

In order to achieve these broad changes, a number of practical measures were needed, which Wilenski summarised under the headings of 'increasing political control' and 'encouraging innovation and changing biases'. Tenure at the senior levels of the public service should be abolished, and people sympathetic to Labor's policies should be appointed. Budgetary processes should be reformed 'to involve ministers more directly in critical decisions'. Equity considerations – 'Who benefits?' – should become a central part of policy analysis. Other measures to be pursued were freedom of information, appeal tribunals, affirmative action, regionalisation and community participation, and lateral recruitment to break down compartmentalisation and create 'permeability' in the public service. In particular, Wilenski defended the need for more roving generalists in the public service, alongside the traditional specialist with professional credentials and accumulated experience. Substantive knowledge and experience in a particular area 'counts for a great deal but it is often not enough (and indeed it may sometimes be a handicap) in facing new public sector tasks in a rapidly changing environment' (Wilenski 1980: 403).

For Wilenski, a reformed public sector would reconcile social democratic principles of equity and public intervention, the idea of efficient administration, and democratic openness with a libertarian purpose. As he later summarised the arguments, reform had the three aims of creating a more efficient, democratic and equitable administration (Wilenski 1986: ch. 9).

Public Choice Theory

A second school of thought on change in the Australian public sector slowly gained intellectual momentum through the 1970s and into the 1980s. It was articulated by New Right intellectuals in various think-tanks. Their proposals were not for reforming, but rather for attacking and eroding bureaucracy and the public sector. Much of the justification came from neoclassical economics and public choice theory, which emphasise the inherent inefficiency and waste of government alongside private markets. Both schools stress principles of individual freedom which, for them, have been undermined by the 'Leviathan' state which has grown up in the Western democracies since the 1940s.

Public choice applies the familiar assumption of modern economics – that most rational action is self-interested – to an analysis and critique of the role of government in modern democracies. From the public choice perspective, government and bureaucracy in the Western democracies suffer from gross inefficiency and waste because they focus narrowly on serving the economic interests both of special-interest groups and of the bureaucrats. For public choice theorists, 'rent-seeking' – the public equivalent of the profit motive – is the main motive behind bureaucratic activity. To tackle these problems, limits on the role of government are required. Proposals included limiting the power to tax; turning to private markets to undertake many of those things traditionally undertaken by government through privatisation, contracting-out and other means; rolling back the power of central government through decentralisation; introducing commercial and market-like approaches within government. These were just some of the ideas articulated and defended by the public choice movement from the 1960s on (see Self 1993; Stretton and Orchard 1994).

Managerialism

Third, a spate of books appeared during the 1970s and 1980s popularising the ideas of management specialists. They put the case for general approaches to management improvement relevant to all sectors of the modern economy, private and public. Although not directly related to public choice and economic rationalist argument, they nevertheless reinforced the view that traditional approaches to public administration were suspect and in need of reform. More flexible and innovative approaches to management were required. The movement to reinvent government is best seen as part of this tradition.

Each of these streams of thought played a role in shaping Australian public sector reform during the 1980s and 1990s. The reforms of the Hawke Labor government reconciled the social democratic, public choice and managerialist criticisms of bureaucratic government. The Australian public sector was gradually harnessed to the Hawke government's priorities along the lines that critics argued were essential if a social democratic government was to succeed. Democratisation, devolved management and new approaches to budgeting all reflected themes in the social democratic and managerialist arguments. Increasingly, the priorities of the Hawke and Keating governments were shaped by economic rationalist and public choice arguments about the need to place limits on government and to pursue greater efficiency, competition and market emulation in public sector activity. The latter aspects have taken greater hold in the Howard government's reforms.

Australian public sector reform has been the subject of much debate. Critics of economic rationalism and managerialism have strongly challenged the foundations of the reforms from a broadly social democratic viewpoint. Some of the managerialists associated with the Hawke–Keating reforms strongly defended the practice and thinking behind them. The debate about the Howard reforms reflects a new phase. Rationalists see them as simply the next stage in the continuing reduction of the role of government in Australia. On the other hand, many see the Howard changes as fundamentally undermining the public institutions essential for good government in Australia. Critics of Howard include some of the managerialists.

The Social Democratic Challenge

By the late 1980s, the public policy change presided over by the Hawke government was attracting strong criticism, much of which attacked economic rationalism. Some have summarised economic rationalism as entailing a commitment to a number of 'mutually reinforcing beliefs', the main ones being the negative concept of freedom, limited government, and free-market economic organisation, themes familiar in public choice theory (Barker 1991).

Economic rationalism also reflects a particular methodology. It seeks to understand economic life in abstract, deductive terms through the use of formal, rule-like models. The kind of knowledge generated by this approach tends to be specialised and positivist in character. Modern micro-economics – which provides much of the foundation of public choice theory – develops knowledge about economic life on the basis of a few assumptions that abstract from real life (for example, that all human action is self-interested, or that markets achieve an equilibrium between supply and demand), and builds pure theory on the basis of those assumptions. The theory provides a framework for approaching problems in the real world without the need to investigate afresh the empirical and other complexities in different arenas of the economy and society at different times.

The critique of the influence of positivism and modern economics on Australian public policy and public life generally has been bubbling away since the early 1980s. For example, Hugh Stretton argued that positivist social science has corrupted Australian public policy debate through its pretence that questions of value and social purpose can be replaced by pure social or economic theory abstracted from the complexities of the real world. Social democratic intellectuals face a formidable, but necessary, task in challenging the positivist view that the social sciences are value-free or that real-world issues can be adequately understood through abstract theory. While social scientists may not like to be reminded of it, value assumptions lie at the heart of their enterprise. And sensitivity to practical problems in different realms of society and economy lies at the heart of good social science (Stretton 1980, 1987b).

Later, Stretton and Tom Fitzgerald criticised important economic policies of the Hawke and Keating governments, in particular financial deregulation and the trilogy. They argued that both of these changes reflected free-market economic doctrine and undermined the capacity of the national government to control and influence the structure of the Australian economy. Under financial deregulation, the flow of finance in the Australian economy became increasingly anarchic. In general, the changes encouraged a whole range of unproductive investment – corporate take-overs and property investment – that Australian society would do better without (Stretton 1987a, b; Fitzgerald 1990).

Michael Pusey, in *Economic Rationalism in Canberra*, extended this social democratic critique of the influence of modern economics on Australian public policy in two ways. First, he provided important empirical evidence showing that people educated in the ways of modern economics have come to dominate positions of power within the Canberra bureaucracy, bringing with them more conservative economic and political beliefs than the postwar generation of Commonwealth bureaucrats. Pusey argued that central economic agencies, in particular Treasury and the Department of Finance, have come to dominate both market-oriented departments like Trade and Industry, Technology and Commerce, and program and service departments like Social Security, Health and Education. This dominance is exercised in two major ways – through central control of budgeting, and through greater reliance on corporate management in program administration. From the viewpoint of central agency bureaucrats, the main aim of this decision-making hierarchy is the most efficient use of resources in the context of a declining public budget. Debate about the social purposes of public policy has been marginalised through this change. In this perspective, the managerialist changes to public administration have become an important means for pursuing economic rationalist ends.

The irony in Pusey's argument is that the reformist quest to replace experience and specialists with generalists, along the lines advocated by Wilenski and other social democratic reformers in the 1970s, had by the late 1980s turned on itself. The new generalist economists were every bit as specialist as those they replaced, except in a narrower, less practical way. (On the limits of generalists in the public sector, see also Encel 1988: 237–8.)

Pusey's second proposition is that the changing of Canberra's bureaucratic guard has fundamentally altered and limited the role of Australia's national government in nation-building. The debate about national purpose and the direct economic role of national government in Australian society is now much more narrow than it was in the past. Rather than allow national government to respond practically to problems, public action must first be assessed against abstract principles of economic efficiency and competition.

Alongside this social democratic critique of economic rationalism, a critique of managerialism also emerged in the late 1980s. This critique highlighted many of the same things – the narrowing of the intellectual perspective for the management of public institutions to questions of outputs, products, the measurable; and capacity for centralised control, authority and integration. Inappropriate private sector models of management were applied to the public sector. Despite the important efforts to decentralise service delivery, the new managerialism was centralist in its stress on control over finance. The tension between these aspects was unsustainable in the long term. The new approaches also denied the essentially political nature of government activity. The stress on measuring and products meant an overemphasis on the 'quantifiable, single-purpose outputs while denigrating claims of worth and effectiveness made on non-economic grounds' (Considine 1988: 4; see also Yeatman 1987).

What would the critics do instead? They defended a range of alternative ideas about both the theory and practice of public policy-making that is best summarised as a defence of the mixed economy and a more open and complex view about the intellectual and institutional resources necessary to build good public policy. Pusey argued that the order and structure of any modern society is provided through some combination of three realms – the market economy, civil society, and the state. The health of any modern society depends upon creative attention to these three realms. This can only occur in a public sphere of open debate. The tragedy of modern ideologies of both the Left and the Right is the pretence that either the state or the market ought to be elevated as the driving force within the public sphere. As a modern ideology of the Right, economic rationalism overplays the abilities of economic markets; underplays the role of the government, particularly in redistribution and the provision of public goods; and assumes that civil society will look after itself. Pusey's three realms of modern society are mirrored in the social democratic defence of the mixed economy. Private, public, and household or domestic economic activity each has a role to play (Stretton and Orchard 1994: ch. 7).

The methodological alternative to economic rationalism centres on the idea of practical reasoning. Policy development and management of public institutions should respect knowledge based upon experience, or what Pusey called the 'slowly acquired feeling for the particularities of social situations in the "real world" beyond Canberra' (1991: 110). The resolution of economic and social problems requires a practical orientation to the complexities, rather than reliance on deductive, reductionist economic models. (On these themes, see Vandenberg and Tregenza 1994: 350.)

The Defence and its Coherence

The critique of the influence of economic rationalism on Australian public policy in the 1980s was strongly rebuffed. Many argued that for both practical and intellectual reasons, the changes of the 1980s and early 1990s were inevitable and sensible. The main reason for that judgement was that the new economic circumstances which faced the country by the mid-1980s required a more outward-looking, business-like bureaucracy. Old approaches were not adaptable, flexible or responsive enough to the range of new demands and pressures faced by the Australian economy. Neither did they enable national government to adequately harness the bureaucracy to serve the objective of building a more vibrant, internationally focused economy (see Boston and Uhr 1996).

The argument that the changes of the 1980s were inevitable, sensible, and variable between different Western societies has recently been defended by Herman Schwartz. He argues that the changes to the role of government in the social democracies since the late 1970s reflect the interests of both business and trade unions in the tradeable sectors of the economy to 'use politics to make the non-traded (public) sector into a traded sector'; that is, to apply the disciplines of the private market economy to the public sector, especially at a time when national economies like Australia's are exposed to the winds of international competition. For him, public sector reform in Australia has gone through two main phases. The changes of the 1970s, motivated mainly by the social democratic arguments of Coombs and Wilenski, focused on changes to organisational structures and were basically incrementalist. The crisis environment of the 1980s produced more wholesale change focused on micro-economic reform and changes to the incentive structures operating in the public sector (see Davis 1997 for a similar argument about the two phases).

Schwartz (forthcoming) draws three main conclusions about the significance of the public sector reforms of the 1980s. First, the changes and restructuring are not transient, but have aimed to change behaviour in the public sector permanently. Second, the changes in Australia are not idiosyncratic nor 'simply an "error" promulgated by [the Labor government] foolishly imitating trans-Tasman or British trends'. The changes transcend political ideology and are best explained as an outcome of the changing balance of interests and class configuration in the societies concerned. Third, 'politics does matter; inevitable changes can come in quite different forms and with different consequences'. There are soft and harsh versions of the changes, with Australia at the soft end of the spectrum. The Australian reforms reconciled economic and social principles.

The underlying structure and logic of Schwartz's arguments raises important questions. The variation in public sector reform in different societies, and the different interests underlying that variation, lead to the sceptical view that the changes may not be as inevitable as they are claimed to be. Further, Schwartz does not account for the important differences in the intellectual underpinnings of the reforms in Australia over time. Those differences point to the contingency and openness in the reform choices that have been made. Schwartz's account explains the changes if you accept the public choice foundation of his argument. He is right to argue that formidable interests on both the Left and the Right lay behind the public sector reforms of the 1980s and early 1990s; but they are just that – interests – and are therefore open to change and can be shaped by political leadership and social processes.

The defence of the public sector reforms of the 1980s has also been taken up by some of the economists who have been directly engaged in implementing them, in particular by Michael Keating and John Paterson. They argue that the triumph and consensus about micro-economic reform and liberal individualism in Australian public policy during the 1980s was inevitable because of the intellectual superiority and coherence of this position, and the vagueness of the alternatives, particularly alternatives based upon collectivist solutions and macro-economic perspectives.

Paterson (1988) argues that the changes to the public sector through the 1980s reconcile better economic techniques of public administration with important ethical and social values. Rather than closing and narrowing the foundations of public administration in Australia, the managerialist changes produced a more open and accountable public service, more attentive to the needs of the society it serves. Centralised control and integration might be a major focus of the reforms, but that has gone with genuine decentralisation of management authority and greater capacity for self-direction and independent judgement by public servants in going about their work. There is also more disclosure and accountability in government.

For Keating, the managerialist label does not do justice to the aims and purposes of the reforms. They were 'directed at better linking of policy formulation, improving decision-making through resource allocation, delivering service to the public, and review, particularly by external bodies'. In his view, the reforms have achieved the aims set for them: to increase political influence over the bureaucracy; to assist decision-making processes focus on efficiency, effectiveness and equity in quantifiable ways; to create a more responsive, flexible, consumer-oriented public service; and to create a more open, less elitist bureaucracy (Keating 1989). Later Keating (1995) suggested that the 1980s reforms reconciled in a positive way the three principles originally defended by Wilenski – democracy, efficiency and equity.

Other templates for understanding the reforms have also been suggested. For example, Anna Yeatman – an early critic of managerialism – has argued that the public sector reforms of the current period in Western societies should be thought of in terms of the emergence of a new post-bureaucratic model of public administration, a model recognising increasing complexity, uncertainty and democratisation in society. Markets, and the competition they foster, may be an important means by which some of the democratic aims of the post-bureaucratic approach can be pursued, but this approach goes well beyond economic rationalist precepts (Yeatman 1997). Others see the 1980s reform as allowing government to produce non-market 'public value' in more sophisticated, imaginative ways, involving co-production with others – private business, clients, third-sector agencies or citizens generally (Alford 1993).

Despite these defences of the 1980s reforms, questions remain whether an economic rationalist undercurrent shapes them. All seem comfortable with the greater private sector role in providing public services in Australia, albeit for different reasons. None seem particularly worried about the loss of nation-building capacity or the shift in the balance of public and private forces shaping Australia's mixed economy, aspects of great concern to the social democratic critics of economic rationalism. Indeed, all seem very sceptical of the notion of the public interest that shapes that concern. As Keating (1995) argues, there is no such thing as the public interest represented independently by the bureaucracy. Such notions are defined politically, and consideration of them should be confined to the political realm (see also Tingle 1995). The suspicion lingers that arguments about the inevitability and sense of the 1980s reforms are crucially linked to the rationalist starting-point of those who defend the reforms.

Continuing Public Sector Reform under Conservative Governments

Public sector reform in Australia entered a new phase in the mid-1990s. Some see the emergence of a hollow state, with a much smaller staff and greater reliance on contractual relationships in the provision of public goods and services (Davis 1997). Others use the term *virtual government* to describe the same process (Sturgess 1996).

At the practical level, rationalist reform of the public sector continues. The Kennett government's program of privatisation and contracting-out in the state of Victoria is the closest reflection in Australia of the New Zealand model of reform. Some of those associated with the Kennett reforms argue that a hollow state needs increasingly decisive strategic direction from the centres of power. Positive principles of institutional design are required, focused on purpose and function. In what is named the 'Westminster heresy', principles of impartiality, meritocracy and permanency of tenure in the public service are regarded as increasingly irrelevant in the new context (Paterson 1997). Nevertheless, the Kennett reforms have been much criticised for undermining basic democratic rights and responsibilities (Alford and O'Neill 1994).

The Howard government's public sector reforms carry on the quest for the hollow state and the attack on the Westminster principles in the Australian public service. Common industrial awards, permanency of tenure and impartiality in the public service are being undermined. The intention is to preserve core functions of the public service – 'managing the processes of government, regulating the economy and providing advice to ministers' – but beyond that, contracting-out, privatisation and micro-economic reform should continue. These changes will make for 'a more focused and responsive Commonwealth public sector' (Moore-Wilton 1996; see also Reith 1996; Schroder 1997).

The Howard reforms have been strongly criticised. For many, they represent the end of an independent Commonwealth public service in which professionalism and political impartiality are respected operating principles (Stewart 1997; Australia Institute 1997). Others support the general direction of the Howard reforms but wonder whether the extension of private sector principles to wage-setting, performance assessment and the writing of contracts in the public service go beyond what is sensible. Wage-setting in the public sector is driven by budgets rather than profits; and contracting-out in some areas – like policy advice – could corrupt good government (Michael Keating, in Steketee 1997a, b). Steketee summarises the key concerns about the Howard reforms:

> the issue is whether the bureaucracy that government now approvingly calls "responsive" has not just bent to the will of its political masters, but is buckling under it ... What we risk throwing out with the drive to greater efficiency and responsiveness to the demands of government are the valued parts of the public sector ethos – a long memory, unparalleled experience and, most importantly, a tradition of providing frank and fearless advice (Steketee 1997a).

The Exhaustion of Economic Rationalist Reform

The key question in the late 1990s is whether economic rationalist reform of the public sector will continue unabated or whether the process has now reached important limits. Has the reform process exhausted itself? The latter view has some support in the Australian debate. Some argue that private sector models ride over the distinctiveness of government, in particular its overall role and shape. The modern public sector is 'one enormous quasi-organisation', raising 'exceptional problems of coordination' that require appropriate institutional responses. Privatisation and contracting-out get in the way of that; indeed, they introduce new problems of monitoring and possible corruption of public policy-making (Wettenhall 1997). Others defend the need for more theoretical eclecticism in public sector management beyond conventional economic models, if the state is to continue to carry the responsibility for the resolution of social and economic problems (Gregory 1997). Even those defending 'virtual government' – a concept designed to encapsulate the much closer and varied relations between government, markets and civil society now emerging – acknowledge that many of the necessary functions of government imply a public capacity to shape society in a universalistic, holistic way. Governing does require the maintenance of an open society, system design and maintenance, regulation and income redistribution (Sturgess 1996). In his comprehensive examination of public sector reform the world over, B. Guy Peters defends the continuing importance of the traditional public service values of 'probity, accountability and responsibility' and 'service to the public as a whole' as crucial, and not to 'be dismissed without adequate reflection' (Peters 1996: 132–3).

In 1980, Peter Wilenski's case for public sector reform in Australia raised questions and expressed tensions that are of continuing importance in the debate between the rationalists and the social democrats. Can the social democratic and libertarian dimensions of the case for public sector reform coexist without one undermining the other? What is the relation between responsiveness, openness, and the need for the decisive exercise of public power in society? Should the bureaucracy simply implement the policies of the government of the day? Or should there be some feedback mechanism whereby the practical experience and legacy of implementing and administering new ideas have some influence in reshaping the government's policy aims? Should there be clearer lines between bureaucratic and political processes which ensure that the former fall in behind the latter? Or should we try to reconcile the traditional public service ethos of political neutrality with an acknowledgment by all concerned – politician, bureaucrat and citizen – that disputed values are central to all public sector activity? What knowledge would good public servants have – particularly key policy-makers and those required to exercise professional judgement – if it is not related to a particular substantive area or to practical experience? Finally, can equity and efficiency aims live happily side by side without loss to either?

The Australian public sector reforms of the 1980s and 1990s represent one set of answers to these questions, but others are now in the wind.

CHAPTER 8

Government and Civil Society
Restructuring Community Services

Deborah Brennan

The relationship between the state and civil society is at the heart of contemporary debates about the nature of democracy and the links between social and economic development in a number of Western societies. Robert Putnam, for example, has attracted considerable attention with his argument that the quality of public life and the performance of a range of social institutions 'are powerfully influenced by the norms and networks of civic engagement' (1995: 66). Putnam argues that high levels of social participation, dense community networks, and extensive relationships of mutual support have a powerful impact on both economic performance and the vibrancy of representative government. Elements of Putnam's thesis, especially the notion of 'social capital', were popularised in Australia by Eva Cox in her 1995 Boyer Lectures. Cox defined social capital as 'the processes between people which establish networks, norms and social trust and facilitate co-ordination and co-operation for mutual benefit' (1995: 15). She called for a reassessment of market-oriented approaches to social policy and for an emphasis on trust, co-operation and mutual support. American democratic theorists Joshua Cohen and Joel Rogers advanced proposals for rejuvenating democracy which depend crucially upon strengthening 'secondary associations' such as neighbourhood associations, parent– teacher groups, women's organisations and unions. The aim of their model is to extend the active participation of citizens in the political process (Cohen and Rogers 1995). Similarly, in the United Kingdom, Paul Hirst outlined a model of 'associative democracy' which depends crucially upon a strengthened and revitalised non-government sector (Hirst 1994).

Such arguments have particular relevance for Australian social policy. Welfare arrangements and provision of community services in this country were founded upon a unique relationship between the state and civil society. From the earliest days of settlement, public authorities encouraged and supported a variety of private and community-based initiatives. Charities and other non-government welfare organisations played a major role in early attempts by government to create a private welfare sector. As early as the 1820s, the New South Wales government used the Benevolent Society as an agent of government welfare, providing up to 70 per cent of its funding and building it an asylum. Thus, rather than organising themselves as a 'hedge against the state', individuals and non-state institutions tended to be drawn into the machinery of government (Webb 1995). To a greater extent than elsewhere, the state in Australia was 'the creator of civil society' (Castles 1989: 42).

During the 1980s and 1990s, the federal and state governments attempted to reshape the provision of community services and thus to reframe one important element of the relationship between the state and civil society. Labor and Coalition governments shared a desire to fundamentally reform public administration and to develop new relationships between the market, the state (or public sector), and the non-government welfare sector. As the Australian Council of Social Service noted in its 1997–98 Budget Priorities Submission:

> New ways of providing and financing community and other public services, new delineations of the role and responsibilities of different tiers of government, and new formulations of the relationship between government and non-government sector, are all on the agenda. At the same time, the broader context is one of fiscal constraint and pressure to more narrowly define the 'core business' of government. [ACOSS 1997: 137]

As Orchard points out in Chapter 7, a radical transformation has occurred in the way that many decision-makers – senior public servants, ministers and service providers – think about and practise government since the 1970s. Public sector change has been driven by several distinct sets of ideas and goals. The notion that the public bureaucracies ought to be more democratic, not only in terms of their own composition, but also in their relationships with civil society, received its fullest expression in the royal commission initiated by the Whitlam government and headed by H. C. Coombs (Royal Commission on Australian Government Administration 1976) and in the writings of public service reformers such as Peter Wilenski. The reformers of this period sought not only to change the composition of the public service, but also to improve the links between government and community through enhanced consultation, participation and accountability. These ideals proved far more difficult to achieve in practice than many had anticipated.

Throughout the ensuing decade a great deal of attention was given to introducing principles of administration and accountability imported from the private sector. Another crucial issue concerned the size of budget outlays and arguments that public expenditure crowded out private initiative. Later proposals focused on 'redefining and rearranging the way [the public sector] works' (Alford *et al.* 1994: 2). This is a far more radical agenda. Its aim is not simply a reduction in the size of government, but a fundamental rethinking of what the public sector does and how it should relate to the private sector and to civil society at large. It also raises major questions about where the users of services (considered now as 'consumers' rather than 'citizens') fit into the overall scheme. The debate about reinventing government, like the debate about social capital is thus, at its core, concerned with the relationship between civil society and government.

One of the most striking features of the literature on reinventing government is that many of its central precepts – such as the importance of having a more responsive bureaucracy and the value of devolving decision-making and resource-distribution to local communities – have clear resonances with the public administration ideals expressed by public service reformers of the 1970s, as well as with the goals of contemporary community organisations, peak bodies and democratic socialists. Issues of profound concern to both camps include: what services should be provided by government and why? what should be the role of the private for-profit sector and the private not-for-profit sector? through what mechanisms should funds be allocated to service delivery organisations and on what basis? The advocates of reinventing government criticise what they call the one-size-fits-all approach of government agencies which deliver services. This critique echoes the frustrations expressed by citizen and consumer groups concerning bureaucracies which are insensitive to local needs, which engage in decision-making from afar, and which apply formula-based responses to complex human problems. In other words, we are not dealing here with a set of ideas driven exclusively by the New Right or economic rationalists. The actual implementation of these ideas in the context of the broader political agenda of the Howard government holds considerable dangers for those who are committed to the notion of the public sector as a set of institutions and services which are owned by the whole community and which remain, through the political process, at least indirectly accountable to all citizens, rather than simply to individual 'consumers'.

The philosophy of reinventing government has had a major impact on Australian public policy. The introduction of a national competition policy (following the Hilmer Report), the drawn-out and inconclusive activities of the Council of Australian Governments in reviewing health and community services, the Audit Commission report into the general functioning of the Commonwealth government, and the legislation concerning the structure of the Commonwealth public service introduced by the Howard government – these have all been informed, in different ways, by the desire to fundamentally rethink what the public sector does and how it relates to other parts of the economy and society.

This chapter seeks to explain these new approaches to government, to explore the vision of society which underlies them, and to consider their implications for funding and service provision within the community services sector. It also asks how consistent these new approaches are with the ideal of active, participatory citizenship, and what effect the implementation of the agenda of a reinvented government might have upon the state's ability to embody our collective responsibility for social justice.

Who wants to Reinvent Government and Why?

The United Kingdom, New Zealand, Canada and the United States, as well as Australia, have all been involved in the project of overhauling the role of government and reformulating the relationship of government to other parts of society. The notion of reinventing government is particularly associated with the work of American writers David Osborne and Ted Gaebler. Their book *Reinventing Government: How the Entrepreneurial Spirit is Transforming the Public Sector* (1993) was described by *Business Week* as 'the new gospel of good government'. In another religious analogy, American Vice-President Al Gore is said to regard this book as the public management 'bible' of the Clinton administration. Gore's own report into the performance of the US federal administration – *From Red Tape to Results: Creating a Government that Works Better and Costs Less* (1993) – is explicitly based on the philosophy and ideas of *Reinventing Government*. Indeed, one of the authors of *Reinventing Government* played a major role in preparing the Gore Report.

Closer to home, the Victorian Commission of Audit, responsible for developing the principles which have underpinned the restructuring of government administration under Premier Jeff Kennett, claims this book as one of its most important inspirations (Alford *et al.* 1994: 13). At a major conference in Canberra in late 1994, *Reinventing Government* was widely praised by senior state and federal public servants, many of whom described how they had drawn upon its framework to come up with new ideas within their own spheres of responsibility (*Canberra Bulletin of Public Administration* 1994).

What is *Reinventing Government* about? At the outset it is important to note the general point that this is a book about government in the United States of America. It begins with the claim that, for many Americans, 'government is dead'. The evidence for this, apparently, is to be found not only in public opinion polls that indicate that Americans have little confidence in government, but also in the widespread failure of public sector endeavour: 'Our public schools are the worst in the developed world. Our health care system is out of control. Our courts and prisons are so overcrowded that convicted felons walk free. And many of our proudest cities and states are virtually bankrupt' (Osborne and Gaebler 1993: 1). None of these statements could be made with anything like equal force in relation to Australia. This is one of the reasons for resisting any simplistic attempt to import the *Reinventing Government* critique into the Australian context.

A second general point is that, for all its attractiveness to radical conservative thinkers such as those behind the Kennett government, *Reinventing Government* cannot be dismissed as promoting an anti-public sector philosophy. It is a more complex book than that. As Emy notes in Chapter 1, its perspective 'is neither statist nor minimalist'. For example, a recurring line of argument in the book is that, while business does some things better than government, government does some things better than business: 'The public sector tends to be better ... at policy management, regulation, ensuring equity, preventing discrimination or exploitation, ensuring continuity and stability of services, and ensuring social cohesion.' Accordingly, government should *not* be run like a business. If it were, say Osborne and Gaebler, 'democracy would be the first casualty'. Similarly, these authors are keen to dissociate themselves from economic fundamentalist ideas such as the desirability of wholesale privatisation of government functions. Privatisation, they argue, *can* be beneficial in certain situations; however, 'those who advocate it on ideological grounds ... are selling ... snake oil' (1993: 22, 45).

The main thesis of Osborne and Gaebler is the need to modernise public administration and bureaucracy in order to make their structures and processes more relevant to the needs of the contemporary world. They argue that hierarchical, centralised bureaucracies might have been appropriate in another era, but they do not function well in today's information-rich, knowledge-intensive society and economy: 'They are like luxury liners in an age of supersonic jets: big, cumbersome, expensive, and extremely difficult to turn around' (1993: 12). The bureaucratic model, they argue, worked in the industrial era because it provided security, stability and a sense of fairness (in that everyone was treated alike). The model was particularly good at delivering 'the basic, no-frills, one-size-fits-all services people needed and expected during the industrial era: roads, highways, sewers, schools'. However:

> We live in an era of breathtaking change. We live in a global marketplace, which puts enormous competitive pressure on our economic institutions. We live in an information society... We live in a knowledge-based economy, in which educated workers bridle at commands and demand autonomy. We live in an age of niche markets, in which customers have become accustomed to high quality and extensive choice. [1993: 15]

Writing in the Australian context, Gary Sturgess (1994: 43) has endorsed the idea that there is a need to reinvent government. He argues that the current wave of change within government represents more than part of the endless cycle of bureaucratic reform. He sees it as a 'generational shift in the nature of government', which has been 'brought about by the shift from an industrial to a post-industrial society'. Sturgess has coined his own phrase – *virtual government* – to describe his vision of the future.

> Instead of ruling from on high, with an imperial and sometimes capricious air, governments of the future will see themselves as part of a global service industry, seeking to add as much value as possible to the goods and services produced by their individual and corporate citizens. Government services will be richly variegated and tailored to the individual needs of their many customers...
> The best way of trying to visualise government in five or ten years time is to think in terms of 'virtual government'. [1994: 45]

Osborne and Gaebler acknowledge that it is not only the public sector which needs to refashion its bureaucratic structures: private corporations, voluntary non-profit organisations and educational institutions also need to transform their practices and structures in order to meet the challenges offered by developments as diverse as the consumer movement and the globalisation of markets. Nevertheless it is to governments (notably the US federal, state and local governments) that the thrust of their arguments is directed. The next section of this chapter considers the implications of these arguments for the community service and welfare sectors in Australia.

Separating Steering from Rowing

According to Osborne and Gaebler, government bureaucracies need to make basic changes in their methods of operation. In a key metaphor (which is used repeatedly throughout the book and which is also echoed by many of their Australian followers) they advocate that 'steering' (making policy decisions) should be separated from 'rowing' (direct service delivery). Such a separation, they argue, would enable governments to focus on what they do best – raising revenue and 'setting societal priorities through a democratic political process' – while freeing the private sector to do what it does best – 'organising the production of goods and services' (1993: 30). Governments need to become more 'entrepreneurial' and to use their resources in innovative ways which will enhance both efficiency and effectiveness.

This notion of entrepreneurialism is explained by reference to a range of alternative service delivery models that depart from the traditional approach, in which public servants employed directly by government departments or agencies deliver public services. Osborne and Gaebler list thirty-six alternatives to the delivery of services by public employees. These alternatives (described as 'arrows in government's quiver') include franchising, public–private partnerships, vouchers, voluntary associations and contracting. At this point, an interesting shift has taken place in *Reinventing Government*. Despite the earlier argument that both government and private enterprise have areas of special competence and expertise, the vocabulary in which these 'alternatives' are discussed relies almost exclusively upon the language of the marketplace – *competition*, *customer focus*, *contracting-out* and *corporatisation* are some of its key words. The strengths of the government model seem to have vanished.

This discussion provides a point of reference from which we can see some specific limitations of the relevance of this critique to Australian social policy. In the first place, the provision of human services by public servants (that is, staff employed directly by government departments or agencies) is the exception rather than the rule in this country. Almost all of the thirty-six 'arrows in government's quiver' are currently, or have been, employed in the delivery of government-funded services to the community. Children's services, aged care, home and community care, women's refuges, and services for homeless youth all provide instances of models *other than* the one-size-fits-all approach said to be characteristic of services delivered by government employees. Hence, we need to be very wary of any attempt to reinvent the administration of these services on the grounds that the traditional bureaucratic model is out of date. The passion for tendering and contracting-out community services which gripped Victoria under Premier Kennett appears to be based, at least partly, on such a misconception. (Of course, there are other motivations behind the changes in public administration in Victoria, such as an ideological commitment to reducing public expenditure and an *a priori* assumption that private sector provision is superior.)

Second, it can plausibly be argued in relation to community services that what is needed is a *closer alliance* between those who are rowing and those who are steering – not *greater distance*. The separation of steering from rowing can leave those who need to influence the direction of service provision without any effective leverage points (up the creek without a paddle, to extend the boating analogy!). Consider, for example, a group of people with disabilities who are concerned about the way a service is operating. Should this group address their concerns to the government agency which provides the funds? Presumably not, since the agency view will be: 'We only make policy decisions. We don't deliver services.' Perhaps, then, they should make representations to the provider of the service? But here the response is likely to be: 'It's not our problem. We are simply providing the service that we have contracted to provide.' What room is there in these structures for social movements, lobby groups and organised groups of citizens to have their say?

For those who fear that having lobby groups in contact with decision-makers and service providers will lead only to the undesirable end of 'budget maximisation', this is a welcome result. The influence of a special-interest group has been curtailed and the interest of the (anonymous) taxpayer in having budgets limited has been served. But is this really the way to secure the best interest of the community overall? An alternative view is that the community as a whole is better served if the needs of its disabled, elderly and otherwise vulnerable members are met as fully as possible. By breaking the ties between policy-makers, service providers, funding bodies and community activists, governments may, in fact, be cutting off an important source of information about the needs and aspirations of some citizens, and thus diminishing the general good of the whole community. Further, when services are constructed as private, contractual relationships between the service provider and the individual client, the expression of collective interests becomes far more difficult.

Another limitation of separating steering from rowing is that there is no discussion of the significance of this principle in relation to different kinds of goods and services. The implication is that the basic principle can be applied equally to the service of child-care and the service of sewage disposal. Yet patently this is not the case. Parents seeking a child-care service, for example, are likely to have a great variety of needs and preferences, depending upon their family configuration, employment status, ethnic background, and other factors. As well as wanting to be involved in the steering of children's services policy, they may be willing to do a bit of rowing themselves. On the other hand, people needing sewerage presumably have a low desire for involvement in any aspect of the service, and certainly they are unlikely to want to row the boat!

Similar limitations apply to the current fashionable belief in the intrinsic benefits of competition. It is frequently claimed that the quality of service improves if service providers compete for the job. An example of this type of thinking, entirely unsupported by evidence, is provided by the National Commission of Audit (which uses yet another sporting analogy):

> There is now a greater appreciation that governments produce better results if they operate more like referees and supervisors, specifying the rules and results required. Delivery of desired outcomes is usually better if opened up to competition, so that suppliers within and outside the public sector can tender for the services required. Those setting the rules and desired outcomes where possible should be separate from those supplying the services. Referees shouldn't be players as well, and vice versa. [1996: viii]

According to this line of thinking, where a monopoly exists, or where consumers have limited choice, poor standards of service are likely to be accepted because there is no alternative. Opening services to competition should result in better-quality service and lower costs to the consumer. Australian experience has not always borne out this theory – especially for the poor. Competition in the banking industry, for example, has led to higher charges for pensioners and low-income earners as the banks increasingly construct their pricing policies to show that they do not wish to do business with the poorer sections of the community.

There are other serious flaws in the application of this theory to the community services sector. For example, before public subsidies were extended to users of private child-care centres, publicly funded child-care was seen as 'monopolistic'. The new system of extending subsidies to the users of private for-profit services while reducing funding to the non-profit sector (initiated by the Hawke government in 1991 and strengthened by the Coalition in 1996 and 1997) was intended to increase choice for parents and to create competition between providers. In fact, the consequence of the new funding arrangements was the closure of many small, non-profit services – leading to *reduced* choices for many parents. The implication that publicly funded services were of the one-size-fits-all variety was also wide of the mark. Publicly funded child-care centres have never been run by public servants and have never conformed to a single model of organisation and service delivery. Generally they are run by parents, together with representatives of the sponsoring body such as the local council or church group. Such services are intensely local and responsive to local needs.

Avoiding Capture by Special-interest Groups

Other management theories which spring from the same school as *Reinventing Government* also insist upon the importance of establishing distance between consumer organisations and the government organisations which fund particular services. Such theories advocate the importance of locking out community organisations, or at least minimising their influence on government decisions. They are also suspicious of the motivations of bureaucrats who become overly committed to the functional area they work in. The budget-maximising theory of bureaucracy states that bureaucrats have an interest in expanding their departments, getting additional funding into their area, and generally building bigger empires (Niskanen 1971). The larger the budget and the number of employees, the greater the remuneration, status and power of the bureaucrat. Bureaucrats therefore have an incentive to maximise their budgets and expand their domain – an incentive which may operate against the public interest, especially if the latter is interpreted in simple economic terms as meaning low taxes and a small public sector. Similarly, interest groups who benefit from a particular arena of expenditure (social security recipients, social workers who counsel social security recipients, unions and public employees) also have an interest in maximising government expenditure in their area. According to this argument, such groups will use whatever access they have to governmental decision-making processes to argue for additional funding and expansion of their area. Governmental decision-making and resource allocation procedures which permit such behaviours are said to be inimical to the broader public interest. Hence, it is advisable to separate policy-making from provision, to establish 'purchaser–provider splits' and to avoid capture by special-interest groups.

Such theories regard all players as motivated purely by self-interest. They deny the existence of any motivation – and any interests – other than self-interest and economic gain. Taxpayers are portrayed as individuals without any social ties or any personal needs, whose sole interest is to keep public expenditure low and thus minimise their personal tax liability. Within such a framework, alliances between user groups and workers in areas of community service provision are seen as particularly insidious.

In Australia we have seen numerous occasions where alliances have formed between the staff working in a particular service or industry and the users of the service. For example, parents using child-care services have banded together with child-care workers to press for improved wages and conditions and thereby achieve a higher-quality service for children. According to Niskanen's theory, this would be an instance of budget maximisation – self-interested unions joining forces with self-interested parents to increase their share of the budget – at the expense of taxpayers. Commentators who concur with this view are not difficult to find. David Clark, writing in the *Australian Financial Review* (5 July 1988), for example, argued that regulations in child-care were devised by early childhood teachers and their friends in order to 'feather their own nests'. It is interesting that these arguments are most often made in relation to areas of service provision such as community and welfare services, where those supposedly feathering their own nests are among the worst-paid members of the workforce.

Blurring the Divide between Public and Private

Another major consequence of the new ways of doing government is that the boundaries between public and private are becoming increasingly blurred. Australian social policy already provides some classic examples. Within children's services, for example, it used to be possible (indeed important) to distinguish between private for-profit services (which were operated by their owners, and did not receive any direct government assistance) and non-profit, community-based services (managed by a committee of parents and workers, and receiving assistance from government). This division is no longer clear. In long-day-care, for example, services which meet state licensing guidelines and which comply with the accreditation process are eligible to apply for federal child-care assistance regardless of whether they are privately owned or community-based. All services receiving child-care assistance are said to be part of the federal government's Children's Services Program. Other areas where boundaries are blurring are tertiary education (where some courses are now sold to full fee-paying students both overseas and at home) and rehabilitation services (where the purchaser of the service is likely to be the Commonwealth, but the provider is a private agency).

Does it matter if we can't tell public from private? This question deserves far more serious attention than it has so far received, especially from the community sector. The question is often approached in a simplistic way, focusing on the views of 'consumers' as the only criterion. Thus, we hear that 'parents don't mind whether the child-care centre they use is private or public, so long as it provides a quality service at a reasonable price'. But, as Eva Cox pointed out in her 1995 Boyer Lectures, some far more profound issues than consumer preference are at stake here. Arguing against the current fashion for promoting competition and deregulation and stripping down the public sector, Cox has stated that 'attacks on the redistributive role of government are not only dysfunctional but positively dangerous. They are part of an oversimplified dogma which can destroy civil society in pursuit of the cashed-up individual' (1995: 4).

Those who wish to reinvent government frequently extol the provision of services by private providers. An intriguing instance is provided by Osborne and Gaebler, who write: 'when Congress passed its first major child-care bill, in 1990, the debate was between those who wanted Washington to fund day-care centres directly and those who wanted to use market mechanisms, like tax credits and vouchers, to give low-income families the power to make their own decisions. *Needless to say*, the latter view prevailed' (1993: 283, emphasis added).

Why 'needless to say'? This is an interesting question for Australian welfare and community service groups to ponder. In this country (so far) tax measures and vouchers have *not* been regarded as the preferred responses to the need for child-care. The Liberal Party has advocated them sporadically, but has not yet moved clearly in this direction. Community-based organisations and most feminist groups have vigorously rejected both vouchers and tax measures to support child-care. The reasons for this are precisely those given by Osborne and Gaebler (quoted earlier in this chapter), namely that the public sector is much better at 'ensuring equity, preventing discrimination or exploitation, ensuring continuity and stability of services, and ensuring social cohesion'. However, having paid lip-service to the idea that public provision may be more appropriate for certain kinds of services, the reinventers forget this notion when the discussion of *actual* services takes place. Then, all of a sudden, the claim that the private solution is better is so obvious that it needs no discussion or justification!

Yet there are some extremely important issues to be considered when human services are provided privately, or are subsidised indirectly through voucher schemes and related measures. Democratic theorist Benjamin Barber has argued that considerable damage may be done to the political fabric of a nation by the introduction of voucher systems in education. Although he acknowledges that voucher systems have many benefits, he claims that fundamentally such schemes are 'inimical to the very idea of a public good and of public judgments politically generated'.

> The voucher system would mobilise individuals, but it would mobilise them via private incentives; it speaks exclusively to their private interests as parents and thus as consumers . . . It permits citizens to think of education as a

matter of private preference and encourages them to dissociate the generational ties that bind them to their own children from the lateral ties that bind them (and their children) to other parents and children. [Barber 1994: 296–7]

Barber also claims: 'Voucher schemes undertaken in a climate of antigovernment privatism will only hasten the death of all public seeing and political judgment, enhancing the private power of individuals at the expense of a public vision of our common world.' In a similar vein, the efforts of the UK government to adopt market-oriented approaches to the provision of public services have been described as effectively depoliticising citizenship (Oliver 1993). It is precisely such concerns which motivate those who argue for a strong public sector and the continued existence of community-managed services in which people have a stake not only because of their own private needs, but also because of their commitment to the needs of their fellow citizens.

Conclusion

The new trends in government discussed in this chapter essentially establish and reinforce the dominance of market thinking in public administration. They reconstitute citizens as consumers whose primary interests are personal and private. Within this framework people are no longer seen as citizens with *collective* interests in services of a decent standard – services which will serve the *collective* interests of children, the elderly and the disabled members of our society. Instead, all are regarded as isolated individuals, each intent on pursuing their own self-interest and maximising their own gains. Notions such as community, solidarity, justice, social capital and equity have no place in these ways of thinking. Such notions are seen either as irrelevant or as a smokescreen for other motives. The philosophies which underpinned the provision of publicly funded services which bind citizens together in common cause with one another have little place in this way of thinking.

> The effect of this reasoning is that the 'consumers' of public goods and services are atomised in relation to each other, and the assumption is made that they can understand and express their preferences independent of any collectively oriented and/or political dialogue about how best to explore, express, and meet their needs in relation to publicly provided goods and services. They are no longer members of a public community of citizens, but become instead private, self-interested actors. [Yeatman 1990: 2]

It is particularly intriguing that these approaches to government and public service provision were initially promoted by a Labor government and that this occurred at the same time as Prime Minister Keating embarked on a campaign to expand our understanding of citizenship and, in particular, to encourage the notion of 'active citizenship'. The Civics Expert Group headed by Professor Stuart Macintyre promulgated a conception of citizenship as 'the basis of an inclusive society' (1994: 13). One of the strongest bases of an inclusive society is the existence of community services which are publicly owned and which serve all members of the society on a fair and equitable basis. Can we really have effective citizenship and a genuinely inclusive society if our most basic human services are only available to those with sufficient cash to purchase them in the marketplace?

The current wave of interest in reinventing government needs to be scrutinised and monitored carefully – especially in relation to community services and welfare policies. In theory, the purposes of this movement appear to be simple and in tune with the concerns of many community organisations about the need for more flexible, responsive and decentralised decision-making. In practice, it can easily slide into yet another set of justifications for cost-cutting, privatisation, and blocking out the voices of citizens. A strong, strategic role for government in planning and funding community services need not in any way diminish civil society; rather it can enhance and strengthen the non-government sector and deepen its capacity for promoting the interests of vulnerable members of the community.

CHAPTER 9

Social Movements, Democracy and Conflicts over Institutional Reform

Jocelyn Pixley

Democratic reforms of the past few decades have been uneven. Contested democratic elections, introduced in an unexpected number of countries, were landmarks of the 1980s. Many other countries still suffer under authoritarian rule. For those of us in 'old' liberal democracies, the situation is simply not comparable. Even so, disenchantment or pessimism about the limits of democracy are not uncommon. Elected governments seem to pursue similar policies even though different parties take office.

In the 1970s, prospects for an expansion of the public sphere and for building additional democratic institutions peaked, then declined. Economic life, that arena over which most of us have least control, spun further away from the possibility of democratic deliberation. Fears about globalisation often paralysed debate. Postmodern diagnoses emerged that celebrated localised identity struggles in a sea of global currents, and eschewed efforts to maintain national democratic institutions. The far more influential neoclassical political economy and public choice doctrines weakened the intellectual defence of public institutions considerably, particularly in Anglo-American countries. According to public choice doctrines, governments neither could nor should respond to popular demands, as politicians and public servants were as opportunistic and dishonest as economic agents. Rather than attempting to render the state more accountable to a critical public sphere, however, this new orthodoxy insisted that the market should be the sole economic co-ordinator.

Few admit that the implementation of market co-ordination mechanisms in the 1980s and 1990s entailed not merely deregulation, but government provision of new regulations. In effect, the International Monetary Fund, international credit-rating agencies (like Moodys), national governments and their Reserve Banks did not foster *laissez-faire*. Instead, they imposed new disciplines and policies – the 'economic fundamentals'. These focused, *inter alia*, on fighting inflation first, cutting back on public spending, and regulating labour though civil law rather than statutory industrial relations institutions.

The muted recognition that such co-ordinating mechanisms in favour of the market have not *reduced* state power, but have constituted state power in new, market-oriented ways, underlines the questions asked in this chapter. Australia is no parochial exception, but for some time was a mild exemplar of the widespread increase in inequality and unemployment, of the breakdown in social cohesion, and of governments' attempts to stifle democratic deliberation and dissent in the public sphere (associated most with Thatcherism). After all, few governments remain popular when their primary aim is to lower the standard of living, as Australia's Labor governments learned during thirteen years of fairly open 'consensus management'. The subsequent conservative Coalition government learned more quickly without it.[1]

In response to the ill-effects of market-oriented government policies, various prescriptions have emerged, calling for an end to so-called *laissez-faire* and proposing a developmental state instead (for example, Marsh 1995; Weiss and Hobson 1995). These proposals for governments to 'manage society' more effectively, in order to foster international competitiveness, are explored in this chapter. Apart from the implicit nationalism, these proposals want governments strengthened by managing in partnership with key economic interests and social movements. Some believe that the concepts of 'settlements' or corporatist 'compromises' are the key to previous institutional reforms. Their ideal is thus a new consensus, reforged or retooled into a 'nationally' competitive settlement of all the 'stakeholders' (Hutton 1997), or through an 'intelligent alliance of state and market' (as *The Economist* argued: in Miliband 1994: 16). At the same time, governments need to foster the sources of social cohesion, which others claim requires a renewal of social capital and trust (for example, Fukuyama 1995; Putnam 1996).

The question asked here is whether these prescriptions for developmentalism, trust and alliances between state and society might further the democratic process, or impose a pseudo-consensus functional for ruling elites (local and global). In considering the sociology of social movements, various functionalist tendencies are equally apparent. Instead of these static views about state collaboration, I suggest that institutional reforms are fragile, and conflicts over their nature and changing purposes are endemic. The strengths and weaknesses of Australian institutions, in one of the oldest democracies in the world, are highly illustrative. Functionalist prescriptions for social movements to help governments restore order, to foster economic change and to provide information to ruling elites are a potential option; but a more democratic alternative is an accountable state, limited by a vigorous public sphere. Similarly, social movements may be urgently needed to render global institutions and multinational corporations more accountable. But we cannot predict whether the elements of such a public sphere, those connected with support for international human rights, social justice and global environmental institutions, will remain significant, both globally and locally, to foster that democratic Australian Way. Such elements are 'only' a normative ideal.

The Sociology of Social Movements

Social movement analyses developed during the 1970s. Their contribution to our understanding of social change is significant, but so too was the context. First to emerge were empirically based criticisms of structural functionalism, the formerly dominant paradigm developed by US sociologist Talcott Parsons, who had extraordinary influence on sociology in the 1950s. American functionalist Neil Smelser (1962), for example, had previously used Parsons's organic system model to dismiss social movements as irrational forms of 'collective behaviour' in response to 'strain', often entailing pathological disturbances of the 'value system'. Such 'uninstitutional behaviour' is at best 'the action of the impatient', which could arise from sources as diverse as trade unions or the Ku Klux Klan. For Parsons, those movements in accord with the 'evolutionary path of modernisation' and the 'progressive' value system (free enterprise, democracy), such as feminism, may be viewed as modernising agents for elites, but collective behaviour may also be suppressed or repressed by the state (Smelser 1962: 1–22, 72; Eyerman 1984).

Smelser's ink was barely dry when American critics responded that the so-called new social movements of the 1960s showed none of these mere behavioural characteristics. The American value system was indeed subject to radical attack, but in the name of an expanded democracy. This was hardly a time of structural 'strain'; moreover Civil Rights, women's liberation and students' movements were neither pathological nor 'irrational', nor could they be regarded as merely functional for modernising elites. They were organised, often middle-class, and caused 'trouble'.

The sociology of social movements also took issue, particularly in Europe, with historical determinism and Marxism's search for a 'revolutionary subject' in the system category of class. These were influential contributions to modern social theory. Other social analyses were also important in these broader debates, yet the sociology of social movements demonstrated (conclusively in my view) that the direction of social change is contingent on the strengths and weaknesses of popular movements in their conflicts with powerful elites. That said, it is only to be expected that there are a number of flaws in this new sub-field of sociology. A popular variant at that time, the New Social Movement thesis, undermined the general impact by emphasising novelty so much that it represented yet another 'retreat into the present' in sociology (Elias 1987). New Social Movement approaches, notably of Touraine, Cohen and Melucci, were ahistorical and excessively optimistic.[2]

On the one hand, they turned too quickly away from the democratising potential in the labour movement, and its normative and utopian elements. Australian sociologists were rightly critical of unions' past sexism and racism, and worried about incorporation into government and business alliances (such as the Accord) and potential dilution of democratic demands from below. But many took for granted the Industrial Commission's protection of marginal, female and migrant workers, and neglected socially oriented union action, such as the Green Bans, a world first. On the other hand, some were naively optimistic for what they saw as a sudden birth of new social movements in the 1960s. Many analysts shared the assumptions of the movements in question, and wanted to envisage a definite trend to greater control from below. Thus the singularity of these movements tended to be seen in their newness and their anti-systemic characteristics, rather than their obvious normative differences from the fascist movements of only a few decades previously.

So, the recourse to a system-anti-system dualism (Holmwood 1996) left Alain Touraine looking, if not for a revolutionary then a unifying subject – in students and later in anti-nuclear protests. Habermas found it instead in feminism. Many argued that new social movements were new because we were in a fundamentally different society – more complex, post-material, post-industrial, programmed, etc. In another optimistic vein, state analysts like James O'Connor predicted a possible fiscal crisis of the welfare state due to escalating demands of social movements, a theme invoked in Habermas's concept of legitimation crisis.[3] That is, governments would lose control of economic policy to movements from below, and a democratic, and possibly radically different, political settlement would ensue from the former, now disparaged, welfare state compromise.

The 1960s and 1970s were exciting times. When the visibility of these social movements declined by the 1980s as the welfare state was dismantled, this vision turned just as quickly to a naive pessimism.

Many *did* argue about a neo-conservative social movement with its backlash against the 'rising tide' of entitlements, citing other counter-movements such as anti-feminist and racist organisations.[4] The broader backlash saw neoclassical economic policies, anti-immigration and authoritarian family policies introduced in many countries. Thus a longer view could retain the analytic insights of social movement as a concept. But social theory's response, overall, was far more deflationary (Alexander 1995). It rejected the fashionable interest in new social movements *and* the analytical insights as well, and turned to postmodern themes of fragmentation and globalisation. These trends were depicted as inexorably taking us away from any potential for more democratic institutions or policy compromises inspired by practical utopian views about the good life. Governments had lost control of economic policy in this view, not of course now to social movements but to global finance capital and the information revolution.

Thus, the conception put forward by Alberto Melucci (1989) of movements as 'nomads' roaming across civil society is a form of romantic functionalism. New social movements for him are primarily cultural, and contest the control over information resources rather than the production and distribution of material resources. Governments are implicitly cast as accessible and accommodating to new cultural identities and discourses. Melucci neglects two major factors here: first, environmental and feminist movements (for example) do make claims for material resources and demand institutional reforms. Second, social movements often face very restricted avenues of influence on the liberal democratic state. This neglect leaves governments in effect liberated from civil society in a merely symbolic relation with social movements (Peterson 1989; Pickvance 1995).

There is a retreat into the present, or short-termism, in both the optimistic and pessimistic variants of the sociology of social movements, and an unwillingness to outline normative criteria.[5] Thus, the major new social movements are committed to social justice, and many (feminism, ecology and peace) are not new but have long opposed old forms of domination such as male power. Other, more repugnant social movements are not committed to social justice, and may even incite hatred and violence against those most oppressed. Where xenophobic movements are concerned, such normative criteria are essential to temper the naive optimism that almost any social movement will democratise the state.

Public Choice Doctrine against the Public Sphere

Indeed, as Holmwood (1996) argues, the model entailed in much contemporary social theory is a simple reversal of functional, closed-system approaches, where any deviant anti-system movement is preferable to the allegedly closed and rigid Keynesian welfare state. However, system categories have proved more open and fragile than the system–anti-system model allows, given the rapid unravelling of the welfare state. The far more promising concept of the public sphere, a key focus of Habermas (1991) and of debates about social movements, is also neglected in this dualistic model. The democratic potential of mediating institutions, where public debate and conflict over reform may render both state and market more accountable, has been criticised on two fronts: in the aggregative model of public choice theorists, and in postmodern arguments. Thus Lyotard in *The Postmodern Condition* suggests the normative ideal of the public sphere is outmoded because the 'condition of postmodernity' entails plurality and incommensurability of 'language-games' (in Markell 1997: 377).

In an analogous attack on the public sphere, public choice theory assumes an aggregate of rational consumers both in economic life and in politics. A major proponent of public choice, Anthony Downs, argues that each political consumer has one eye on 'the gains to be had, the other eye on the costs' (in Stretton and Orchard 1994). Nevertheless, Downs actually recognises that *Homo economicus* is far less adequate in explaining political behaviour than the sociological concept of primary social groups, which he admits is more crucial to individuals' 'adjustments', namely their motivations, values, belief-systems, and the prior formation of their 'preferences'.

Despite this, Downs refuses to accept that orthodox economics should be a 'mere adjunct of primary-group sociology' (in Stretton and Orchard 1994: 131). What this dogmatic refusal indicates is that today's impact of public choice theory against public life is to *vacate the field* – not to rational consumers but to 'primary groups'.[6] That is, the attack on public institutions, with programs of privatisation, reduction of public goods, diminution of influence of non-government organisations and generally of democratic debate has reduced the extent of 'secondary', less personal links between citizens. This means that instead of a mediating public sphere to provide broader sources of recognition, people are left with their *immediate* primary groups. But primary groups are fertile ground for the Mafias, the racist, xenophobic gangs, the political parties making appeals to isolated people who only trust those exactly like them. (The emergence of Pauline Hanson's One Nation Party in 1996 is an Australian example.) Without public arenas, supported by the rule of law, and public institutions like Australia's Industrial Commission and other statutory bodies, social identities become narrow, uni-faceted and parochial. Groups of workers are pitted against each other and against other marginalised groups. There are few possibilities for reconciliation, let alone any dialogue about the public good. There are limited chances for the collective shaping and reshaping of plural, multifaceted and interlocking social identities (Fraser 1992: 140).

A Developmental Mode of Governance

By the mid-1990s, increasing doubts were expressed about the pursuit of market liberalism. In Australia the long Labor years came to an end in acrimony against Paul Keating's global market-oriented vision. The Coalition government, elected in 1996 on promises of reassurance, turned instead towards a similar, but much more divisive, line. Complicit as it was with the populist opposition to globalisation (such as the One Nation Party), but also dogmatically committed to market liberalism, contradictions for the Coalition emerged rapidly. Public attacks on market liberalism took a nasty turn towards racism, as East Asian immigrants and Australia's most disadvantaged, the Aboriginal peoples, became scapegoats for the economic insecurity imposed by elites. The Coalition government became increasingly hypocritical in trying to maintain trade and tourism with Asian countries while flirting with this populism, stifling dissent everywhere else, and dismantling or weakening public institutions that defended multiculturalism, women's rights, workers' conditions, and so forth.

Apart from this alarming trend, intellectual opposition to market liberalism is varied. From a managerial view, some claim that the results of following the Thatcher and Reagan models are a lack of economic co-ordination and investment failures, which have required a stronger 'police state' to manage the conflicts stemming from economic decline, reduced living standards and social chaos. Instead, Australian economic policy should be interventionist and co-ordinated, with national directions tempered by democratic debates and negotiation with social movements. This focus on interventionist economic policy and its relation to social movements – not from protesters but from a managerial elite – is worth examining and comparing with the authoritarian populism outlined above.

The managerialist, state-centred interest in what is called a developmental model of governance sets up social movements as functional for economic regeneration by an interventionist state. A developmental state would collaborate with movements and interest groups, thereby enabling it to foster competitiveness *through* society. Social cohesion is meant to be restored in this process. The sociological question is whether such manipulation of civil society might only liberate the state from its present incapacities and leave unchanged the existing, unequal power hierarchies. Is this concern more about the state's crisis of lack of direction, or about the state's interest in democratising processes?

Ian Marsh (1995) provides a clear example. *Beyond the Two-Party System* provides an economic perspective on 'issue movements' to foster 'competitive and collaborative' policies. Marsh urges Australia to move beyond the two entrenched parties to a political model like that fostered by the new mixed-member proportional electoral system of New Zealand. There, over half the members of parliament are elected in single-member districts, and nearly half by means of a second 'party vote' from closed lists supplied by political parties. This latter method tops up the party share of seats proportional to the overall distribution of votes cast (Lamare and Vowles 1996: 322). According to Marsh, cross-party alliances would enable governments to regain directive capacity through responding to interest groups.

In justifying the move beyond the two-party system, Marsh posits a Golden Age, not the postwar boom but 'perhaps the most fertile and creative in Australia's brief political history', the 1901–09 era of a 'cameo multi-party system', when neither free-traders nor protectionists nor Labor could govern the new Commonwealth in their own right (1995: 272). Here we have another single-factor explanation based on a so-called Australian Settlement, a period that frequently carries the burden of Australia's history, as Maddox points out in Chapter 3. But instead of the former inward-looking society of Deakin's 'protection, arbitration, fiscal equalisation and welfare' (Marsh 1995: 355), we need a new, internationally competitive agenda.

Marsh presses the familiar line that skills, work organisations and wage bargaining should be enterprise-based. He notes (only) that the 'producer-emphasis' in South Korea entailed violent intimidation to break up industry unions (1995: 303, 173, 177). Pointed criticisms of Australia's weak industry policy are allied with calls for the education system to move away from fostering 'personal development and citizenship' to being the 'keystone to national competitiveness'. Likewise, welfare rights currently have 'little regard to the links to competitiveness'. Payments are too rigid and dysfunctional for a competitive economy, because they encourage geographic and occupational immobility and the 'preservation of wages above market clearing levels' (Marsh 1995: 203, 206–7).

Market language prevails, despite the insistence on more democratic governance. Marsh's extensive listing of interest groups and social movements assumes that compromises over conflicts between interest groups take place on a level-playing-field. So, the trade union peak body, the ACTU, is likened to the Business Council of Australia; and welfare and church community provider and client groups operate on the same field (Marsh 1995: 57–68). The likely views of 'issue movements' (1995: 71–80) on Marsh's particular vision for Australia are apparently not relevant. The unemployed would be represented by welfare organisations and 'some trade unions' and, at the phase of 'problem solving and interest mobilisation' where policy is being clarified, even the 'women's movement or the gay movement *may have stakes*' (1995: 219–28, my emphasis). So much for 'issue movements' or, by contrast, major corporations that curiously play a minor role. Even so, this recalls Melucci's position, since Marsh suggests that social movements merely raise 'issues' and bring new ideas to elites.

Linda Weiss and John Hobson in *States and Economic Development* (1995) and Weiss (1997) offer a broader view of developmentalism. They similarly reject public choice arguments about the state's role, drawing on specialists on the East Asian success story. For them, public choice approaches are misguided in attributing economic decline (in say the United kingdom or the United States) to the postwar rise of allegedly growth-retarding interest groups that weakened free-market co-ordination in the liberal democracies. Instead, Weiss and Hobson explain economic decline as due to a lack of a strong co-ordinating role for the state. Their thesis is that a 'governed inter-dependence' between the state and industrial capital, and the other functional categories in a country, is the key to industrial growth and competitiveness. A developmental state, identified with the 1960s–1990s in South Korea, Japan and Taiwan, does not shy away from governing the market in collaboration with society. On this they cite the major land redistribution to peasants in these countries, and subsequent agriculture and industry policies. Instead of state power *over* society, they suggest, the key to economic development and competitiveness with high standards of living in a country is state power *through* society (Weiss and Hobson 1995: 148–97).

In order to foster economic regeneration, consent is required to a strong state that displays what Weiss and Hobson call 'Central Co-ordinating Intelligence'. Like Marsh's, these approaches are functionalist: not just private enterprises but also social movements and functional categories with their representative interest groups should be accepted, even welcomed, as partners with the state and provided with institutional spaces, in order to circulate elites, oil the machinery of government and get things done. This is because the market is incapable of acting as a co-ordinator to make a country competitive in the international economy.

Weiss and Hobson contrast decline in the United Kingdom with the postwar co-ordination achieved through private–public agencies in Germany, Italy or Sweden, which act as quasi-national correctors to the market (1995: 200). For them, imperialism, 'the pursuit of greatness', explains UK decline, for it led to close government liaisons with financial and commercial institutions rather than with domestic industry. They argue that economic failure is above all a political failure, not due to a weak state but to weak links with key economic groupings (1995: 218–19).

These arguments for an economic role for an interventionist state certainly undermine the faith in a self-regulating market. Nevertheless, what lessons should Australia draw, as we always seem to do, from elsewhere? Australians have always gained much stimulus from a multitude of ideas and policies from overseas. Yet why, for example, should social movements turn to this interventionist state, with its Hegelian 'Central Co-ordinating Intelligence' (or CCI as the ominous acronym)?

The developmental state of Marsh or Weiss is one where governments take a strategic interest in collaboration with social movements and functional interest groups. But what would prompt policy-makers to compromise with a broader public and social movements? A metaphor for this well-meaning, yet functionalist approach inadvertently emerged in the following story.

In considering the terrible fires that swept South-East Asia during 1997, there is no doubt that the great suffering might have been avoided if Indonesian and Malaysian ruling elites had paid attention to public dissent from environmentalists, instead of detaining them in prisons. Yet a commentator wrote 'as with canaries in coal mines, these [home-grown environmental movements], which include many indigenous activists, are early-warning systems against economic developments boomeranging back on the welfare of the region' (*Sydney Morning Herald*, 1 October 1997).

Here the public sphere is instrumentally likened to a canary in a coalmine, used only to see if it lives or dies. Better than repression and the devastation, of course, but the canary metaphor highlights these top-down approaches. For if the market is unjust and inefficient, so is Leviathan. Instead of liberating the state from the public sphere in a form of pseudo-collaboration with the mere canary, the problem is how to limit and subject both state and market to rigorous public scrutiny. This requires criticism of existing liberal democracies, vigorous political discussion about reform, and more difficult efforts to call international institutions to global public account.

Where are Social Movements These Days?

There is, however, considerable dispute about whether a vigorous, well-informed political culture with which governments might be forced to compromise actually exists now. In the United States, Robert Putnam argues that individuals are now 'bowling alone'. A decline in civic engagement has occurred with a loss of 'social capital', by which he means the networks, norms and trust that enable people to act effectively to pursue shared social goals (Putnam 1996: 34). Putnam attributes this civic disengagement to the electronic revolution, particularly television, in decentralising and fragmenting society and culture, and fostering pessimism, passivity and even misanthropy (1996: 48).

Putnam's alarmist diagnosis of a decline in 'sub-political' activism is entirely congenial to the market-oriented model. Indeed, many public choice theorists cannot understand why collective action occurs at all (as they regard free-riding not as an empirical question of 'slackers' but an *a priori* assumption of all rational action: Wolff 1990). That is, a rational actor allegedly rides free on the efforts of others without putting in any effort. Even if this certainly happens, free-riding is far from universal: co-operation prevails in nearly every social activity from a picnic to an armed invasion. Francis Fukuyama, in *Trust: The Social Virtues and the Creation of Prosperity*, as the title suggests, contests this neoclassical view. He suggests the debate between free-marketeers and industrial policy proponents fatally neglects cultural differences as a crucial factor in a country's economic competitiveness. Accepting Putnam's diagnosis and adding rising divorce as evidence of decline in social trust, Fukuyama argues the loss of these cultural virtues is the cause of America's economic decline (1995: 10–11, 50–1).

Such a diagnosis is easily disputed. Social capital originally referred to a resource of individuals (not nations), based on advantages and privileges accruing to particular community memberships. For Pierre Bourdieu, those possessing social or cultural capital can inflict 'symbolic violence' on excluded groups, but equally it can refer to Mafia families, youth gangs and ghetto survival strategies (Portes and Landolt 1996: 18–21). Moreover, divorce and television are rather simple explanations for people's declining interest in associations of a past era, not least for those who dispute Putnam's thesis that civic participation *per se* has declined.

Even if one accepts the diagnosis, the proposed remedy to social disintegration, namely replenishment of social capital, may not be so easy, as Emy suggests in Chapter 1. In many respects, the diagnosis is not asking for an increase in trust, but looking for ways to augment loyalty, argues Jack Barbalet (1996a: 86–7, 1996b). Any simple corrective strategy – say to increase trust – requires some promotion from a political elite; but under conditions with few grounds for people to trust government organisations, the more likely emotion is loyalty.

Ulrich Beck has an opposing diagnosis. He sees an explosion of sub-politics, partly due to electorates' boredom with conventional class parties and associations. He is also optimistic that the impact of social movements is 'withering away' the 'authoritarian' state. He cites how even athletes are organised, not just the trade unions and churches; so too the disabled, arms dealers, tax evaders, conservationists, motorists, the divorced, terrorists and parents (Beck 1994: 38–9), which all contradicts Putnam's thesis. Indeed the United States also boasts anti-consumerism, cultural environment and public journalism movements, which directly aim to strengthen the public sphere. Beck suggests that this activism influences state institutions to become oriented to negotiation, in situations where none of the negotiating partners 'wins' and where the capacity of an authoritarian state to 'act' is simply obsolete (1994: 37–9). Beck introduces the concept of a self-limiting state to explain this potential relation, a model quite different from a developmental state.

Beck's idea of self-limitation is, however, only one, rather optimistic, view of governments' likely relations with social movements. Quite different outcomes are envisaged when social movements and a renewal of social trust are posed as functional for economic regeneration and the restoration of social cohesion. This is not to deny evidence that social movements and interest groups regularly make noisy demands on policy-makers. But it is worth remembering that many find collaboration with specific parties and state agencies more congenial than others.

Thus far, the idea of a developmental state may in practice be more democratic than leaving private enterprise, finance capital and market-oriented governments to decide our futures, but perhaps developmentalism is meant to impose loyalty on an apathetic, ill-informed public or on a public fragmented in myriad competing associations and lobbies. Given that some economic regeneration is essential, at least in the sense that all societies must have a satisfactory economic organisation, the democratic issue is how regeneration could be shaped by social movements. A non-authoritarian version of a developmental state would necessarily cede more control, even some control, to the 'democratic public' and feminist, human rights, union and environmental movements, than most statist versions permit. The next section explores the concept of a self-limiting state in relation to social movements.

Are Social Movements the Answer?

Some social movement analysts (for example, Macintosh 1993) suggest the developmental model of the state is required to accede to the public sphere more than the old bureaucratic state or the market-oriented state. In the market or competitive model, there is an enforced fragmentation through privatisation and contractual arrangements and the exclusion of any co-ordination of services and broader objectives. By contrast, a developmental state accepts the need for intervention to foster economic development, and this entails opening up to pressure and forming alliances with outsiders. Such working across boundaries, despite unequal power and resources, can challenge the bureaucratic model of administration between top politicians and senior officers. A developmental state thus accords public status and authority to outside groups, but also where the more militant groups maintain broader interaction with their own constituencies (for example, the unemployed), governments often find themselves in relationships that they cannot 'unimpededly control, but nevertheless need' (Lustiger-Thaler and Maheu 1995: 160). This of course suggests a self-limiting, negotiating state (similar to Beck's model), clearly more democratic and open to vigorous sub-politics from below.

Such a view may be too optimistic about this potential devolution of state power, and normatively too benign about both the state and social movements. As I have argued, sociology has moved well away from evolutionist and teleological theories of social change, to emphasise 'human agency, the contingency of events and openness of the future' (Stzompka 1993: xiv). Social movements as analytic constructs remain important additions to understanding the kinds of social changes that are agent-driven and originate from below (Stzompka 1993: 274–5). These are non-determinist approaches which give movements a potential influence on long-term change and policy directions, whose democratic legitimacy depends on the vigour of the public sphere. But rather than using static concepts like settlements, conflicts over institutional reforms should be seen as endemic. We can be neither optimistic *nor* pessimistic about the role of social movements, for the future is unknowable, contingent and non-determined.

In mapping out a typology of change, Piotr Stzompka correctly gives movements a limited role. Change can be either imposed from the top or generated from the bottom. Governments, corporate elites and administrators often implement successful changes based on intentional plans, but latent change is just as likely from top-down actions that produce unintended side-effects or backfire. In comparison, intentional change originating from below is the role of *effective* social movements, when organised masses are able to enforce political reforms or form mass parties. Unintended changes that emerge from below are most usually the consequences of aggregates of disparate individuals acting and coping in everyday life, protecting themselves and making choices (the topics of demographics and economics). These may unwittingly bring long-term changes or macro-trends in customs, demographic upheavals and economic shifts (Stzompka 1993: 274–5), changes which may have broader, perverse effects, a problem played down by public choice theory.

Even among the liberal democracies, there is a great deal of variation in activities and visibility of social movements. Differences are partly due to the extent that political parties are open to new ideas or to claims for social justice, and to the extent of government controls on free association and protest (Pickvance 1995: 134). Thus Barbalet emphasises potential state suppression or repression, citing the century of violence against the US labour movement inflicted by the state and by employers, who were free to use private police (the role of Pinkerton's detective agency), espionage forces and arsenals. This continued until a 'legalistic amelioration' was introduced in 1935–37, flawed and undermined as early as 1947 (Barbalet 1989: 249–56; Gersuny 1994: 212–13).[7]

Touraine, despite his dubious identification of one oppositional movement with 'industrial society' (labour), does suggest a more conflict-ridden role for social movements, in the idea of continual contests for control over cultural and economic patterns. The state is not a mere tool of dominant forces, but provides the principles of economic organisation, where governments may defend the power of some 'partly archaic dominant class' or draw support from the 'thrust of new forces' (Touraine 1977: 366). Change is unpredictable and its direction depends on the form of the social structure or, as in Gramsci's conception, on the types of historical alliances. Alliances are defined not by objective sociological categories, but by their concrete political expressions in specific historical periods, and how these impact on the state (Touraine 1977: 411; Gramsci 1971: 83). The qualitative kinds of change (or order) imposed by the state depend on relative strengths and weaknesses of popular movements. To be sure, many movements are today international in scope, and nation-states are increasingly dependent on international credit ratings, the International Monetary Fund and world trade agreements. But whether the state is more open to dominant forces (at national and international levels) or to movements for 'self-management' which may make international appeals, the state will still manage change or maintain order.

So, in considering the role of social movements at the end of the nineteenth century in Australia, the changes by the 1900s cannot be characterised as a simple Settlement, or a compromise of capital and labour or, as in political science, due to a 'cameo' of multi-party governments (for example, Marsh 1995). How did Australia haltingly begin to industrialise as well as become one of the most democratic countries of the time in the world? Well, women were not handed the vote, they struggled for it, as the history of feminism and the mass organisation of the women's temperance unions show (Pixley 1991). Women opposed the pastoral industry's control over national directions as much as unions, represented by women's vote for Federation and opposition to the male culture of itinerant rural wage labour. And, in contrast to the United States, the Australian Labor Party emerged partly as an unintended consequence of colonial governments' attempts to repress unions – the plans backfired.

Federation and New Protection are better understood as arising from short-lived, loose and cross-cutting alliances between a weak industrialising class, the labour movement, and numerous women's organisations. Equally important, the pastoral industry's dependence on British finance was disrupted by the 1890s depression, and momentarily reduced its considerable influence on colonial governments and on the public sphere (Pixley 1992, 1993: 46–50; Cryle 1989).[8] A temporary defeat of pastoralism, notably in the labour movement's demand that pastoralists be prohibited from importing cheap indentured labour, partly resulted in the repellent Immigration Restriction Act. Women's struggles against the male culture of drunken violence, desertion and enforcement of conjugal rights brought women the vote. Yet men gained the family wage, and excluded women from earning half that wage.

As in any time and place, the period can be characterised by short-lived gains and losses, unintended consequences, setbacks and subsequent backlashes, as Maddox also suggests. Some institutional reforms made Australia more socially just and democratic, yet elements of these very same reforms fostered the opposite. Arbitration was an immense setback for women – and unskilled men. Yet after years of struggle by feminists, and after significant influence in international arenas on these matters, Australia's centralised wage-fixing in the Arbitration Commission, later the Industrial Relations Commission, helped to reduce the gendered wage gap, to defend workers' rights, conditions and family responsibilities, and reduce ethnic tensions (Pixley 1996). It was thus hardly surprising that the commission was so disliked by the private sector and the Coalition government, but more disappointing that the Labor government had previously started reducing its statutory powers.

Such reforms, even century-old ones, always cause dissension. Rather than seeing a future lost to globalisation, it seems more important to put energy into defending the public sphere. Whenever the public sphere is dominated by powerful market players, and whenever social movements not inspired by social justice are more visible than those which are, it is important to remind ourselves of alternative traditions, which gave rise to the more open and cohesive democratic institutions in Australia. The sociology of social movements reminds us that we cannot predict the outcome of struggles in advance. New historical alliances will always be forming. Some may oppose Australian governments' openness. Others may manage, even briefly, to foster an economic policy that is sustainable, both in international environmental terms and for the sake of over-burdened family life everywhere. Who knows?

Notes

1 Karl Polanyi (1957) pointed out the massive growth of bureaucracy and state power in Britain after 1832, the first time a 'fanatic faith' in the self-regulating market became government doctrine. Paul Pierson (1994) shows the difficulties faced by Thatcher and Reagan governments in dismantling the welfare state, especially in the area of old-age pensions and health care, an early stumbling-block for the Coalition Prime Minister Howard.
2 There is a large body of literature of note on this point: see Touraine (1981), Cohen (1982, 1985), and Melucci (1989). Compare recent work, e.g. Rootes (1995), Pickvance (1995), Bagguley (1992, 1995).
3 See Touraine (1971), Touraine et al. (1983), Habermas (1981), Eyerman (1984), O'Connor (1973).
4 Ian Marsh has written extensively on the neoliberal movement in Australia, e.g. Marsh (1989).
5 Mottl (1980), for example, defines movements and counter-movements, where the latter try to maintain the status quo against 'progressive' reforms of 'movements'. But this provides no way of defining a counter-movement that may oppose the injustices of economic rationalist 'reforms', and may try to maintain the status quo. For example, Australian public funding and regulation of community child-care centres, a relatively recent gain by feminists and the child-care lobby, was undermined by market 'reforms' of the Howard government in 1996. Another way of understanding social movements is through their function of contesting the uniform and pre-defined needs entrenched in social policy, by raising new needs to light and offering new definitions of needs (Hewitt 1993). As Meehan suggests, a non-authoritarian social policy can never be certain there are correct solutions 'for all people at all times'. Yet it may be difficult for policy makers to be 'fair' but not neutral to the more repugnant opinions and demands (Meehan 1994: 75).
6 This idea was suggested to me by a postgraduate student, Shaun Wilson.
7 Compare this with countries with established parties of labour in Europe and Australasia, or social democratic and socialist parties influenced by unions. There is hardly a welfare state in the United States to even speak about. Also compare the Labor Party's transformed approach to feminism since the Whitlam government, in comparison with the Howard government or, for that matter, the Reagan and Bush administrations. Of note, see Sawer and Groves (1994), Watson (1990). It made a difference, too, that the ACTU took up the feminist agenda during the Labor Governments.
8 There are more detailed analyses in Pixley (1993, 1996). Cryle (1989) points out that pastoralists continually attempted to gag public debate about land settlements with Aboriginal peoples and indentured labour, throughout the nineteenth century, either by suing newspaper proprietors or editors or by purchasing shares in newspapers. These problems facing a vigorous public sphere or the idea of the Fourth Estate are not unfamiliar today.

PART IV

Transformations of Economy and State

CHAPTER 10

Economic Restructuring in Australia
Policy Settlements, Models of Economic Development and Economic Rationalism

Stephen Bell

History tells us that a large economic crisis is likely to re-scramble the political and economic policy egg. In Australia and elsewhere, for example, the deep depressions of the 1890s and 1930s were critical ingredients that helped topple established political coalitions and usher in new patterns of economic policy (Gourevitch 1986). On both occasions the structure of relations between the state and the economy was transformed in the direction of greater state intervention in the market.

This chapter argues that a similar process of crisis and transformation has been under way since the 1970s, not only in Australia but in a range of other advanced economies. Unlike the resolutions of the 1890s and 1930s, however, this time the centre of reformist gravity has shifted back towards the market. Such has been the scale of the shift that few would disagree with the claim that the world economy is now more capitalist in terms of the dominance and spread of market forces than at any time in the twentieth century, and certainly so since the 1930s. This claim is especially true for Australia. For a country with relatively statist political economy traditions, the market-oriented neoliberal transformation of the 1980s and 1990s is nothing short of extraordinary. This chapter traces these developments and uses the concepts of 'policy settlement' and 'model of economic development' to help organise the discussion. The former refers to the political coalition and political compact that underpins a given model of economic development, which, in turn, is broadly defined as the mix of state intervention and market forces that structures political economy in any given era. In this sense, policy settlements form the policy and political underpinnings for given models of economic development (see Bell 1997a: ch. 4). Also, economic structuring needs to be considered in the round: and we need to explore, in an interconnected way, how states and markets structure political economy, from the micro level of production arrangements right up to arrangements at the level of the world order.

This chapter explains the rise and decline of two models of development (underpinned by two distinct policy settlements) that structured Australian political economy for much of the twentieth century – the 'domestic defence' model and the Keynesian full-employment model (Bell 1997a: ch. 4). The former was the triad of tariff protection, centralised arbitration and immigration controls that were established in the first decade of this century, which protected high wage labour and the manufacturing sector. The latter was the national macro-economic policy in the period after World War II: full employment, underpinned by Keynesian demand management and an associated system of international financial regulations, aimed at stability and expansion. The collapse of these arrangements and their replacement since the 1970s by an economic rationalist model, with its emphasis on market forces, is discussed at some length. It is argued that the economic rationalist order has created or failed to fix a range of economic problems, and that a new pattern of winners and losers is emerging. After examining aspects of the policy settlement that underpin this economic rationalist model, the chapter concludes by suggesting that it will be difficult to dislodge in the short to medium term.

The Collapse of Domestic Defence and the Full-employment Order

In the final analysis, Australia's domestic defence model collapsed because its microeconomic system became untenable. In a world increasingly dominated by high-value-added manufactures and services trade (Drucker 1986), Australia's protectionist import-substitution industrialisation never produced much more than a mass of infant industries. In part, manufacturing industry's lack of competitiveness reflected the kind of 'truncated industrialisation' often associated with high levels of foreign investment. It also reflected a pattern of state micro-economic neglect whereby protection was dispensed without much oversight or accountability (Bell 1993: ch. 1). The result was an uncompetitive, fragmented and inward-looking manufacturing sector. The upshot has been that Australia still remains heavily dependent on commodities and low-value-added exports. The problem with such an economic structure in the late twentieth century, is that the world economy is increasingly driven by high-value-added manufacturing and service industries, not by commodities (Bell 1997a: 83).

The wash-up has been a secular deterioration in Australia's terms of trade, a weakening dollar, current account problems and burgeoning foreign debt. Indeed, Australia now has the worst current account situation in the OECD, a product of attempts to balance a First World society atop a Third World commodities/resort economy (Ravenhill 1994; Emy and Hughes 1991: ch. 2; Emy 1993: ch. 3; Fagan and Webber 1994; Bell 1997a: ch. 6).

On top of this, trauma of a second kind – essentially a crisis of the postwar order – afflicted not only Australia in the 1970s, but also other advanced capitalist economies, particularly in the Anglo-American countries (Armstrong *et al.* 1991). By 1974 the golden years of the postwar boom were over (Marglin and Schor 1990). Orthodox accounts of this stress exogenous shocks – commodity prices, oil-price shocks, the break-up of the Bretton Woods monetary order in 1971, and so on (McCracken 1977). While useful, such an account can be extended by arguing that the onset of major economic problems in the 1970s was also caused by more systematic institutional causes lodged in the mounting internal tensions of the postwar order.

The key issues here can be defined as the labour problem and the state problem. First, by the late 1960s, Australia and most other Western economies were confronted by a classic Kaleckian labour problem. Relatively full employment in the postwar decades led to the growing strength of labour's bargaining power relative to capital. As Kalecki had predicted in 1943, in a capitalist system:

> The maintenance of full employment would cause social and political changes which would give new impetus to the opposition of business leaders. Under a regime of permanent full employment, the 'sack' would cease to play its role as a disciplinary measure. The social position of the boss would be undermined and the self-assurance and class confidence of the working class would grow. Strikes for wage increases and improvements in conditions would create political tension. [Kalecki 1943: 326]

By the late 1960s these tensions were evident: a number of advanced economies experienced an outbreak of worker militancy and industrial conflict (Armstrong *et al.* 1991: 192–6; Crouch and Pizzorno 1978). The militancy, strikes and wage demands washed through Australia. Strikes and industrial militancy rapidly increased and the wage share of national income grew rapidly while the profit share fell (Bell 1997a: 93).

When the capitalist world became bogged down in deep recession from late 1974, the strength of labour was even more starkly revealed this time helping to drive an entirely new phenomenon – stagflation. Besides the inflationary factors associated with the OPEC oil-price shocks, commodity price pressures and the loose monetary policies of the early 1970s, a key additional factor driving the new inflation was the cost-push pressure of intense distributive conflict (Eichner and Kregel 1975; Gilbert 1981; Heilbroner 1979; Goldthorpe 1978).

In this view, inflation represents the monetary expression of the economy's incapacity to meet the distributional demands placed upon it. In past eras, recession has normally blunted intense distributive conflict, particularly in terms of the capacity of workers to fight for wages amid the constraints imposed by unemployment and the discipline of the labour market. By the 1970s, however, changes in Western political economies had seen the growth of stronger power-blocs in the economy (more monopoly, oligopoly and administered pricing in business, higher unionisation, stronger more assertive trade unions, etc.), enabling powerful economic actors to fight for wage or price increases, even in a recession (Skidelsky 1979: 68; Hirsch 1978).

The labour problem was also evident in growing strains within the postwar system of production and work organisation. Although long criticised by reformers as needlessly alienating, mindless and inefficient (McGregor 1960; Wrenn 1982), management in most Western countries extended and expanded production systems based on Taylorist management principles, not least because this appeared to offer firmer control over the labour process (Zimbalist 1975; Wright 1995). By the late 1960s, however, growing alienation and resentment on the part of workers was reflected not only in the militancy and strike action noted above, but also by a rising tide of absenteeism and falling productivity. Labour productivity growth in OECD countries averaged 3.7 per cent between 1960 and 1973, but this rate fell to only 1.6 per cent for the fifteen years to 1989 (Armstrong *et al*. 1991: 240). In Australia, there was a similar pattern. Labour productivity in the years 1960–73 averaged 3.4 per cent, but this fell to 2.3 per cent in the years 1973–79 and dropped again to an average of 1.2 per cent in 1979–93 (OECD 1995). Of course, various factors contributed to this fall-off (e.g. slowing public and private investment), but, as Armstrong *et al*. note, the productivity slowdown generally predates the investment fall-off of the 1970s (1991: 73).

If labour had begun to pose a threat to capital under the postwar model of development, so too did an increasingly expansive state. Business interests, in particular, held this view. In the mid-1950s, for example, public expenditure averaged about 28 per cent of gross domestic product in OECD countries. By the late 1960s, it was 34 per cent, and by the mid-1970s it was averaging about 41 per cent of gross domestic product across the OECD countries (OECD 1978; Thomas and Meyer 1984). In general, the view of business and other critics was that the state had become too big, too expensive and too intrusive. As Schwartz argues: 'Coalitions of politicians, fiscal bureaucrats and capital and labour in the sectors exposed to international competition allied to transform what they saw as a major factor contributing to declining international competitiveness: the state' (1994: 531).

In response, business interests and a wider constellation of economic rationalist critics campaigned against 'excessive' regulation. There were also claims of an excessive state policy focus on wealth-distribution, rather than on supply-side concerns and wealth-creation. The state was also accused of diverting investment funds away from business. A key aspect of this was the so-called fiscal crisis of the state: a structural gap between limits on revenue and pressures for expenditure that has led many governments since the early 1970s to go into substantial debt, which, it is alleged, has been crowding out the private sector in credit markets and raising the cost of capital. The problem stems largely from the fact that key societal interests demand more from the state than they are willing to pay for through taxation. Business interests, in particular (but well supported by middle-class voters) have campaigned against the tax 'burden' of the modern state. One result has been that, across the OECD countries, as revenue has been constrained, state debt as a proportion of gross domestic product has more than doubled: from 16 per cent in 1973 to over 33 per cent by 1986 and to 40 per cent by 1993 (Armstrong *et al.* 1991: 256; OECD 1994).

To be sure, many have argued that these business and economic rationalist complaints about the state have been exaggerated (for example, Wilenski 1984). The point, however, is that, whether the problems are real or imagined, they may well affect business sentiments or behaviour and, in turn, economic performance. The importance here of business confidence – particularly any potential to dampen what Keynes called the animal spirits of capitalists to invest and expand the economy – should not be underestimated (Offe 1984: 151).

The arguments above have explained the mounting difficulties of the postwar order largely in terms of domestic *tensions within* the advanced Western economies. Yet there were also powerful changes occurring in the world order by the late 1960s and early 1970s. Heightened competition in the international economy was one aspect of this. Essentially, business was being caught in a pincer movement between rising domestic costs and constraints, and the rising competitive pressures of the international economy. Beyond this, the very nature of the international economy was radically changing, in a way that would that would further enhance the capacity of business interests (particularly mobile ones) to challenge and eventually help overthrow the postwar full-employment model. One aspect of this increased capacity of business is the increasingly transnational character of production: a key implication is the scope it provides for capital flight as a mechanism either to escape or to challenge postwar arrangements in the advanced economies (Gill and Law 1989). Another, arguably even more important, development was the rapid escalation of global financial markets in the 1980s and 1990s. There is no space here to explore the explanations for the growth of international financial markets, although weakening US postwar hegemony and the subsequent collapse of the Bretton Woods system by the early 1970s were major factors (see Block 1977; Gowa 1984; Pringle 1992; Helleiner 1994a).

Economic Rationalism

In response to the problems outlined above, the 1980s and 1990s were dominated by a largely successful attempt to jettison both the domestic defence and postwar models of development. Economic rationalism has been the ascendant policy paradigm and model of development. The major economic rationalist policy shifts in Australia need no reiteration here but, in brief, they have included the abandonment of high protectionism in favour of international and domestic free-trade policies, together with micro-economic reform policies aimed mainly at competition and cost-reduction. Labor's 1983–96 corporatist wages policy with the unions has also been jettisoned in favour of more market-oriented enterprise bargaining. At the macro-economic level, postwar policies aimed at full employment have been abandoned in favour of policies of 'sound finance' aimed at low inflation and fiscal consolidation (Bell 1997a).

These policy shifts appear to be an Antipodean version of a much wider movement towards economic rationalism across the globe (Gourevitch 1986; Garrett and Lange 1991). While this is still an uneven process, both across countries and across policy arenas, economic rationalist policy convergence has certainly been a major facet of contemporary political economy. This has been particularly apparent in the Anglo-American countries, but economic rationalism has also challenged and largely overturned social democracy in Northern Europe (Pontusson 1992; Kurzer 1993), while radical free-market policies are being applied in Eastern Europe and the former Soviet Union (now with support from the International Monetary Fund), as well as in India and much of Latin America. Economic rationalism is also challenging economic nationalism in East and South-East Asia. Whether economic rationalism will overturn the distinctive attributes of the co-ordinated market economies of countries such as Japan or Germany is at present a moot point (Berger and Dore 1995).

In Australia's case, economic rationalism is underpinned by a new policy settlement backed by a very powerful political coalition, featuring globally oriented business sectors (particularly in the financial sector), actively supported by political leadership in the major parties who have been able to win electoral support on an economic rationalist platform. Dominant political forces almost always win by building effective coalitions (Gourevitch 1986). Bernard describes the membership and broad aims of the currently prevailing political coalition as one in which:

> neo-liberal politicians, internationally competitive industries, finance ministries and central banks and private financial institutions emerged within and across states . . . The coalition fostered support by tapping deep-seated middle-class feelings that taxes were too high and government too large, and that the 'natural' solutions entailed a reduction in the size of the state, control of inflation, and promotion of international competitiveness. (1994: 225)

In Australia's case, as Kaptein argues, many urban professionals, together with increasingly powerful media corporations and externally oriented farming, resources, tourist and banking sectors, have broadly supported economic rationalism (1993: 104–5). In major shifts, such as the ending of national protectionism, for example, the change represents a fall in the political power of manufacturing interests and the policy ascendancy of globally oriented economic sectors long disadvantaged by domestic insulation and protection. In this sense, policy privilege has been reallocated. Financial interests have benefited by deregulation and free movement of capital, while for the first time this century, trade policy directly reflects the interests of the commodity export sectors (Duncan 1993).

Beyond this, in a departure from the *nationally* rooted systems of political economy established under the postwar order, a key feature of the economic rationalist era is the degree to which *international* pressures now impinge on (or even override) domestic arrangements and options (Bell 1997b). Such trends have been associated with the increasing power of those state agencies charged with managing the international interface (such as central banks, ministries of finance, etc.), and a corresponding decline in power of agencies linked only with domestic groups or clients. It also appears that state elites are increasingly outward-looking: they take their cues from what is now a globalised process of economic rationalist elite discourse and consensus formation; its vehicles are G7 summits, institutions such as the OECD and the International Monetary Fund, and magazines such as *The Economist* (Panitch and Miliband 1992: 12). Writers also point to the proliferation of transnational agreements and governance arrangements that increasingly limit domestic policy options in areas such as trade and industry policy (Marshall 1996).

Perhaps the most important shift, however, particularly at the international level, has been the effects of increased financial integration and the rising power of financial markets. There are a number of issues here. For example, increased openness and financial integration have weakened the effectiveness of national policy instruments (Schor 1992;

Radice 1984). Financial integration and openness make it more difficult for policy-makers to define or measure monetary and credit aggregates, and they enhance private sector opportunities for evasion of national monetary regulations. It is also true that any attempted fiscal stimulus may leak abroad through the effects of higher levels of cross-border integration (Akyuz 1995: 76). Moreover, the market reaction to a fiscal stimulus is likely to be negative, possibly leading to an increase in long-term bond rates which, in turn, will reduce the impact of the fiscal stimulus. As Argy points out, 'In judging the likely impact of a fiscal policy change, the authorities need to "second guess" financial market responses – yet the complexities are such that they cannot do this with any confidence because financial markets respond to fiscal changes in ways which are often perverse, wayward and erratic ... often swayed by technical factors rather than economic fundamentals' (1995: 23). Not surprisingly, as Schor writes, 'there has been a marked shift towards governmental passivity in the face of financial markets' (1992: 10). This is a shift in power relativities that perhaps constitutes *the* major change in international political economy of the 1980s and 1990s. It has seen financial capital become ascendant over both labour and the state, marking a reversal of political tendencies apparent under the postwar order. Increasingly, it seems, national economies have not one but two forms of governance: one lodged in parliamentary institutions, the other in the discipline imposed by financial markets.

Outcomes

As far as business interests are concerned, the broad aims of the economic rationalist model of development have been cost-reduction, disciplined labour, profit restoration, the taming of inflation, and greater market freedom and openness. Beyond this there has been an ideological commitment within business and wider economic rationalist circles to restructure the state and, more broadly, to rebalance the political scales put out of alignment by the extraordinary conditions of postwar full employment, labour empowerment and state growth.

Broadly speaking, most of these aims have been achieved. The lion's share of power, mainly because of high unemployment, now lies with business, not labour. In this environment, inflation has also been beaten. The postwar trajectory of state growth has been halted or severely restricted. Economic openness and integration are proceeding rapidly, and profit shares and profit rates have been rebuilt (Bell 1997a: 93, 99). In short, the advanced capitalist economies (and their states) have become much more business-friendly.

As governments scramble to establish competitive business environments able to attract or hold increasingly footloose capital, it is clear that the greatest beneficiaries of the new order have been large, globally oriented blocs of capital in the industrial, service and financial sectors. Of these, as reflected in financial hegemony over other sectors and in burgeoning profits and growth, the financial sector has clearly been dominant. Indeed, as noted above, a major shift in the 1980s and 1990s was the sector's liberation by global financial deregulation from the second-class status it endured under postwar controls (Helleiner 1994b). Hence, greater financial *laissez-faire* in recent decades represents a return to pre-1940s versions of capitalism as normal, in which the financial sector is typically in the driver's seat of the world economy.

The results of such financial liberalisation have been staggering. The power of the financial sector is based on the capacity to mobilise vast economic resources. For example, after starting from a very low base in the early 1970s, trading in the currency markets alone by the early 1990s had reached approximately $US900 billion a day, a value about forty to fifty times greater than the level of international trade. More recent estimates put the level of currency market trading (most of which is speculative) at $1.3 trillion per day, with annual growth rates in trading approaching 30 per cent (*Economist* 7 October 1995).

However, the various areas of business triumph noted above have incurred substantial costs in other areas, and it is clear that new alignments of winners and losers are emerging under the new order. For example, one cost has been a pattern of slow economic growth, at least compared to the postwar era. Across the OECD and in Australia, average growth rates since the mid-1970s have been only half that achieved during the postwar era (Bell 1997a: 88–9). A number of factors have been responsible for this, but many analysts point to the prevailing climate of restrictionist macro-economic policies and the impact of two major policy-induced recessions (in the early 1980s and early 1990s) as an important part of the explanation (Armstrong *et al.* 1991). If low inflation has been a major gain for such a policy stance, many analysts (though certainly not all)[1] also point to high and persistent unemployment as a major disadvantage of such policies (Eatwell 1995). It is also becoming clear that less-regulated forms of capitalism, involving big top-end profit opportunities and less-regulated labour markets (and restricted welfare payments), will inevitably generate greater inequality and social polarisation (*Economist* 1994). This trend is apparent seemingly everywhere. Much discussed in this respect has been the United States. There, according to one study, the 'growth in the incomes of the richest one per cent of Americans has been so large that just the *increase* between 1980 and 1990 in the after-tax income of this group equals the total income of the poorest twenty per cent of the population' (Goldsmith and Blakely 1992: 20). As Figure 10.1 shows, on one key measure of inequality, Australia is not far behind the United States.

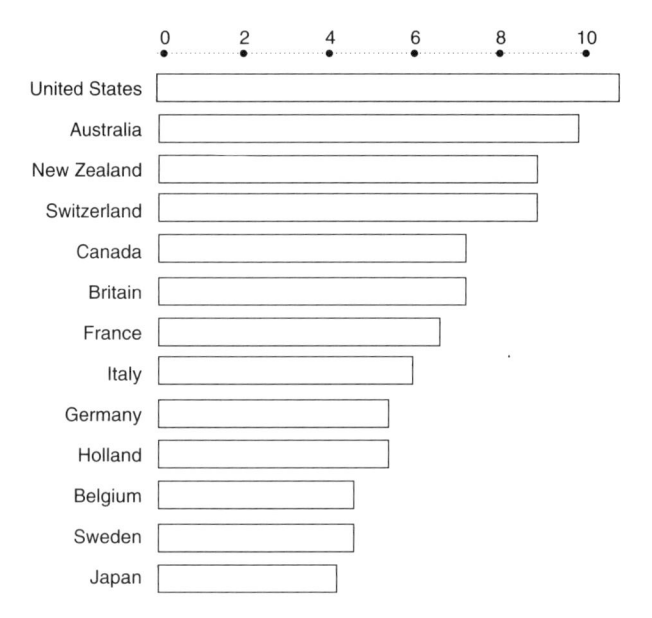

```
                    0     2     4     6     8    10
  United States
      Australia
    New Zealand
    Switzerland
         Canada
        Britain
         France
          Italy
        Germany
        Holland
        Belgium
         Sweden
          Japan
```

Figure 10.1 Income inequality in various countries: ratio of income of richest 20 per cent of households to poorest 20 per cent, latest year available
Source: *Economist*, 5 November 1994

Analysts point to the huge costs that unemployment and inequality impose on the real economy in terms of inefficiency and the large fiscal welfare burden on the state (Corry and Glyn 1994). These problems, and sluggish growth, also weaken business and consumer confidence and place significant demand constraints on the economy.

More broadly, globalisation, especially as reflected in financial market activity, has also made economies more vulnerable and insecure, and increased economic volatility (Argy 1996). Many analysts point to increased short-termism in investment patterns in both financial and industrial sectors, and continuing difficulties that many innovative small and medium-sized firms have in obtaining 'patient' financial support (Brain 1992). These problems have promoted increasing criticism from firms and associations in the real economy; even, in some cases, about an excessively restrictionist policy fixation by central bankers on low inflation. To be sure, industrial and financial sectors joined in the 1980s and 1990s in the battle against inflation. Yet as far back as 1977, the Victorian Chamber of Manufactures complained that 'It would indeed be a tragedy if the battle against inflation were won only to find that industry had died fighting the battle' (VCM 1977). More recently the Australian Business Chamber has advocated a pro-growth economic strategy, and questioned the Reserve Bank's policy strategy. At a broader level, industrial leaders such as Akio Morita, the head of Sony, has complained about financial volatility, arguing that what the markets really do 'is impose the irrationality of the speculator's culture on the daily lives of business people and consumers' (in Toohey 1994: 199).

In part, the problems above connect with another set of problems in the real economy, especially the major fall-off in productivity growth mentioned above. In Australia, this has reflected the displacement of labour by capital equipment and a major trend decline in private and public sector capital formation (Bell 1997a: 237). US research indicates that as much as 75 per cent of the fall-off in private sector productivity in that country can be attributed to the decline in public sector infrastructure investment (Aschauer 1989, 1992).

These problems are both a symptom and a cause of a more fundamental problem, especially in Australia: namely, the failure during the 1980s and 1990s to restructure the economy effectively. If this project is defined as reducing Australia's dependence on the increasingly vulnerable commodities sector or on low-wage sectors such as tourism, then the project has clearly failed (Bell 1997a: ch. 10). In the 1980s and 1990s private sector strategies combined with an uncertain and lacklustre industry policy framework to produce a situation where Australia is *increasingly* dependent on commodities and tourism exports (Bell 1997a: 246). This situation results from the failure of an increasingly exposed manufacturing sector to hold its own in Australian and world markets (Bell 1997a: ch. 10). Indeed, manufactures import penetration has overwhelmed any export growth, while the sector has lost market share internationally. Increasingly, Australia shows signs of being pushed onto the 'low road' of economic development, featuring low innovation, low skills and low wages (Marceau, *et al*. 1997). One key indicator here is that the loss of jobs through manufacturing deindustrialisation in Australia has been much worse than the OECD average (Marceau *et al*. 1997: 7.6). Also, virtually all of the jobs created in Australia in the 1990s have been part-time, while the fastest areas of job growth in the economy have paid below-average wages. Indeed, Gregory (1993) shows that of the 1,379,000 jobs created in Australia between 1976 and 1990, 983,000 (or 71 per cent) were in the lowest income quintile.

Conclusion

Economic rationalist capitalism, much more so than the postwar system, is a capitalism of winners and losers. The latter include the weak and vulnerable, of course, but increasingly large parts of the middle class are also feeling the effects of employment insecurity, while some sectors of business have also fared badly. Hence, in dealing with the problems generated by earlier models of development, economic rationalism has helped generate a new set of problems. In this environment, the unemployment issue has (finally) attained a good deal of political bite, although coherent solutions remain elusive. On the restructuring front, reflecting growing disillusionment with the level playing-field, activist industry policy is again on the political agenda.

If economic rationalist policies have failed in some respects, is a return to some form of managed capitalism politically feasible? Perhaps, if the problems of unemployment, inequality and insecurity force a shift, much like a rerun of the 1930s. But the impediments to reform here are immense. A high-growth, full-employment economy (for Kaleckian reasons) is not something the financial markets look forward to. The economic rationalist coalition identified above also remains intact, powerful and committed to further market-based reforms. Beyond this, the majority of losers from the current system also happen to be relatively weak politically. And even if a new reformist electoral coalition could be forged, any significant shift back to a full-employment macro-economic regime, for example, would be an uphill battle without major reform of the international economy and a reregulation of financial capital. This, however, would be sternly resisted. As Hutton argues:

> Capitalism may need to be managed and regulated to give its best; but that implies that the business and financial elite give up some of their autonomy of action – the very autonomy that their economic and personal inclination demands should remain unimpaired. In addition, policies that produce more output and stability of employment benefit the labour interest – and so again directly constrain business power. From the elite's point of view, it may actually be preferable to run the economy more unstably and inefficiently if the alternative is any reduction in its autonomy of action. [1994: 54]

Hence, although periods of economic trauma have in the past re-scrambled the policy egg, a post–economic rationalist model of development seems some way off yet.

Note

1 The alternative view focuses on labour market rigidities as a major source of unemployment.

CHAPTER 11

Economic Rationalism
Social Philosophy Masquerading as Economic Science

J. W. Nevile

Future economic historians will note three major themes in economic policy in Australia in the last quarter of the twentieth century. They are deregulation of the financial system, privatisation, and micro-economic reform. The last covers a range of measures, including tariff reductions, taxation reform, and changes to Australia's traditional and unique labour-market institutions. In all three cases, great changes were made in the 1980s and the 1990s. The financial system was transformed. The exchange rate was floated and exchange controls abolished. There were mergers among Australia's large banks; building societies transformed themselves into banks; foreign banks entered the Australian retail banking market. There were also important technical changes which altered the way monetary policy was conducted and put great weight on interest rate changes as the major instrument of monetary policy. Both federal and state governments engaged in what seemed like an orgy of privatisation. Government enterprises were sold to the private sector, including overseas buyers; some, such as Qantas and the Commonwealth Bank, had been icons of pride in public assets; others were state banks originally set up to help rural Australia. In the name of micro-economic reform, tariffs were drastically reduced. There was almost continual discussion of taxation reform, and major changes were introduced, such as dividend imputation, fringe benefits tax and capital gains tax. The award system was shifted from centre stage in the wage-fixing process, and enterprise bargaining was encouraged.

The election of the Howard government extended change even further. The Prices and Incomes Accord, the major exception to the policy trend, was immediately abandoned and enterprise bargaining given a boost. The first stage of the privatisation of Telstra passed through the Senate, and one of the first acts of the Howard government was to set up yet another inquiry into the financial system.

All these changes were the visible result of the ascendancy among both politicians and bureaucrats of the ideology known as economic rationalism in Australia and market liberalism in other English speaking countries. The term *economic rationalism* has become a catch-all term of abuse in some circles, but since it is so influential it is important to realise what its tenets actually are. Economic rationalism is not a tightly knit school of thought, but it has an essential core which is outlined in the second section of this chapter.

The success of economic rationalism has been remarkable, turning many previously held verities on their heads. This is not the result of advances or of new discoveries in economic theory. All around the world there was a deliberate political campaign to change the prevailing political ideology to that held by economic rationalists. This is spelt out in the third section below.

One of the tricks of many economic rationalists is to present their policy recommendations as no more than the logical consequences of orthodox economics. This is far from the case. The fourth section of this paper shows that the policy prescriptions of economic rationalism depend more on the values held by economic rationalists than on the theorems of economics. In any case orthodox economics is very clear that policy recommendations must rest on both economic analysis and a set of values.

The changes resulting from the implementation of economic rationalist policies were widespread. However, the most important was the loss of full employment as a goal of public policy. The unemployment rate rose from an average of 2.0 per cent over the five years ending in 1974 to an average of 9.4 per cent over the five years to 1994. Economic rationalism was not the only cause of this increase in unemployment but it certainly contributed to it, in ways which are discussed in the fifth section. The most important is the abandonment of a commitment by government to maintain or restore full employment. The Howard government has an explicit quantitative target for low inflation. It has no quantitative goal for reducing unemployment. Economic rationalism has reversed the priorities of the ideology it replaced.

The Definition of an Economic Rationalist

Non-economists tend to define economic rationalism in too sweeping a fashion. For example, Battin, a political scientist, maintains that the key tenet of economic rationalism is 'the belief that the market is the only legitimate allocator of goods and services in *society* at large not just in the *economy*' (1991: 296, original emphasis). I know of no economist who believes this, or even believes that the unfettered market is the only legitimate allocator of goods and services in the economy. For example, economic rationalists do believe that society should keep from starvation those whom the market leaves without income, whether this be done through the state or voluntary organisations. They do believe that the government should intervene to prevent, or at least discourage, private enterprises from polluting the environment. They do believe that the state, not the market, should provide public goods[1] such as defence, and so on. A better description of an economic rationalist is one who believes that there are very few exceptions to the rule that the market is the best way of deciding what is to be produced and how it is to be produced. Moreover, an economic rationalist holds that, even when market failure exists (that is, when the market is not the best way of deciding what is to be produced and how it is to be produced) the consequences are usually of less importance than those of the government failing in this respect, and are easier to correct.

This definition of an economic rationalist places emphasis on production, on what is to be produced and how it is to be produced. While some economic rationalists argue that unequal income distribution is important to create the right incentives, generally in Australia economic rationalists say little explicitly about income distribution, about who gets, and who should get, the goods and services that are produced. Certainly, they argue that market incomes should be determined by the market – for example, that wages should be fixed by market forces with no interference in the form of minimum wage laws or award wages and conditions laid down by the Conciliation Commission. However, they tend not to comment on the role of social security or the social wage, and hence on the final pattern of income distribution, except perhaps to leave a vague impression that social security will take care of those whom market forces leave living in poverty.[2]

In the past, many economic rationalists argued that the adoption of the policies that they advocated would raise total production so rapidly that even those at the bottom end of the income distribution would secure rises in real income (through market forces), and hence poverty would be a diminishing problem. Those with intellectual honesty now acknowledge that counter-examples, such as the cases of the United States and New Zealand, show that this is unlikely to happen, at least for a generation or two. All that is left to counter poverty is the social security system, but economic rationalists do not, in general, discuss how this role for the social security system is to be reconciled with the push for low taxation and minimal government. Overseas writers, who have inspired Australian economic rationalists, do make comments on how income should be distributed; but in Australia economic rationalists tend to focus on production, arguing that in general the questions of what is to be produced and how it is to be produced should be left to the market.

One further point about economic rationalism should be noted. Those in this camp are almost always more concerned to keep inflation at a very low rate than to reduce unemployment substantially. Perhaps this is because economic rationalism downplays the existence of market failure, and involuntary unemployment is traditionally associated with market failure; whereas inflation can, if one wishes, be blamed on government failure. One school of economists, the new classical school, even argues that involuntary unemployment does not exist and that it is possible through tight monetary policy to reduce inflation without affecting the level of unemployment; though to be fair I can only think of one economist, among those responsible for giving advice to those determining economic policy, who ever believed in the new classical school of economics. In any case, the conventional wisdom now is that it is not possible to avoid a short-run trade-off between unemployment and inflation when monetary policy is used as the principal anti-inflationary instrument.[3] Economic rationalists are opposed to using incomes policy as a weapon against inflation because it requires substantial intervention in market processes. Hence, their emphasis on keeping the rate of inflation very low does involve a cost in higher unemployment. This is discussed in the fifth section below.

Economic Rationalism as a Political Program

Economic rationalism is the Australian version of a political movement known in other English-speaking countries as market liberalism. As Marginson (1992) points out in his study of the works of Hayek, Friedman and Buchanan, the father figures of this movement wrote not primarily to increase knowledge but to change the world. They were laying the foundations of a political crusade rather than trying to establish a new school in economics. Hayek's best-known work is not that for which he received the Nobel Prize in economics but his 1944 classic in political philosophy, *Road to Serfdom*. In the next few years he saw that society after World War II was indeed moving away from individualism, and lamented that 'under the sign of "neither individualism or socialism" we are in fact rapidly moving from a society of free individuals towards one of a completely collectivist character' (Hayek 1949: 1). Hayek acknowledges that this movement away from individualism was due to politicians' implementing what the public desired, but argued that therefore public opinion should be changed through the writings of himself and like-minded economists and political philosophers: 'what to the politicians are fixed limits of practicability imposed by public opinion need not be similar limits to us. Public opinion on these matters is the work of men like ourselves, the economists and political philosophers of the past few generations who have created the political climate in which the politicians of our time must move' (1949: 108).

In his Nobel Prize acceptance speech, Buchanan criticised the economists of his time as 'ideological eunuchs'; elsewhere he stated that the only purpose of science is to assist in developing propositions about how the world ought to be (Marginson 1992: 7). Friedman drew inspiration from Hayek, whom he praised for his 'influence in strengthening the moral and intellectual support for a free society'. In turn Friedman threw himself wholeheartedly into the movement to change public opinion, with numerous magazine articles, television appearances and the famous book *Free to Choose*, written with his wife, in which he exulted that the tide of public opinion is turning (Marginson 1992: 7).

In Australia, economic rationalists are equally open about the fact that their objective is to change society. For example, King and Lloyd describe economic rationalism as 'a microeconomic *agenda* that focuses on reducing government intervention in markets' (1993: ix, original emphasis).

The political program called economic rationalism, or market liberalism, is firmly based on a social philosophy sometimes called libertarianism. This social philosophy places great emphasis on the freedom of the individual. To quote Friedman: 'As Liberals, we take freedom of the individual, or perhaps the family, as our ultimate goal in judging social arrangements' (1962: 12). And he makes it quite clear that freedom has nothing to do with freedom from want, etc., but with freedom to do as one wishes without restraints imposed by other people. Constraints imposed by lack of means do not raise problems of freedom. Robinson Crusoe could have no problem of freedom while he was alone on his island, even if he starved to death. (The example of Robinson Crusoe is taken from Friedman himself, 1962:12.) Monopolies are thought of as limiting freedom, but not lack of resources or capabilities or talents. Consequently, for Friedman the role of government is strictly limited.

> Its major function must be to protect our freedom both from the enemies without and from our fellow citizens: to preserve law and order, to enforce private contracts, to foster competitive markets. Beyond this major function, government may enable us at times to accomplish jointly what we would find it more difficult or more expensive to accomplish severally. However, any such use of government is fraught with danger. We should not, and can not avoid using government in this way. But there should be a clear and large balance of advantages before we do. [Friedman 1962: 2, 3]

This political philosophy, rather than economics, is the basis of the economic rationalists' crusade for minimal government.

Economic Rationalism is Not the Logical Conclusion of Mainstream Economics[4]

Due usually to lack of caution, rather than a desire to deceive, a number of prominent Australian economic rationalists have stated that their policy prescriptions follow inevitably from standard economics, and depend only on the propositions of economics and not on the values of the particular economists advocating the policies. For example, Sloan describes those opposed to the ideas of economic rationalism as 'anti-economists' (1993: 132), and Anderson and Blandy describe an assault on economic rationalism as 'an assault on economics itself' (1992: 36). This identification of particular policies with the conclusions of an objective study of economics is not only wrong: it is counter to the whole tradition of economics, which states firmly that any policy prescription must rest on values. There is almost always a cost as well as a benefit, and the relative weight given to each depends on one's values.

Mainstream economic thought around the world divides economics into two streams: positive economics, which is the study of what is; and normative economics (including all policy advice), which is concerned with what ought to be or what is desirable. Since normative economics takes into account what is considered desirable, it depends on value judgements on which men and women may continue to differ, however intelligent and knowledgeable they may be. On the other hand, according to conventional wisdom, positive economics is value-free, so that any two intelligent people should be able to reach agreement on the correctness or otherwise of a proposition in positive economics, through rational discussion and empirical observation.

Even if the analysis of economic rationalists was no more than orthodox positive economics, it would not be true that the policy recommendations they draw from that analysis are no more than orthodox economics, with the implication that those who oppose them are either ignorant or irrational. Virtually every policy recommendation, if implemented, involves both winners and losers. The gains of the winners may be greater than the losses of the losers, but this, in itself, does not mean that economic analysis supports the implementation of a policy change. For example, most people, including many economists, would argue that the policy change would not be justified if all the winners were already wealthy and all the losers were living in poverty even before the proposed change. Any discussion of changes is normative economics and hence rests on assumptions about values as well as economic analysis.

This alone is enough to demonstrate the falsity of any claim that opposition to the policy recommendations of economic rationalists is either irrational or ignorant; but two further points can be made that strengthen the argument against such a claim. First, the claim that positive economics is value-free can be contested. Second, some eminent orthodox economists contest the proposition that, once questions about distribution of income and wealth are put aside, orthodox economic analysis argues that a minimal state is beneficial.

Although most economics departments teach that positive economics is value-free, this can be and is challenged. I argue that positive economics rests on value judgements in at least two respects. Deductive reasoning should conform to the rules of logic, which are certainly value-free. But in general positive economics is not just a matter of deductive reasoning. It also requires an appeal to empirical studies. Moreover, the facts that an economist studies are not facts produced in carefully controlled conditions in a laboratory. They are facts thrown up by real-world situations and some judgement is required in interpreting them. This judgement is heavily influenced by the values of the person making it. The case for reducing government regulation of, and intervention in, the economy rests on the empirical judgement that cases of market failure are uncommon; that is, if the market is left to itself, it almost always produces an efficient outcome. Economic rationalists who place a high value on political and personal liberty are suspicious of government intervention and regulation, which they see as reducing personal liberty. It is perhaps not surprising that such economists generally make the professional judgement that market failure is rare. Given the values that they hold, the costs of unnecessary government intervention are high. From this viewpoint, it is responsible to be very cautious in claiming that market failure exists.

Other economists are more concerned about the costs of not intervening when to do so will be beneficial to the economy. If there is market failure, the people who suffer are usually the economically weak, who may well experience real poverty. This is particularly true of the labour market, where a major symptom of failure is involuntary unemployment. Economists who put a high value on economic security for all, on preventing anybody falling below a certain level of income, are far more likely to make the professional judgement that market failure is an important problem in an unregulated capitalist economy than are those with a libertarian social philosophy.

For those who know statistical jargon, it is all a matter of type 1 and type 2 error.[5] Economic rationalists, and others, who believe that positive economics is value-free, forget that there is no objective way of deciding whether type 1 or type 2 error is more important. It is a matter both of the consequences of each type of error and one's value judgements about the relative undesirability of each set of consequences. It is entirely proper for economic rationalists to allow value judgements about freedom to influence their policy prescriptions. It is improper and, more importantly, incorrect for them to claim that these policy prescriptions flow simply from the laws of economics. It is crucial for the rest of us to realise that their policy conclusions flow as much from their social philosophy as from their economics.

The second reason why positive economics is not value-free is the human tendency to give more weight to empirical observations that tend to support one's preconceived ideas than to those that tend to disprove them. If you doubt this, consider how often media commentators who are economic rationalists point out that in the United States, where there is a deregulated labour market, there was only a small rise in unemployment in the 1980s; whereas they never mention that when Thatcher deregulated the labour market in the United Kingdom there was a very large rise in unemployment in that country.

In many circumstances, this tendency to give more weight to observations that support a position already held is not improper. It may be appropriate, especially when one's preconceived ideas rest on a firm empirical foundation. But it is important to realise that in practice one's preconceived ideas often rest on the values that one holds, as well as on deductive reasoning and empirical observation. Because many economic rationalists transfer some of the value they place on freedom to the market itself, they often discount evidence that the market does not work well.

In short, the policy prescriptions of economic rationalists do rest to a large extent, more in some cases than others, on the values held by economic rationalists. And the overriding value, which greatly influences the results they obtain, is the worth given to individual freedom from so-called arbitrary restraint on individuals by other individuals, notably those in government.

I have spent some time presenting the argument that positive economics is not value-free. However, it is a controversial point, and it is necessary to emphasise that the proposition – that the policy prescriptions of economic rationalists do not flow automatically from mainstream economics – does not depend on whether or not positive economics involves value judgements. If it does, the case for the misleading nature of economic rationalists' claims is even stronger. But irrespective of that, it is clear that economic rationalist policy prescriptions are not just orthodox economics. They are not necessarily implied, even by a positive economics that ignores questions of income distribution. In case you think that the strength of this statement comes from my ideological bias, let me quote Geoff Brennan, who is the most eminent Australian economist among those espousing the Buchanan school of economics. Brennan argues that 'there is no presumption in . . . economics in favour of a minimal state', concluding that: 'Welfare economics after the public-goods revolution is as much a catalogue of possible market failures as of general market success. To argue that mainstream economics argues for a minimal state is in that sense simply a mistake' (1993: 7).

Economic Rationalism and Unemployment

The dramatic rise in unemployment of the 1980s and 1990s was noted at the beginning of this chapter. Economic rationalism is implicated in many ways in this. In the short run, micro-economic reform has increased unemployment; this has also proved to be true in the longer run. Financial deregulation has reinforced pressures to give priority to low inflation, except for brief periods where unemployment is unusually high; and progressive deregulation of the labour market makes necessary increasing reliance on unemployment to control inflation.

The fundamental problem is the emphasis on low inflation as a policy goal that is a feature of economic rationalism. It is natural for an ideology which downplays the existence of market failure to be less concerned about involuntary unemployment, which is a consequence of market failure, than about inflation, which, if one wishes, can be blamed on inappropriate economic policies.

It was pointed out above that it is impossible to avoid a short-run trade-off between unemployment and inflation when monetary policy is used as the principal anti-inflationary instrument. The argument is whether there is also a long-run trade-off. There is increasing evidence for hysteresis, that is, the proposition that not only is unemployment determined in part by the level of unemployment last year, but that the equilibrium level of unemployment is also determined by past levels of unemployment. Hence, many economists are coming to the view that there is a long-run trade-off between inflation and unemployment when monetary policy alone is relied on to control inflation. It is no longer possible to take the easy way out and maintain that tight monetary policy to reduce inflation will not also increase unemployment. Nevertheless, there is continual pressure from financial markets to make low inflation the overriding policy goal.

Economists employed in the financial sector and financial journalists do not necessarily argue that reducing inflation is costless. Sometimes they argue that interest rates should rise to reduce the rate of growth of employment because falling unemployment is producing unacceptable inflationary consequences (see, for instance, Max Walsh in the *Sydney Morning Herald*, 10 March 1995). More often they omit consideration of unemployment. Indeed, some financial journalists and some spokespersons for the private business sector believe that this is not a proper concern of macro-economic policy, but should be tackled through micro-economic reform, which in this context is largely a euphemism for cutting wages for the less skilled. For example, in the *Sydney Morning Herald* (15 May 1997) Padraic McGuiness wrote that 'the chief task of normal macro-economic policy [is] the control of inflation'.

It may be that institutions in the financial sector always placed much more weight on controlling inflation than on reducing unemployment. The point is that, because of financial deregulation driven partly by technological change but also by the ideology of economic rationalism, financial market institutions now have much more power to impose their views on the government. Financial deregulation has both hastened and heightened the decline in power and influence of governments, and of authorities like the International Monetary Fund, in global financial markets. Governments have lost control over the exchange rate for their currency – probably the most important single price in the economy.

The Economist (14 January 1995: 48–9) speaks of a government being punished by financial markets, and similar language is used by Australian financial journalists. The language may be extravagant, but the underlying point is correct. The exchange rate has such a widespread influence on the economy that governments must be constantly looking over their shoulder with concern about the effects of policy actions on financial markets.

The corollary to this is obvious. The priority given by financial institutions to anti-inflationary policy now has a strong influence on government actions and is an important factor in the persistence of unacceptably high levels of unemployment in Australia. Moreover, it has prevented unemployment caused by other economic rationalist policies from being reduced. In particular, structural unemployment caused by micro-economic reform, especially the removal of tariffs and the corporatisation of government business enterprises, has not been effectively tackled for fear of inflation. The situation was summed up in a speech by Bernie Fraser, the former governor of the Reserve Bank of Australia. As reported in the *Sydney Morning Herald* (16 August 1996), he said that monetary policy was becoming the hostage of influential financial markets with a vested interest in making the Reserve Bank give greater weight to low inflation than to employment and growth. Fraser said it would be 'ironic . . . if the short-termism of politicians were to be replaced by the short-termism of the financial markets'.

Moreover, the situation has become worse with the demise of the Accord, the increased emphasis on enterprise bargaining, and the consequent removal of centralised constraints. In the 1980s centralised wage-fixing under the Accord enabled a marked decline in both unemployment and inflation, and laid the basis for the very low levels of inflation in the early 1990s. This restraint on inflationary wage pressures will become much less potent as the labour market is further deregulated and enterprise bargaining further developed. It is to be replaced by the fear of unemployment. Unemployment will have to be high to make that fear credible. There could not be a more pointed contrast with the commitment to maintain full employment in the era when Australian governments had a Keynesian ideology.

Conclusion

Economic rationalism is often described as gross intellectual imperialism, as economists apply economic ideas to social issues to such an extent that social and political ideas are excluded from the discussion. While superficially this may be true, when one probes below the surface the reverse is true. Economic rationalism is the result of economics being taken over, hijacked one might say, by a particular social ideology. As it happens, I think some of the policies advocated by economic rationalists are very good, some are appalling, and some will not make a great deal of difference, one way or the other, to general economic welfare if they are adopted. But while it is important to evaluate individual policies, it is also important to look at the nature and characteristics of economic rationalism as a whole. I have tried to show that the term *economic rationalism* is a misnomer. Economic rationalism does not, in any fundamental way, spring from economics but from social philosophy. Thus, the distinguishing characteristic of the state that emerges when thoroughgoing economic rationalism is applied is that it is a libertarian state. Moreover, it is a state which has explicitly rejected a previous fundamental social contract: a social contract to maintain full employment.

Notes

1 In this context a public good is defined as a good which cannot be provided to one person without simultaneously providing it to others.
2 This is the major difference between economic rationalism in Australia and the writings of those who inspired it. Milton Friedman, for example, states: 'The ethical principle that would directly justify the distribution of income in a free market society is "To each according to what he, and the instruments he owns, produced"' (1962: 162).
3 In summing up the discussion at the conference reported in Adrian Blendell-Wignell (1992), Max Corden stated that 'Consensus did exist on three crucial matters . . . [of which the first was] you can not deflate without some cost' (p. 341).
4 This section is a revised version of material previously published in Nevile (1994: 30–2).
5 For those who do not know statistical jargon, type 1 error is that of rejecting a true hypothesis and type 2 error is that of accepting a false hypothesis.

CHAPTER 12

The Accord and Industrial Relations
Lessons for Political Strategy

Roy Green

Australia's traditional consensus on the role of industry policy in long-term growth and job creation has unravelled. However, it is now in the process of being remade in response to changing global markets and technologies. What shape the consensus takes is not yet determined, but it is sure to be influenced by the failure of micro-economic reform to bring about sustainable improvements in the structure and performance of the Australian economy (Quiggin 1996). The lessons drawn from this failure have been very different. The main advocates of micro-economic reform treat the economy as a self-regulating mechanism which left to itself would produce optimal outcomes. The problem for them lies not in the theory but in its practical execution, particularly the lack of political will on the part of politicians to pursue deregulation and free markets. The alternative view, which forms the basis of this chapter, is that the theory itself is flawed and that failure was therefore inevitable. The main purpose of the chapter is to address the issue of whether industry policy in Australia is simply to become a continuation of the failed micro-reform agenda under a new name, or whether the opportunity will be taken to combine active demand management with more interventionist supply-side measures in a new consensus on employment, growth and social justice.

Industry Policy Defined

The earlier consensus was based on the now familiar nexus between compulsory arbitration and tariff protection for the manufacturing sector. This nexus was established formally in the 1906 Excise Tariff Act, which made protection conditional on the payment of a 'fair and reasonable' wage, to be set by the new Conciliation and Arbitration Court as the basic wage. The consensus was reflected most explicitly in the 1929

Brigden Report, which stated that 'the maximum income per head for Australia would probably be obtained by reducing it to one large sheep-run with the necessary subsidiary and sheltered industries', and then went on to point out that 'there is more to be said for protecting an industry because it employs labour at good wages than for any other reason' (Brigden 1929). In other words, the substance of industry policy at this time was import substitution, whose role was to redistribute Australia's huge commodity surpluses to manufacturing. While the consensus was further sustained by the postwar Keynesian full-employment objective, it became untenable with the gradual but irreversible deterioration in the terms of trade for Australia's primary producers. A series of reports – Jackson in 1975 and Crawford in 1979 as well as reports of the Tariff Board itself – made the case for reductions in tariff assistance, but generally in the context of industry development policies to facilitate structural adjustment in the economy and labour market and to increase manufacturing competitiveness (Bell 1997a).

The tariff reductions, begun in 1973 and accelerated in the 1980s, were accompanied by industry plans but, without a coherent policy framework, the emphasis shifted in the 1990s to micro-economic reform. Specifically, this involved the removal of impediments to the operation of markets, including product and labour markets. For example, according to the Industry Commission, micro-economic reform would eliminate inefficiencies that cost the Australian economy a total of $22 billion a year (IC 1992). However, even if this estimate were correct – and it has since been revised downwards by the commission – it ignored and still ignores the much greater economic costs of unemployment, both in terms of output forgone and the Budget costs of increased benefit outlays and lower tax revenue, let alone the social costs of ill-health, crime and domestic violence (Junankar and Kapuscinski 1992). Nor does the commission's approach suggest any mechanism by which jobs will be created and unemployment reduced, except through cutting the costs of inputs, such as wages, so that new market activities can emerge spontaneously in place of those that became uncompetitive in the absence of tariff protection. Consequently, the problem for this approach is twofold. First, it does not incorporate any significant role for demand management in employment generation; and, second, it rejects supply-side policies which are needed to identify and foster new sources of competitive advantage, and which must increasingly be based on superior knowledge and skills rather than wage costs in the new global environment.

If a new consensus is to be forged on industry policy, there must be an agreed understanding of both its content and its interdependence with other areas of policy, such as fiscal and monetary policy, training and skill formation, and the program of industrial relations reform and workplace change (Genoff and Green 1998). The current resurgence of debate has pointed to the wide range of meanings implied by the term. According to the Australian Chamber of Commerce and Industry (ACCI), 'Industry policy should encompass the full range of activities of government which affect the competitiveness and operating environment of business.' This generic definition is taken further in a policy sense by the Business Council of Australia (BCA), which argues for 'a comprehensive and integrated action program to raise Australia's international competitiveness'. More specifically, the Metal Trades Industry Association (MTIA), in its report *Make or Break*, states that 'the aim of industry policy is to secure investment in high value-adding industries based on leading technologies, world cost competitiveness and strong integration with global markets, so that Australian industry is able to generate high quality jobs'. The Australian Manufacturing Workers Union (AMWU), in *Rebuilding Australia*, calls for a National Economic Development Strategy, which recognises the need to 'strengthen the tradeables sector, particularly our manufacturing industry, so that net exports make a stronger contribution to growth than has occurred in the past'.

Essentially, these reports are seeking a new set of social compromises, though with a robust and sustainable economic basis, to go beyond both the original Settlement on tariffs and arbitration and the more recent preoccupation with micro-economic reform. Indeed, the Australian Business Foundation argues in its formidable study *The High Road or the Low Road?* that a new mindset is required: 'We must move beyond the current obsession with national, non-discriminatory policies which make no distinction between sector or size type of firm, and the total opposition we seem to have to all initiatives which tend towards "picking winners".' The study maintains that we should question 'the idea that we have only *one* industry policy and recognise that we need *many* industry *policies*'. It emphasises the role of knowledge and innovation in economic performance, building on the OECD finding that 'Competitiveness in high-technology industries is mainly driven by technology factors and much less by wage and exchange rate movements, while the reverse is true in low-technology industries' (OECD 1996: 12). In further research on 'national innovation systems', which has proved influential, the OECD proposes 'additional structural reform, which can increase innovation and the diffusion of technologies within and among national economies', but this is acknowledged to be a complex process:

> At the level of national innovation systems, industrial clusters with links to local and regional innovation networks have been associated with accelerated diffusion of technology and know-how. The pace at which technologies are

diffused within national innovation systems depends on the country's industrial structure and technological specialisation, institutional set-up, corporate governance regimes, degree of economic openness and the flexibility of firms' organisational and managerial structures. [OECD 1997: 4, 48]

The significant factor in the present debate in Australia is the breadth and intensity of the clamour for a new kind of vision, leadership and policy activism to be exhibited by Australia's governing institutions. The question remains, however, whether there is a strategy just waiting to be picked up, or still to be formulated in a more receptive political environment? So far, no such strategy has emerged, though the Labor Party in its new policy platform is closer to formulating one in opposition than it was in government. The activism of the early 1980s, encompassing the development of ambitious industry plans, had largely dissipated by the 1990s, with the micro-reform agenda shifting the focus to across-the-board programs designed to 'improve competitiveness'. The election of a Coalition government in 1996 brought an ideological commitment to 'fiscal consolidation', allied with market-driven growth and investment. This resulted in the winding back of industry assistance programs, particularly export assistance and research and development, and a populist rhetoric opposed to business welfare. However, recommendations by the Industry Commission for further tariff reductions in the automotive and textiles, clothing and footwear industries raised the stakes. While the response precipitated a backdown by the government, it also exposed a damaging policy vacuum, which was highlighted by continuing high unemployment and large-scale downsizing by major corporations. Public anxiety about the future of Australian manufacturing, having been awakened, could no longer be ignored, particularly after BHP's decision to close its steel-making operation at Newcastle after eighty years of operation (Green 1997).

The government commissioned two inquiries, one headed by David Mortimer to review business programs delivered by government departments and agencies, and the other by Ashley Goldsworthy to examine ways of building Australia's capacity in information technologies. The Mortimer report, *Going for Growth*, is an attempt both to make sense of the multiplicity of existing programs and to accommodate the pressure for a more coherent approach to the structure and direction of industry policy. The generally favourable response to the report from all sides of the debate has been interpreted as a signal that the desired consensus is forming around a positive, even interventionist, approach to the task of increasing the rate of economic growth in Australia, with a specific focus on improving the performance of manufacturing industry. However, the policy paralysis immediately following publication of the report suggests that, far from there being a consensus, the debate has simply shifted to a new terrain. As already indicated, the different perspectives on the future role of industry policy reflect fundamentally opposed assumptions about the efficacy of markets in achieving efficient resource allocation, employment generation and sustainable development. Just as President Nixon's announcement in 1971 that 'we are all Keynesians now' simply disguised these differences, so industry policy has become an umbrella term for a range of perspectives which must be clearly demarcated and identified.

Theory Governs Practice

The dominant perspective is that of neoclassical economics, which asserts that optimal efficiency and consumer welfare is achieved by markets approximating most closely to the assumption of perfect competition. In this approach, prices and quantities are determined simultaneously in all commodity markets, including those for factors of production. If imperfections or impediments to the operation of markets exist, then it is the purpose of the neoclassical version of industry policy to remove such impediments. However, the impediments here turn out to be exactly the things which were themselves previously condemned by the same economists as comprising the *core* of industry policy, namely tariffs and subsidies, as well as the familiar labour-market imperfections, such as trade unions and minimum-wage regulation. In other words, alert to the changing political landscape, the neoclassical orthodoxy has repackaged and retitled its increasingly marginalised preoccupation with micro-economic reform and called it 'industry policy'. To the extent that the Mortimer Report shares this preoccupation, the subscribers to orthodoxy have been prepared to endorse it; but this should not be taken as a road-to-Damascus conversion to industry policy as understood by its proponents. Rather, it is clever tactical repositioning in response to being caught offguard by what the Mortimer Report refers to as the 'widening of the debate' (Mortimer 1997: 24).

The alternative view of industry policy questions the efficacy of markets in achieving an optimal structure for the Australian economy, which must include full employment and an equitable distribution of income. This is the overall perspective of industry policy advocates. It is a strength, as well as a weakness, of this perspective that it is not unified but comprises a number of theoretical components. First, there is the post-Keynesian tradition, derived from Keynes's *General Theory*, which challenges the conceptual basis of neoclassical orthodoxy (Burgess and Green 1997). In particular, it demonstrates that the equilibrium level of output may fall short of full employment and that unemployment is therefore a result of the operation of the market mechanism itself, not imperfections which supposedly prevent markets from clearing. It also identifies 'co-ordination failures', where, for example, the returns from investment are so low or the returns demanded by finance capital so high that investment remains stuck at low levels (Cooper and John 1995). The favoured neoclassical prescriptions of cutting wages, balancing budgets and reducing interest rates are consequently shown not to produce the intended effects. Cutting wages does not reduce unemployment, but may increase it through the negative impact on effective demand, as well as stifling technological change through substitution of labour for capital. Nor does cutting public spending and lowering interest rates automatically generate private investment, since this also depends primarily on the level of demand. It was for this reason that Keynes likened lowering interest rates to 'pushing on a string', when economic growth could be stimulated more directly by the use of demand management.

The second contribution of the alternative approach takes as its starting-point the rich analytical tradition of the Institutionalist economists, such as Veblen, Commons, Mitchell and, more recently, Galbraith, who also reject the neoclassical framework; though, rather than offering a theoretical alternative, they pursue a more empirical understanding of market structure and performance. As a result, the approach usefully supplements post-Keynesian thinking, which tends to focus on economic aggregates at the expense of the micro-economy and hence does not address the structural dimension of the limits to growth established on the supply side of the economy through the balance-of-payments constraint. Historically, as most economists are willing to acknowledge, demand expansion in Australia has been accompanied by unsustainable increases in the current account deficit. It is unsustainable because the deficit reaches a point where it can be financed only by attracting ever larger capital inflows with higher levels of real interest rates. This in turn applies the brakes to expansion, which may even be forced into reverse, perpetuating the stop-go cycle of boom and recession. The question posed by Institutionalists and their successors in the current industry policy debate is how to devise a supply-side strategy aimed at overcoming the balance-of-payments constraint, and hence boosting long-term growth and jobs, by increasing exports and replacing imports. The answer, more so now than at any previous point in our history, lies in the development of a high-skill, high-productivity manufacturing sector.

The fact is that elaborately transformed manufactures have for some time been the largest and fastest-growing segment of world trade (Green and Genoff 1993). While international trade in services is also increasing rapidly, it is insignificant by comparison, and in many cases is related closely to the growth of manufacturing technologies. As the evidence clearly demonstrates, the economies that are locked into primary commodity exports are those which have experienced the sharpest falls in their terms of trade in the 1990s. They have also been vulnerable to an overvalued exchange rate, which in turn has reinforced the domination of resources production by pricing even the most efficient manufacturers out of both domestic and international markets. The old doctrine of comparative advantage, based on a country's factor endowments, has been superseded by the notion of competitive advantage, which may be *created* through the concerted application of knowledge and ingenuity (Porter 1990). This parallels the findings of the 'new growth theory', which, by contrast with standard comparative static models, treats knowledge and associated spillover effects as an endogenous component of dynamic growth models (Dowrick 1995). It is the pursuit of competitive advantage, not textbook orthodoxy, which has underpinned the postwar miracle of Germany, France and Japan, and more recently, notwithstanding the financial crisis, that of East Asian economies such as South Korea and Taiwan (Rodrik 1995). While Australia's manufacturing export performance has also improved dramatically since the mid-1980s, the balance of trade in high-value-added, knowledge-intensive elaborately transformed manufactures continues to deteriorate (see Figure 12.1).

The third contribution to this approach further elaborates the role of innovation, especially in the development of knowledge-intensive industries. This approach, which has come to be known in the literature as 'evolutionary economics', may be traced to Schumpter's notion of 'creative destruction' in the growth cycle of capital accumulation (Freeman 1994). It seeks to understand the dynamics of the economic system and industrial structure in relation to three key observations, elaborated by the Australian Business Foundation in its report: 'that innovation drives the growth of nations; that the free market alone will not maximise innovation performance; that policy needs to focus on generating knowledge and promoting the efficacy of the flows of knowledge' (1997: 2–4). The cumulative and self-reinforcing effects of innovation are often highly concentrated and integrated into industrial districts. For example, the investment pull of Silicon Valley and other high-technology nodes continues unabated. National and regional economies with sophisticated physical, educational and information-technology infrastructure, as well as governments that encourage investment in research and development and leading-edge industrial and service sectors, directly build the fundamental characteristics of

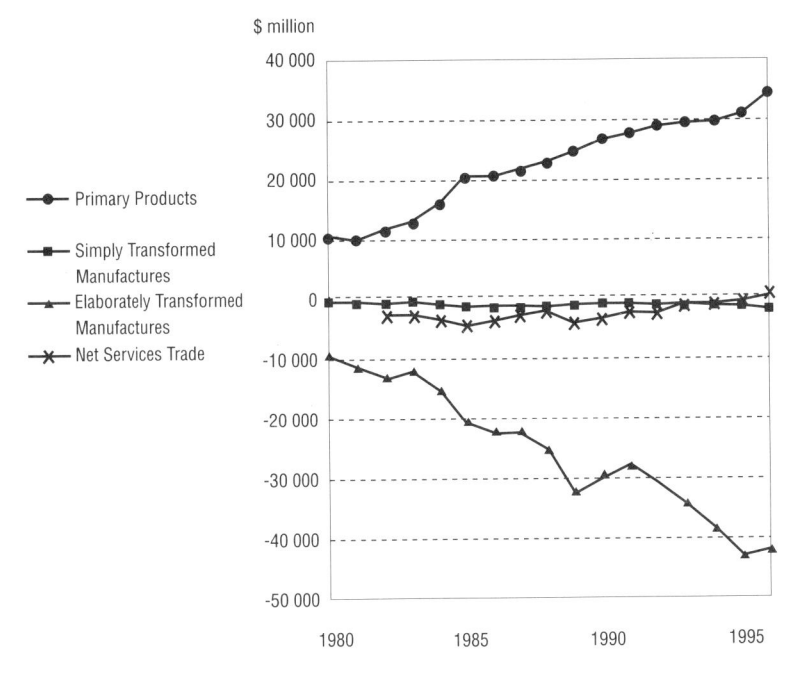

Figure 12.1 Australia's balance of trade, 1980–95
Source: ABS, DIST, Mortimer (1997).

long-term growth paths and crucial first-mover advantages (Green and Genoff 1993).

These competitive advantages consolidate investment opportunities that feed back into banking and finance and marketing and innovation. In the south-western suburbs of Paris, the European Silicon Valley, more than 100,000 people work or study in the 10,000 technologically advanced firms in electronics, data-processing, telecommunications, energy and biotechnology – investment synergies which have been promoted by the Ministry of Industry and Research. As Cohen and Zysman have pointed out, 'high tech gravitates toward state-of-the-art producers', and that means a vibrant manufacturing sector, since embedded within manufacturing is a knowledge infrastructure essential to a dynamic economy. In this sense, 'we are experiencing a transition not from an industrial economy to a service economy but from one kind of industrial economy to another' (Cohen and Zysman 1987: xiii). While jobs growth in the future will be in services, it must have links into state-of-the-art manufacturing, because without it these service jobs will be by definition poorly paid. Moreover, net additional employment in services will in any case be limited by the balance-of-payments constraint on growth to the extent that it reflects manufacturing competitiveness via the trade balance. What the new growth theory, post-Keynesian, institutionalist and evolutionary economics demonstrates is that policy-makers need a new economic tool kit. As Sheehan has argued:

> The central empirical task is not to determine which of this vast class of models constitute the true universal theory. Rather it is to use this large and growing kit of tools to explore the complex dynamics of individual economies, having regard to the fact that the models themselves suggest that relevant mechanisms and their efficacy might vary greatly from country to country, given variations in initial conditions, technology and firm structure, expectations and ambitions... [Sheehan 1996: 391]

Future Policy

What course should industry policy take in Australia? The gains from securing competitive advantage in elaborately transformed manufactures should not be taken as implying that globalisation is uniformly and inexorably driven by the shift from high-volume, low-cost mass production to high-skill, high-wage, flexible specialisation. Newly industrialising countries have been relegated by the international division of labour, or have in some cases relegated themselves, to a growth path based on low-wage competition, especially in markets for products that are labour- and resource-intensive. However, the implication of the new thinking is that industrialised economies should respond not by attempting to lower wage costs, which is economically futile as well as socially divisive, but rather by co-ordinating, facilitating and adapting to high-skill products and processes. The dilemma of Australian industry policy is that the choice has not yet unambiguously been made by leaders in either government or business. Nor is the dilemma peculiar to this country. The 1994 OECD *Jobs Study* attributed the 'appearance of widespread unemployment ... and of many poor quality jobs [to] the same root cause: the failure to adapt satisfactorily to change' (OECD 1994: 30). The Mortimer Report seeks a commitment to a consistent 3.4 per cent growth rate, but provides no mechanism by which this is to be achieved, other than measures to reduce costs to industry. In this, the report is reminiscent of the United Kingdom's ill-fated 1965 National Plan, which set ambitious growth targets in a policy void, only to see them overtaken by a devaluation crisis and subsequent abandonment of the plan by Treasury. Although it must be acknowledged that Mortimer's terms of reference were confined to a review of business progams, the opportunity was missed to break the orthodox policy mould.

Indeed, if anything, the Mortimer Report reinforces orthodoxy by justifying intervention only in cases of a demonstrated market imperfection, that is, 'where the market does not deliver the optimum output' (Mortimer 1997: 71). This assumes, as already indicated, that the market, but for this imperfection, would deliver the optimum output. The report contains many sensible proposals to introduce greater coherence and accountability to the array of existing business programs. Yet there is little understanding of the scope to create competitive advantage through a co-ordinated long-term strategy of investment in research, innovation, organisational learning, design and marketing, or in the development of global and regional technology networks, industry clusters and customer–supplier chains. The flagship proposal for a $1 billion Invest Australia fund to attract investment and minimise regulatory barriers is not a strategy but a substitute for one. It is based on the idea that industry policy consists of incentives to attract footloose capital, when the evidence clearly shows that locational decisions by all but the very footloose are determined by other factors, such as workforce skills, transport and educational infrastructure, growth opportunities and access to markets. The other feature of industry policy in the report is the continuing emphasis on programs to create a 'competitive environment', along with an unsubstantiated desire to 'avoid the creation of industry specific assistance packages' (Mortimer 1997: 164). Again, this ignores evidence of the superior performance of a sector-based strategy, even one as uncoordinated and narrowly focused as that of the 1980s, in promoting investment in elaborately transformed manufactures and exports (see Figure 12.2).

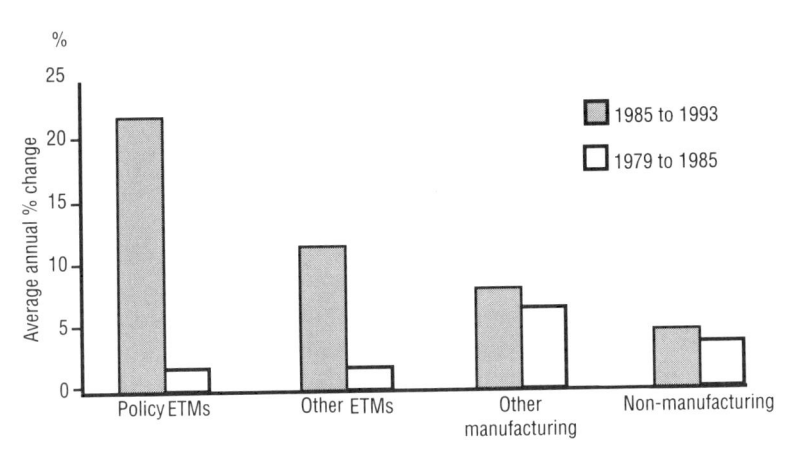

Figure 12.2 Components of Australia's export growth, 1979–93
Source: Sheehan *et al.* (1994).

Far from being concluded by the Mortimer Report, the debate on industry policy in Australia has just begun. In the first place, the survey conducted by the Economist Intelligence Unit for the MTIA's *Make or Break* finds that manufacturers are generally reconciled to the tariff reform program of the 1980s and early 1990s, though there is little support for further tariff reductions in the absence of reciprocal actions by other countries and a broader, more coherent approach in Australia. Moreover, the report argues that firms and organisations are 'now looking for a new phase in industry policy', and they are not disposed to overlook the 'striking achievements' of the 1980s industry plans:

> The pharmaceutical, automotive and IT&T industry sector programs have led to a dramatic surge in Australia's exports of elaborately transformed manufactures as well as significant levels of local R&D activity. It is worth noting that, without the surge in manufactured exports achieved through these programs, Australia's trade deficit on manufactured goods would be much larger. These programs have also supported much higher levels of investment and employment, particularly of highly skilled workers, than would otherwise have been the case. Clearly government programs that focus on specific industries, and provide appropriate incentives, are able to produce good outcomes for the community as well as for the companies involved. [MTIA 1997: 23, 107]

How should a sector-based industry policy be structured for the new millennium, and what kind of institutional arrangements would be required for its support and implementation? While the MTIA recognises the importance of 'establishing strong institutions for delivering industry policy' (1997: 118), its recommendations are not set out in detail at this stage, beyond the commitment to a 'powerful investment agency'. On the other hand, the AMWU report *Rebuilding Australia* does point to some possible directions for institutional reform, including the replacement of the Productivity Commission with a new policy research and review unit, the 'National Development Authority', the creation of a 'National Centre for Workplaces of the 21st Century' and the reinstatement of the Australian Manufacturing Council (AMC). The significance of the AMC is that its industry-sector working parties, constituted on a co-operative, tripartite basis, have the capacity not only to develop a vision for their sectors but also to translate the vision into reality. This is done through a combination of top-down advisory and assistance measures, and a bottom-up extension of enterprise bargaining beyond wages to encompass investment strategy. In the past, the problem with adopting successful models of industry policy from other countries has been that they are often too centralised, even coercive, for Australian conditions. A tripartite approach may be able to address this problem by providing the opportunity for workforce involvement at all levels of policy, from the enterprise to the sector and national levels.

Remarkably, there is no mention of tripartism in the Mortimer Report, which may reflect a view that it has gone out of fashion in the harsh, anti-union climate of the 1990s. However, there is a case for revisiting the concept as part of a fresh look at industry policy and the future role of trade unions in the Australian workplace and society. Already, some progress has been made in the development of partnerships between unions and management in Australia as part of company programs for the design and implementation of best-practice work organisation, but it is widely acknowledged that these programs have been limited by a lack of direction and diffusion of the concepts on an economy-wide basis. The industry-sector working parties of a tripartite AMC would be able to provide a frame of reference for such programs – not, of course, through the discredited methods of state control found in the former Soviet bloc and even some East Asian economies, but on the basis of well-grounded principles of democratic involvement and accountability that in turn define a shift in policy approach from the prescriptive to the 'enabling' state (Hutton 1995). They would also make it unnecessary to return to incomes policies of the traditional kind, since the extension of industrial democracy should encourage employees and unions to take a responsible long-term view of the balance to be struck in workplace bargaining between consumption and investment. Paradoxically, in this era of downsizing, work intensification and the fragmentation of labour markets, the role of industrial democracy has become more, rather than less, relevant to the future of the economy, especially when allied to new developments in pay setting, skill formation and equal opportunities.

The reinvigorated AMC could begin its task with a national stocktake of Australian industry. It is impossible to develop sound industry policy instruments when we can only guess the resources and capability of Australian industry. The ABS data can tell us the number of people employed in the economy and how much income is generated, but this is only the first step. Informed policy-making is critically dependent on the quality of research and information about a nation's industrial structure and its system of innovation. As the Australian Business Foundation has pointed out, a co-ordinated national effort is required to map institutional structures, human resource flows, industrial clusters and innovative firms. At a regional level, such work is being undertaken in a national pilot study of the Lonsdale industrial district in Adelaide, South Australia. The study will map the industrial capacity of manufacturing networks and use geographic systems information technology and industry auditing techniques to develop a spatial model; this will help policy-makers and business to identify opportunities for investment in strategic industries and employment. Such industry intelligence can target industry development measures to grow emerging exporters and new networking opportunities (Genoff 1997).

Australian examples of cluster development and networking are emerging on a regional basis, as for many regions around the world, like Emilia–Romagna, Baden–Wurttemberg, Cambridge–Reading and Route 128 (Boston, Mass.). For example, in the Hunter Valley region of New South Wales, twenty-three clusters have been identified through an integrated regional strategy, and logistical support will be given to firms that seek to combine the advantages of small-firm flexibility with the global economies of scale that flow from effective networking arrangements and producer–user links (HEDC 1997). One such network is Hunternet, consisting of twenty-eight high-value-adding engineering companies, which have defined areas for co-operation as well as competition, particularly in the development of new technologies and skills and the pursuit of market niches. A recent report on business linkages and networks by the Bureau of Industry Economics found that 75 per cent of firms participating in cooperative arrangements achieved 'major' or 'critical' benefits in terms of increased profits/sales and market knowledge (BIE 1995). These examples also illustrate how research and development and innovation underpin the uptake of advanced manufacturing technology and production of elaborately transformed manufactures. As research by the OECD (1996) suggests, the uptake and diffusion of new technology is path-dependent (that is, it depends on the path already taken), and increasingly defines competitive advantage in the world economy. Furthermore, the process is cumulative and, as Dodgson (1996) observes, 'what you do today depends in part upon what you did in the past'. Hence,

> A quarter century after German battery maker Varta went to Singapore, drawn largely by cheap labour, it plans to close operations there and transfer production to a country with the highest labour costs of any industrial nation – Germany. Varta is not alone. German firms, from giants such as Daimler–Benz AG and Siemens AG, to smaller companies such as Sennheiser Electronic GmBh & Co KG, a maker of microphones, are deciding a highly trained workforce in Germany, though expensive, is worth the cost if it keeps quality high. [*Australian Financial Review* 22 October 1997]

Does Australia have a future, as Dr Ohmae of Japan's McKinsey suggests, as the 'brains trust of Asia', with new ideas for sustainable jobs and industries; or are we destined to become locked into a downward spiral of low wage, resource intensive competition? Will we accept the advice of Laura Tyson, President Clinton's former economic adviser, that because high-technology industries 'violate the assumptions of free trade', we should pursue a 'cautious activism' in industry policy? The Australian Business Foundation accepts this view and recommends that 'Governments should shift their policy emphasis from cost minimisation per se towards innovation and technology development strategies. This should apply both to the domestic and international sectors' (1997: 10, 11). There is little doubt that it represents the emerging consensus of recent reports on the future of industry policy in Australia, though there are inevitable differences in scope and detail. Nor is the validity of this approach undermined by the present slowdown in East Asian economies, whose political structures and financial systems are still in the process of being integrated into world markets. The next steps in industry policy are being discussed and implemented in Europe, Japan and the United States; Australia, currently at the margins of these developments, has the opportunity to identify potential gains from first-mover advantages and then to pursue them in a coherent and co-ordinated way. Essentially, as we have argued, this will require a new, more interventionist approach to economic policy at the national level with a new understanding of the role of industry and regional policy.

Tool for Change

In conclusion, it has been a central theme of this chapter that Australia's economic problems can no longer be addressed by a quick fix, whether by attracting capital inflows, necessary though they are, or changing the tax system or reducing business costs. The real issue is to identify and develop the competitive advantage that already resides in people working in thousands of enterprises across the country, and construct a policy framework to realise the potential wealth of talent and ingenuity. This requires arrangements not only to support the involvement of employees and unions in decision-making, but also to co-ordinate the plans and priorities of enterprises through a sector-based industry policy and, just as importantly, to accommodate the specific needs of Australia's regions. The task is a complex one; it cannot be reduced to any single prescription. Industry policy is a powerful tool for change and improvement, but it should be treated as part of an integrated approach to economic growth, employment and environmental sustainability. The approach must include the revival of a Keynesian approach to macro-economic policy, active labour-market programs, a major regional development initiative, and a shift in industrial relations policy to emphasise fairness and job security on the one hand, and involvement by the workforce in change on the other (Green 1996a). Above all, its success will depend upon the training and education of Australia's workforce and management, opened to critical scrutiny in the pioneering but already largely forgotten Karpin Report on leadership and management skills. Will the Mortimer Report share the fate of its predecessor? The report may in some ways be a false start in the new round of industry policy debate, but it is at least a start.

PART V

The New (In)compatibilities: The Welfare State and Competitive Markets

CHAPTER 13

Is Australia Particularly Unequal?
Traditional and New Views

Peter Whiteford

The Traditional View

For many years there has been a widely held view that Australia was characterised by an egalitarian approach in social affairs and a relatively equal distribution of income.[1] Indeed, egalitarianism has been seen as one of the distinctive features of the Australian Way. This view goes back to the turn of the century, and partly springs from the position of Australia (and New Zealand) as pioneers in social legislation. As early as the 1880s, visitors to Australia remarked on the greater equality of the distribution of wealth, with the lack of a poor class, comfortable incomes being in the majority, and millionaires few and far between (Twopenny, in Garton, 1990: 1). Members of the British Fabian Society, Beatrice and Sidney Webb, who visited Australia in the late 1890s, stressed the greater achievement of democracy and commitment to equality compared to the situation prevailing in Britain.

Residents expressed similar views. In the *Melbourne Review* of 1882, Henry Gyles Turner asserted:

> It may be safely said that there is no country in the world where the material prosperity and substantial comfort of the working classes are so assured as in Australia. In the United States and California wages may nominally rule a little higher, but the cost of living is fully fifty or sixty per cent higher than here. In Canada the season of active outdoor labour is so limited by the severity of the climate that there is no room for comparison. In the Cape Colony wages are low and work is intermittent . . . But compare the condition of the skilled mechanic, the artisan and the labourer here with that of his prototype in the old settled countries of Europe, and especially Great Britain, and we find his wages ranging from half as much again to quite double, his hours of labour substantially shorter, and the cost of his living from one third to one half less. [in Turner, 1968: 105]

This characterisation was given semi-official expression by Coghlan, the Government Statistician in New South Wales between 1886 and 1905, who stated that 'wealth is widely distributed, and the contrast between rich and poor, which seems so peculiar a phase of modern civilisation, finds no parallel in these Southern Lands. That there is poverty in these colonies is undeniable and inevitable; but no-one in Australia is born to poverty' (in Raskall, 1992b: 9–10).[2]

This view of the relative standing of Australia has been supported by historians. According to Ian Turner, 'By the 1880s . . . the Australian colonies were stable communities, wonderfully prosperous by old world standards, free of the most obnoxious of old world inequalities, professedly democratic, self-governing and well ordered' (1968: xv). Russel Ward's assessment goes even further:

> Seventy-five years ago the wage earning majority of the population in Australia and New Zealand were politically, socially and economically better off than their counterparts in other countries. National income was much more evenly distributed: class distinctions were less marked and social mobility was greater. Democratic institutions ensured that political power was shared among adult men and women more evenly than in contemporary Britain or France or the United States. Of course Australia remained a thoroughly capitalist country . . . Yet poor men and ethnic minorities in other countries were at least as badly off, and relatively, more numerous. It remains true that in Australasia the welfare state had developed further and faster than anywhere else in the world. When contemporaries spoke of the Antipodes as 'the workingman's paradise', they were aware of exaggeration in the figure of speech but not, usually, of irony. [Ward in Métin 1977: ii]

Although the scope of social policy experimentation in Australia varied over time (Roe, 1976; Castles, 1985), there continued to be evidence suggesting that the distribution of income was more equal than in similar societies, at least until the 1960s. A survey of the literature on income inequality by Sue Richardson (1979) noted the severe problems in making international comparisons, but concluded that most studies consistently showed Australia had 'a relatively very equal distribution of income'. Lydall (1968) concluded that, among twenty-five countries surveyed, Australia, New Zealand, Czechoslovakia and Hungary had the lowest degree of dispersion of (pre-tax) employment income in 1959–60. A study by Paukert (1973) of fifty-six countries found that Australia, the United States and the Scandinavian countries were the group in which the top 5 per cent of households had the smallest income share. A well-known study of twelve countries by Sawyer (1976) for the OECD concluded that Australia, Japan and Sweden had the least unequal post-tax income distribution. The survey by Stark (1977) for the UK Royal Commission on the Distribution of

Income and Wealth concluded that Australia and the United Kingdom had the lowest pre-tax income inequality of eight countries surveyed, while the Gini coefficient[3] for post-tax income was lowest in Sweden and Australia. Kakwani (1980) in a sample of seventeen developed countries found that only in Hungary was the income share of the top quintile less than in Australia, or the share of the bottom 40 per cent greater.

The view that Australia had a relatively equal income distribution has been quoted by social scientists such as Broom and Jones (1976: 42–59) and Encel (1970: 61), and not unexpectedly was accepted by politicians. Harold Holt in 1967 said he did not know of any free country in the world where 'what is produced by the community is more fairly and evenly distributed among the community than Australia' (in Raskall, 1980: 73). Again, W. C. Wentworth concluded in 1969 that Australia was 'probably the country in the whole world where the impact of poverty is least' (in Garton, 1990: 1).

This conclusion was given support by Richard Downing in the first chapter of *People in Poverty: A Melbourne Study*. After noting that the study found 7 per cent of income units in Melbourne in poverty, with closer analysis suggesting a minimum of 4 per cent in need, he went on to say:

> the survey confirmed our expectation that the incidence of poverty and need in Melbourne would be low. . . . International statistical comparisons are always dangerous, especially in this field of poverty . . . It is nevertheless worth noting that, on the basis of not obviously very different criteria, it has been estimated that 14 per cent of the people are in poverty in the United Kingdom . . . in the United States, by far the richest country in the world, 20 per cent of families have been found to be in poverty. The incidence of poverty in Melbourne, and by inference in Australia, can be confidently asserted to be much less than in those two countries. Only New Zealand and Scandinavia, with which countries Australia enjoys roughly comparable living standards, are likely to have as little poverty. [Henderson *et al.* 1970: 4–5]

As late as 1979, Mendelsohn in his history of social welfare in Australia, *The Condition of the People*, wrote:

> The issue of equality is a prime one in Australia. There is a potent sentiment of egalitarianism, and Australians are intolerant of privilege and in theory wishful of moving towards equality. . . . While Australian mythology has exaggerated the degree of equality, the absence from the colonies of an hereditary aristocracy and the circumstances of a fresh start in a virgin country fostered egalitarian aspirations . . . economic institutions lent mild encouragement to the translation of myth into fact. . . . All the information available indicates that the distribution of Australian incomes, always rather equal on international standards, has recently grown more equal. [1979: 63–4]

The New View

During the 1980s and 1990s this view of Australia was radically reappraised. Scarcely a month now goes past without gloomy media reports of trends in income distribution or comparisons with other countries. We are variously told that there is an ever-rising tide of poverty, that the rich are getting richer and the poor poorer, that the middle class is shrinking, or that there is a 'new middle class', and that there is an emerging underclass living in ghettoes. We are said to have the second-highest rate of child poverty in the developed world. It is also said that, although Australia was the wealthiest country in the world in the nineteenth century, we are now slipping in the national income stakes, and it has been claimed that about one in eight Australians suffer from hunger.

The new evidence includes the United Nations *Human Development Report 1993*, which shows that among twenty industrialised countries in the period 1985–89 the income share of the lowest 40 per cent of households was smallest in Australia, and the ratio of the incomes of the highest 20 per cent to those of the poorest was greatest. *The Economist* cites similar figures, giving the United States, Australia, New Zealand and Switzerland the highest income inequality among thirteen countries, and Sweden and Japan the lowest (5–11 November 1994: 19–23). More recently, Atkinson *et al.* (1995) estimate that Australia was the seventh most unequal of seventeen countries. Income inequality was greater in the United States, Ireland, Switzerland, Italy and the United Kingdom, with inequality in France about the same as Australia; the least unequal countries were Norway, Sweden and Finland.

Within Australia, Raskall (1980, 1992b, 1992c) argues that Australian egalitarianism has always been a myth, noting that the statements by Coghlan quoted above were never supported by empirical evidence. Wheelwright states that 'enough evidence has now accumulated to substantiate the view that Australia is one of the most unequal societies in the developed world' (1990: 199), citing the *Luxembourg Income Study* (*LIS*) and the work of Saunders and Hobbes (1988). Sharp (1991), Connell (1991), Carter (1993), Stilwell (1993) and Thompson (1994) reach similar conclusions. The starkest expression of the new view is given by Raskall, who states: 'Let's get a few facts straight. Australia is one of the most unequal societies in the world' (1992a: 9).

There have been contrary views. In commenting on Carter (1993), Nevile points out that the *LIS* data include only a dozen or so of the richest and most equal countries in the world, so that Australian income inequality falls towards the middle of the pack (1993: 90). Travers and Richardson (1993) take exception to the new view, specifically citing the article in *Modern Times* by Raskall (1992a), but their discussion is brief. While accepting that the distribution of income in Australia was the second most unequal after the United States, Travers and Richardson (1993) point to differences in survey timing and the sensitivity of results to the choice of equivalence scales, as well as noting that the *LIS* countries are among the most equal of countries.

On balance, there has been an extraordinary turn-around in opinion about inequality in Australia; despite the contrary views, it seems fair to say that the new consensus is that Australia is very unequal. There are four possible explanations for the difference between the traditional and new views:

- The traditional view is incorrect, and Australia was not particularly equal in the first part of the twentieth century.
- The traditional view is correct, but Australia has become more unequal over the course of the century.
- The traditional view is correct, but other countries have reduced inequality more rapidly than Australia.
- The traditional view is correct, and the new view is incorrect.

Determining which of these explanations is more accurate – and why – is of considerable importance in debates about the future of social policy. Australian commentators are increasingly looking for alternative models for social reform. In the past Sweden was seen as the exemplar of an alternative social democratic model, pursuing the path to greater equality through increased welfare state spending. Most of those cited above as arguing that Australia is particularly unequal can be broadly described as coming from the political Left, who in general propose higher taxes and public spending, or direct control over economic institutions. These policy solutions assume that existing institutions have failed to reduce inequality.

Conservative commentators have also argued that the welfare state has failed to reduce inequality, primarily because welfare provision has undermined work incentives, thus increasing poverty (Murray 1984). These views have influenced Australian commentators, who have identified the United States, the United Kingdom and New Zealand as models for achieving lower unemployment through cuts in welfare and increasing wage flexibility. Thus, for differing reasons, analysts from the Left and the Right both argue that Australian institutions have failed to reduce inequality and therefore deserve radical reform. From this point, their prescriptions diverge: on the one hand, social protection should be expanded; on the other, it should be wound back.

If the Australian Way was never very successful at reducing inequality, then its demise may not be regretted. If, however, Australian institutions have failed only recently, identifying the causes of these failings is essential in developing appropriate responses. If other countries have more effective solutions to the challenge of incorporating greater social justice into the distribution of income, then to the extent possible we should consider moving away from current Australian arrangements towards these more successful approaches. If, however, the new view is incorrect, we may need to identify what aspects of the Australian approach to social protection remain effective, so that these institutions can be supported, while considering what policies do require reform.

It is not possible to assess all alternative explanations in detail. Determining what has happened to income inequality in Europe or North America over the past century is clearly too large a topic. Attempting to reconstruct a picture of the distribution of income in Australia in the earlier part of this century is also extraordinarily difficult. Fortunately, we have a number of careful reviews and analyses of the available data – Richardson (1979), Ingles (1981), McLean and Richardson (1986) and Saunders (1993). Unfortunately, these studies reach rather different conclusions. McLean and Richardson argue that 'inequality has decreased unambiguously and by a substantial amount ... over the period 1933 to 1979' (1986: 80). This mirrors Jones's well-known comment, when comparing the 1915 Census and the 1968–69 Income Survey, that 'it would require a mind peculiarly resistant to evidence to deny that over the last half a century there has been a significant reduction in inequality of income distribution among men' (1975: 32). This contrasts with Encel's reading that 'the distribution of income appears to have remained largely unchanged during this century' (1970: 115), which in turn resembles Aaron's remark for the United States that tracking changes in income distribution 'was like watching the grass grow' (1978: 17). In a further variant, Saunders (1993) concludes that there has not been a unidirectional trend in income inequality over the last eighty years, with inequality likely to have fallen between the Depression and World War II and risen afterwards, so that the distribution of individual gross income was very similar in 1989–90 and 1942–43.

Whatever the precise trends in income inequality over the course of the century, if the traditional view is accurate, then a change in Australia's comparative ranking implies either that other countries have become more equal more rapidly, or that the trend to increased inequality in the 1980s identified by Saunders (1993) was greater in Australia than in other countries. This latter possibility does not seem to be the case. Atkinson *et al.* (1995) identify a broad trend to increased inequality in OECD countries over the first part of the 1980s, most strongly in the United Kingdom and the United States, but less strongly in Scandinavia and the Netherlands. However, in Australia some indicators of inequality were ambiguous, so that it is not possible to say definitively that inequality increased. A 1998 OECD study finds that Australia had the third-lowest increase in disposable income inequality among ten countries in the period 1975/76 to 1992/93: inequality rose between 1976 and 1984, but fell in the next decade, although not sufficiently to offset the earlier rise. This suggests that, if Australia moved from relative equality to relative inequality, the switch occurred before the 1980s.

Moreover, the new empirical literature using the *LIS* and other sources also shows that the distribution of earnings in Australia is still among the least unequal of developed countries,[4] a conclusion apparently consistent with the traditional view. In addition, the Australian tax and social security systems are among the most progressive in the OECD.[5] Put another way, in Australia we appear to have less middle-class welfare than any other OECD country.

Given the relatively compressed nature of the Australian earnings distribution and the progressive profile of Australian tax and social security arrangements, why then is measured income inequality so high? The main argument offered by some analysts is that the Australian welfare state is less effective at reducing inequality than higher-spending welfare states, paradoxically, precisely because we have less middle-class welfare than other countries (Barr 1990; Korpi and Palme 1994). That is, although taxes and benefits in Australia are progressive (*efficient*), they are not very *effective* at redistribution. Other countries reduce inequality to a greater extent than Australia, because their tax and social security systems take a larger share of national income. This implies that, as a country, we simply fail to spend enough on social security transfers or raise enough in taxes to reduce underlying inequality significantly.

A Residual Welfare State?

It is often taken as a given in Australia that our non-contributory, flat-rate and means-tested social security system is more effective at reducing poverty than the more expensive and less-targeted social insurance systems of other countries. This is because, by definition, for a given level of expenditure, a means-tested system provides more generous benefits to the poor than a universal or earnings-related benefit.

The counter-argument is that the degree of redistribution achieved by a benefits system depends on the 'quantum' of benefits as well as the progressivity of the formula for allocating benefits (Barr 1990). A means-tested program with a highly redistributive formula may achieve limited redistribution if spending is low. That is, while the Australian system is more efficient than others, it is not as effective at reducing poverty (Mitchell *et al.* 1994b) or inequality. In contrast, a high-cost, earnings-related system may achieve greater redistribution by providing more generous basic benefits (Korpi and Palme 1994; Saunders 1994).

A political explanation for this process is given by Baldwin:

> In nations where the state became the main insurance broker of the bourgeoisie ... the disadvantaged gained from clinging to the coattails of the favoured. The middle classes arranged things first and foremost for themselves, the unfortunate were the beneficiaries of a comparatively successful trickle-down. ... In the long run, the unfortunate have gained most from those welfare states securely anchored in the interests and affections of the bourgeoisie. [1990: 298]

Similarly, Castles and Mitchell (1992a) suggest that means-testing may dissuade the better-off from supporting adequate benefits for the poor. Gelbach and Pritchett (1997) also ask, 'Does more for the poor mean less for the poor?' They find that the redistributive efficiency gains of indicator targeting may fail to outweigh the resulting reduction in funds available for redistribution.[6] A related argument is that non-targeted benefits produce more egalitarian overall outcomes than means-tested benefits, because even more unequal forms of private provision are crowded-out (Palme 1990; Kangas and Palme 1990).

These arguments are of considerable significance to debates about the future of the Australian welfare state. They imply that, if we wish to reduce inequality, we should increase the level of taxes and welfare spending. Moreover, they suggest that we can achieve greater redistribution between rich and poor even if we have a less-progressive tax system (for example, by introducing a broad-based consumption tax) and a less-targeted social security system (more universal or even earnings-related benefits).

There are a number of obvious problems with such an analysis. In the first instance, it is crucial not to confuse the amount of redistribution with the size of welfare state spending. Logically, it is the quantum of redistribution, not the quantum of taxes or benefits separately, that determines the redistributive effects of a tax-benefit system. Redistribution is a function of the difference between taxes and benefits as a proportion of income. In this context, the redistributive profile of taxes and benefits is important, since proportional taxes and benefits – no matter what their size – do not change the distribution of income.

Reflection also suggests that the political explanation for the benign trickle-down to the poor in large welfare states does not stand up to scrutiny. In fact, it is Baldwin, in his analysis of *The Politics of Social*

Solidarity, who shows the main flaw in his own argument for a benign trickle-down:

> For a member of the middle class, average in both fortune and risk, social insurance of sufficient actuarial orthodoxy was not especially distinct from private efforts at risk redistribution. It offered no particular advantages beyond certain considerations of efficiency and administration, and threatened no fearsome disadvantages. For such a person, it mattered little whether public risk redistribution was limited to the poorest, leaving the self-sufficient to their own devices, or whether statutory intervention broadened in scope, with the bourgeoisie both the main source and primary recipient of reallocation. For the average middle classes the distinction was largely a matter of indifference: *whether they insured themselves or paid taxes for statutory provision was materially inconsequential.* [1990: 297, emphasis added]

If it is materially inconsequential for the middle classes in large welfare states whether they insure for themselves or pay taxes for public provision, then income redistribution cannot be occurring. The central problem with the benign trickle-down is that real redistribution to the poor means that the financial costs to the middle class cannot be the same whether they provide for themselves or socially insure. According to Baldwin's argument, the middle classes in large welfare states must either become more altruistic than those in small welfare states, or be more afraid of social disorder, or they have less political power, or they do not notice that more of their taxes and contributions goes to the poor; in other words, some of the people – the middle classes – can be fooled all of the time.

It does not matter that the middle classes also benefit from being part of a large welfare state – redistribution is redistribution. In the static framework of international inequality comparisons, redistribution can only be interpreted as a zero-sum game – if the poor are better off, then the middle class must be worse off.[7]

In the real world, redistribution need not be a zero-sum game. On the one hand, conservatives may argue that it is a negative-sum game, with everyone worse off than they would be without redistribution. On the other, greater equality may have positive effects on national productivity and economic growth (Persson and Tabellini 1995). While this is a possibility, it does not resolve the logical problems inherent in the benign trickle-down theory, for it still requires the middle class to be content with a smaller relative share of a larger cake.

There is a further explanation for the apparent failure of the Australian approach to redistribution to reduce inequality substantially. This is that the failure is apparent and not real: the results that influence the new view are an artefact of the methods used to measure inequality and income redistribution. The discussion that follows argues that bigger is not necessarily better when it comes to welfare state spending. In particular, most international comparisons have an inbuilt bias to overestimate the redistributive impact of large welfare states, because the methodological framework used to reach these conclusions is incomplete.

The Standard Approach and Its Problems

While these issues can be approached from historical, political and ideological perspectives, recent international comparisons all rest on a restricted set of numerical indices. It is essential therefore to understand the strength and weaknesses of these measures. By definition, any numerical assessment of income inequality must deal with a range of technical questions (Gruen 1989; Whiteford 1997), including the concept of living standards, the measure of material resources, the treatment of wealth, the period over which income is measured, the unit assumed to share income, and the treatment of families or households with differing needs. All income-distribution studies must make precise decisions about each issue. For many issues there is no one correct answer, so the choice of a particular approach is arbitrary in the sense that there can be good reasons for making different choices. But results can differ significantly if different decisions are made about any issue.[8]

The problem with much recent research, as well as with many early studies supporting the traditional view, is that different technical choices have been made. For example, the figures for Australia quoted by *The Economist* make no adjustment for household size, while the results for some (but not all) other countries do. Thus, these results are simply not comparable. Such problems have been substantially remedied with the development of the *Luxembourg Income Study*, which now offers the most consistent source of comparable international data on income distribution. Nevertheless, while the *LIS* undoubtedly provides the best data for international comparisons, there is a set of fundamental conceptual problems with the measurement of income across countries.

Virtually all the studies cited above adopt 'the standard approach' (Ringen 1987) to analysing income distribution data. As set out in Figure 13.1, essentially this is an accounting framework for relating different income components and for deriving aggregates such as gross income and cash disposable income. Within the *LIS* and other microdata, this framework is applied to each household's income to produce the four income measures identified. These household or income unit accounts are aggregated and analysed to produce measures of

Wages and salaries
+
Self-employment income
+
Property income
   = 1. Factor income
   +
Occupational and private pensions
   = 2. Market income
   +
Social security cash benefits
(universal, income-related, contributory)
   +
Private transfers
   +
Other cash income
   = 3. Gross income
   −
Income tax (and employee social security contributions)
   = 4. Cash disposable income
   x
Equivalence scales
   = 5. Equivalent cash disposable income

Figure 13.1 The income accounting framework

distribution and redistribution. The redistribution achieved by taxes or transfers is calculated by comparing income shares, Gini coefficients, or poverty indexes at different stages in the process outlined.

While this framework is used by virtually all international studies, there are obvious limitations that invalidate statistical measures based on it. These problems affect analysis of the degree of underlying inequality; they affect the measurement of the effectiveness and efficiency of the welfare state itself; and they affect the measurement of the final outcomes of redistributive policy. Consequently, they also impact on any policy inferences drawn from international comparisons.

First, any assessment of the distributional impact of the welfare state involves a comparison of the observed distribution with a counterfactual – the hypothetical distribution existing in the absence of the policies evaluated (Pederson 1994). Figure 13.1 relies on a counterfactual in which the welfare state has no behavioural effects on the underlying income distribution. The framework is linear, implying that the distribution of market incomes precedes the operation of the tax-transfer systems, and there have been no interactions between them, apart from the direct effect of government programs in reducing inequality.

Crucially, it is also assumed that the wide variations in the scope of different welfare states have had the same (zero) behavioural impact in each country.

This is completely unrealistic. As argued by Layard (1977) and Reynolds and Smolensky (1977), to the extent that the welfare state displaces private savings or other activities,[9] the standard approach exaggerates underlying income inequality and then exaggerates the amount of redistribution achieved by the welfare state.

Second, the standard framework is incomplete. Most income surveys include information only on cash transfers and direct taxes, which form different fractions of overall government activity in different countries.[10] Most comparative studies ignore the impact of broad-based consumption taxes and government non-cash benefits such as health, education and public housing. Consumption taxes tend to be regressive by income, and are much higher in large welfare states than in small welfare states. Non-cash benefits tend to be less progressive than targeted or universal cash transfers, but vary in significance by less than cash benefits. For example, spending on cash transfers in Australia is only 56 per cent of the OECD average, while spending on welfare services is 84 per cent, on education 88 per cent, and on public health about 98 per cent of the OECD average (OECD 1996).

An even more significant gap in the standard framework is the complete absence of employer social security contributions. Given that these taxes pay for most social security spending in some countries, but do not exist in Australia or New Zealand, and are very low in Denmark and relatively low in the other Anglo-American countries, their absence from welfare state comparisons is particularly problematic (Whiteford 1995). Employer social security contributions can be considered as deferred earnings similar to employer-provided superannuation. The United Nations *Provisional Guidelines for Income Statistics* (1977) advocate the inclusion of employers' contributions to social security schemes as part of wage and salary income in income surveys such as those in *LIS*. Adoption of the UN guidelines would have a massive effect on measured income inequality and relative poverty in many OECD countries, but no effect in Australia.

For example, an average manufacturing worker in Australia appears to earn about 30 per cent more than a similar worker in France or Sweden, when gross earnings are adjusted by purchasing-power parities to a common currency, even though France and Sweden are about as wealthy as Australia. In France and Sweden employers pay social security contributions of around 50 per cent of gross wages, so that total wage costs are similar to those in Australia. Because employer contributions are not included in the standard framework, the measured gap between those receiving benefits and those in work is artificially narrowed in countries with high levels of employer social security contributions.

In fact, the apparently low level of benefit replacement rates in Australia is the primary basis for the view of Esping-Andersen (1990) that the Australian social security system is residual. This simply reflects incomplete accounting of the taxes paying for social security benefits in most large welfare states. Indeed, when the purchasing power of benefits for the poorest is compared rather than their replacement rates, Australia proves to be significantly more generous to the poor than the OECD average. For example, Whiteford (1995) shows that the Australian single age pension in 1991 was higher than comparable minimum benefits in twenty OECD countries (apart from Canada, Iceland, Luxembourg, and the Netherlands). Eardley *et al.* (1995) also found that basic means-tested benefits in Australia (averaged across nine household types) were 24 per cent above the average for OECD countries. This suggests that, if an alternative set of measures is used, Australian targeted benefits for the poorest are relatively generous, not residual. But if Australian benefits for the poorest are actually relatively generous, the basis of the argument for redistributive failure becomes shaky.

Third, there is a related complication relating to the accounting period over which redistribution is measured. Transfers have both an insurance and a redistributive element, so that their redistributive element cannot be examined using only annual income data (Creedy 1992). This point is important, since the mix of elements differs significantly between countries. For example, Falkingham and Harding (1996) estimate that in Australia, on average, 38 per cent of lifetime benefits received by individuals are paid for at another stage in their life, with 62 per cent being redistribution between individuals – hence the relative lack of middle-class welfare. In the United Kingdom only 38 per cent of benefits is redistribution between different individuals. This means that the quantum of redistribution (Barr 1990) is not the same as the quantum of spending. In fact, applying the ratios of Falkingham and Harding to actual social security spending in Australia and the United Kingdom would imply that the quantum of redistribution in the two countries would be virtually identical, even though the quantum of spending in the United Kingdom is 70 per cent higher. Other higher-spending OECD countries achieve even less redistribution between income groups, because their earnings-related formulas in retirement pensions are even less progressive than those of the United Kingdom (Palme 1990). In contrast, the United States has both lower spending than Australia and a less progressive benefit formula.

Fourth, in a single-year accounting period, taxes and social security contributions are treated as a redistributive burden, rather than as a source of future income entitlements to those paying them. These future entitlements are completely ignored, even though they have many of the features of private wealth (although they are not realisable except in the form of an income stream when required). This contributes to the apparent result that middle-class families in large welfare states appear worse-off than similar families in small welfare states. The benefits accruing to middle-class households are not counted because they are future entitlements or substitutes for private expenditure. In the standard approach, middle-class households in large welfare states are treated as if they have plunged into poverty on retirement, simply because the government provides their pensions. Because benefits to the middle- and high-income groups are not fully measured, low-income groups appear to be relatively better-off in large welfare states. In contrast, a greater proportion of lifecycle redistribution in small welfare states such as Australia is through private means, including home purchase, private superannuation, endowment insurance and other forms of private savings. These private costs are not included in the standard framework, even though they are largely equivalent to public social insurance, as specifically pointed out in the above quotations from Baldwin (1990).

Overall, these arguments show that the standard international comparisons that are the basis of the new view of Australian inequality contain fundamental flaws that overestimate the degree of redistribution achieved by the welfare state. This is also true in Australia, of course, but the degree of error is less marked than it is in countries with higher but less progressive social spending. Thus, the standard framework is systematically biased to make high-taxing welfare states that emphasise redistribution across the lifecycle look more equal than low-taxing countries, such as Australia (Ståhlberg 1985, 1986).

Broadening the definition of income to take account of some of these factors narrows the difference between measured outcomes in different countries (Smeeding *et al.* 1992; Whiteford and Kennedy 1995), but the methodology of comparative analysis of welfare state outcomes still requires considerable development. It follows that strong conclusions about welfare outcomes should be tempered by an appreciation of weaknesses of the analytical frameworks producing these outcomes.

Conclusion

The new view that Australia is one of the most unequal of developed countries rests on an incomplete methodological framework. Indeed, the weight of evidence supports the conclusion that, if a fully comprehensive framework for measuring income inequality were used, Australia would remain among the least unequal of developed countries, although probably not as equal as the Scandinavian countries or the Netherlands. In reaching this conclusion, I emphasise the consistent findings that Australia continues to have a relatively compressed earnings distribution, that the Australian taxation system has one of the most progressive structures of all OECD countries, and that the social security system is the most progressive of all OECD countries.

Underlying many of the conclusions reached here are some exceptional institutional arrangements in Australia – notably in relation to the system of wage-fixing, the apparent high level of employee wages, and the financing of the social security system (Roe 1993; Cass 1998; Castles 1985, 1997) – together with the provision of social protection through regulation of wages and working conditions, including sickness coverage under industrial awards rather than government cash benefits (Castles 1991a). The relatively high level of wages received by employees (and not deferred), in combination with the relatively low level of direct taxes, requires Australian workers to save privately rather than publicly. This has been achieved through comparatively high levels of home-ownership (Yates 1991) and through high levels of private savings in the form of investments and property (Whiteford and Kennedy 1995), complicated by the unusual habit of allowing lump-sum pay-outs from superannuation schemes.

A number of broad policy implications follow from this analysis. As noted above, Australia probably has less middle-class welfare than any other developed country. This reflects different political choices in different countries, but does not mean that middle-class welfare is undesirable, unless substitution between public and private provision reduces aggregate community welfare. Correspondingly, if targeting works in Australia to a degree that is greater than usually shown using the standard framework, this does not mean that the approach is easily transferable to other countries, not least because the social security system is only one among a number of interrelated institutions which have developed over a long time. It may appear relatively easy to change the rules of social security systems, but it is not easy in the short run to change the patterns and levels of home-ownership or other forms of private wealth.

To the extent that welfare state institutions redistribute less than they appear to, this gives greater significance to the underlying degree of income inequality in different societies. The arguments above suggest that this is not correctly measured in international comparisons either, but on balance the degree of earnings inequality in any society must remain one of the primary determinants of overall inequality, although substantially modified by the impact of unemployment and non-participation in the labour force. The weight of international evidence suggests that the United States is one of the most unequal of the developed societies, primarily because of the high degree of earnings inequality. While the extent of unemployment is now lower in the United States than in many other developed countries, this overlooks the proportion who are outside the labour force, which is closer to the OECD average. Most importantly, the high degree of earnings inequality and the substantial number of working poor also means that Americans of workforce age receiving benefits are much worse off in absolute terms than similar groups in most other OECD countries (Eardley *et al.* 1996).

Perhaps the most striking feature of the material presented here is the sheer contrast between the extreme optimism of the traditional view and the extreme pessimism of the new view. What explains this reversal? Much of the new view, particularly the journalism, seems to reflect a virulent expression of the cultural cringe. The traditional view resembles 'the cringe inverted, the God's-Own-Country-and-I'm-a-better-man-than-you-are great Australian bore-ism syndrome' (in Roe 1993: 116). The new view at times captures the true essence of the cringe – 'the urge to make unnecessary comparisons and unsubstantiated denigration of the local product' (Roe 1993: 115). If Australia cannot be the most equal country in the world, then it must be the most unequal. As J. F. Archibald – probably – wrote in 1907, 'In part such charges are due to the persistence in this new country of the good old British habit of national self-slander as a means of political argument' (in Turner 1968: 267).

To argue that Australia actually may not be one of the most unequal countries in the developed world has a range of political implications, but it does not imply that the level of inequality in Australia is acceptable. There is considerable evidence that indigenous Australians are as a group extremely disadvantaged, as are some sub-groups of immigrants. Australia's unemployment record deteriorated in the 1980s and 1990s, as did that of the OECD generally, and the increase in the extent of long-term unemployment was marked. In addition, the dispersion of earnings has widened since the late 1970s. While there is evidence that the social safety-net in Australia is set at a higher level than in many other developed countries, the relative position of sole parents and private renters is less favourable (Eardley *et al.* 1996).

Most of these conclusions do not require international comparisons for justification. The real problems faced by disadvantaged Australians are not improved one whit by the conclusion that Australia is not strikingly unequal; nor, indeed, are they worsened if one accepts the opposite argument. The solutions to these problems lie in action within Australia, not in misleading comparisons. If we misunderstand the nature of these problems, then our solutions will be even less effective than they have been in the past. To put it another way: if the new view is correct, then Australian institutions are remarkably ineffective at reducing inequality and may well deserve radical change. If the new view is wrong, then the unmaking of Australian institutions and attempts to recast them in the American mode will markedly increase inequality.

Notes

I am grateful for comments from Bruce Bradbury, Bettina Cass, Stein Ringen and Peter Saunders. The views expressed are my own.

1. Note that this discussion concentrates on income inequality, ignoring questions of the relationship between economic inequality and social equity. It does not make conclusions on whether Australia is or is not a just society. This is a statistical analysis, not a philosophical one. Nor do I consider the gender dimensions of inequality, nor the position of immigrants or indigenous Australians.

2. Garton (1990) shows that the experience of poverty was a continuing reality for many Australians over the period from white settlement, although he does not compare the extent of poverty in Australia with other countries. Jones also questions whether Australia was an early leader in social welfare provision, but quotes figures for Victoria suggesting that the population in charitable institutions was much lower than the corresponding proportion receiving Poor Law assistance in Britain (1990: 8–9). In *War Aims of a Plain Australian* (1944), C. E. W. Bean also criticised those who claimed that all Australian children faced equal life chances (in Turner, 1968: 317).

3. The Gini coefficient is a measure of inequality which ranges between 0 and 1, with a higher figure implying greater inequality.

4. One of the most cited sources for the traditional view was Lydall (1968), which concluded that among twenty-five countries, Australia had one of the lowest dispersions of earnings. Recent data continue to show Australia as having a relatively compressed male earnings distribution (Green *et al.* 1990; Saunders and Fritzell 1995; Bradbury 1993; Gottschalk 1993; OECD 1993), with a relatively low inequality between male and female wage rates (International Labour Office 1993; Blau and Kahn 1992), and lower inequality between full-time and part-time workers (Gornick and Jacobs 1994). Smeeding and Coder (1993) find that after Sweden and the Netherlands, Australia had the least dispersed distribution of overall household earnings. The explanation of Gornick and Jacobs (1994) is that Australia's wage-fixing institutions continued to compress wage differentials in the 1980s and early 1990s.

5. The OECD study of income distribution (Atkinson *et al.* 1995) shows that direct taxes and transfers are more progressive in Australia than in any of the other countries covered. Mitchell *et al.* (1994b) estimate that the

Australian social security system has the highest degree of target efficiency among countries in the *LIS*. A prominent American observer has gone so far as to describe the Australian pension system as radically redistributive (Aaron 1992).

6 This is in the context of the welfare of the poor in developing countries, with analysis based on economic rather than political or sociological arguments.

7 Alternatively, lower lifetime poverty (but not lower lifetime inequality) might be achieved if benefits were more effective at redistributing across the lifecycle for the working class. This would imply that the working class were paying for their own benefits in retirement and unemployment, through high levels of taxation when in work. This process is plausible, but it is inaccurate to describe it as trickle-down, since this redistribution would be horizontal rather than vertical.

8 Whiteford and Kennedy (1995) estimate that the proportion of older Australians in 'relative income poverty' varies between 14 and 37 per cent, depending on the choice of equivalence scale. Broadening the income concept to incorporate health, education and public housing and imputed income from owner-occupied housing reduces the extent of relative poverty from 30 to 5 per cent. On the basis of cash disposable income, relative poverty in Australia is three times higher than in Germany; on the broader income measure it is about 80 per cent of the German level.

9 *LIS* data show that in large welfare states more individuals apparently have zero or extremely low market incomes, while older people in Australia, Canada, and the United States have the lowest receipt of government transfers, but the highest level of income from property and investments, as well as much higher levels of home ownership (Whiteford and Kennedy 1995).

10 For example, according to the *LIS* the average transfers received by Australian households are just over half the average taxes paid. In France, in contrast, transfers are around 2.75 times the taxes measured as being paid by households in the *LIS* data – French households are apparently getting nearly two-thirds of their social security system free!

CHAPTER 14

A Competitive Future
The Industry Commission and the Welfare Sector

John Ernst

The importation and adaptation of ideas from overseas has always been part of the Australian Way, and the history of social policy in this country reflects a clear derivative strain. From the creation of the national social security system in the late 1940s through to the formulation of participatory approaches to social development in the early 1970s, Australian policy-makers have looked to the United Kingdom and North America, in particular, for inspiration.

The tradition of policy borrowing continued apace during the 1990s, with Australian governments of all political persuasions drawn to the idea that market mechanisms provide an omnibus solution to many of the problems confronting contemporary government. The current obsession with market models and metaphors in Australian public policy – whether in the guise of neoclassical economics, or formulas for reinventing government – mirrors the movement of ideas and policy fashions in the Anglo-American countries.

Imported policy ideas, however, require local institutional support and a strong local voice in order to take hold and to progress. During the 1990s, the Industry Commission played a pivotal role in Australian public policy as a purveyor of market alternatives to traditional public intervention and public administration. The function of the Industry Commission as an influential promoter of market theory was similar, in some respects, to that performed by free-market think-tanks such as the Adam Smith Institute in Britain and the Progress and Freedom Foundation in the United States. However, the Industry Commission occupies a formal and highly strategic place in the institutional fabric of national government; this, along with its ability to attract bipartisan support for its work, makes it unusual and possibly unique.

The first section considers the influence that the Industry Commission has exerted over Australian public policy and its recent excursions into the field of social policy. The application of a competitive model to the welfare sector is critiqued in the second section.

The Industry Commission's Policy Template

The Industry Commission was set up by the federal government as 'its review and advisory body on industry matters' (IC 1994: 33), out of the remains of its predecessor, the Industries Assistance Commission, in 1990. Since that time it has become a key intellectual participant in the project to reform the Australian economy. The primary role of the commission is to conduct inquiries into significant areas of public policy, at the behest of government. This inquiry and investigation mandate of the commission has given it considerable strategic influence over the content and direction of the micro-economic reform program being pursued by federal and state governments.

In the seven years of its existence, the Industry Commission carried out about sixty inquiries into areas of the economy ranging from horticulture to computer hardware, from tobacco-growing to tourism accommodation and, most recently and controversially, the automotive and textiles, clothing and footwear industries. In managing its diverse inquiry program, however, the commission has been criticised for managing to be somewhat less than diverse in the conclusions that it reaches. For, whatever the field of inquiry, the tenor of the commission's findings and the policy thrust of its recommendations bear, in almost all cases, a striking resemblance and a familiar imprint.

Quiggin, in a paper on the Industry Commission's activities during the early 1990s, attributes the one-dimensional character of its inquiry findings to the commission's unwavering attachment to a fixed worldview, or frame of reference, built essentially around the nostrums of neoclassical economic theory:

> One of the most important features of the IC approach to policy is that a single framework is applied consistently to a wide range of policy problems. ... The IC approach is essentially a priori in nature. It is difficult to conceive of any empirical evidence that would lead to a change in the Commission's deeply held view that free markets are superior to intervention and that private ownership is superior to public. [1993: 1–2]

From this overarching frame of reference, a policy template is readily constructed. This consists first, of a set of axiomatic objectives, such as economic growth, economic welfare, efficiency, international competitiveness, and the reduction of business input costs; and second, of a limited field of possible policy actions that range narrowly across options such as the introduction of market disciplines, economic pricing (and removal of 'distorting' cross-subsidies), competition, deregulation, corporatisation and privatisation. The apparent inability of the commission to open its collective mind to ideas beyond the prevailing economic orthodoxy is all the more curious, given its rhetorical, and often practical, commitment to consultation and due process in the conduct of its inquiries.

Largely as a result of its inquiry work, the Industry Commission has forged a formidable reputation as a strident voice of economic rationalism and public sector reform. If Keynesian economic theory, public enterprise, government regulation and traditional public management approaches can be viewed, in the metaphor of Christopher Hood (1994), as 'economic policy dinosaurs', then the commission is the exact opposite of some antipodean Spielberg nostalgically recreating a Jurassic past!

Interestingly, this use of one template for all seasons and policy fields, along with a penchant for making recommendations-by-formula, have not deterred governments (and increasingly this includes Australian state governments as well as the federal government) from making references to the Industry Commission. If anything, the reverse seems to apply, for the certainty of the commission's (neoclassical) instruments and the predictability of its findings appear to have drawn governments to it. The inquiry schedule of the Industry Commission and its successor under the Howard government, the Productivity Commission, is more congested than it has ever been.

The Industry Commission and Social Policy

Over recent years, as the lens of micro-economic reform has widened, so has the scope of the inquiry activity of the Industry Commission. In the words of the commission, as 'structural reform inevitably broadens to embrace a wider range of issues in social as well as economic fields, the Commission finds that it has a role to play in explaining to a wider cross-section of the community the potential net gains from structural reforms' (IC 1994: 35). Given the economic importance and public policy prominence of the so-called charitable organisation sector – with an annual expenditure of $5 billion, of which over $3 billion comes from direct and indirect government support (IC 1995a: xvii) – it was probably inevitable that the commission's attention would be directed to the sector sooner or later. Prior to the inquiry into charitable organisations, the Industry Commission had carried out one other inquiry into a mainstream field of social policy – public housing – which was completed in 1993. But these journeys into the heartland of the welfare state by no means represent the first excursions by the commission into the field of social policy (see Table 14.1). In the first half of the decade, the commission was involved in seven inquiries (excluding the latest inquiry into competitive tendering) into areas that intersect with major issues of social policy, including inquiries into public utilities, urban transport and workers' compensation.

From its earliest inquiries, the Industry Commission expressed an interest in equity matters. In general, however, this self-declared interest was rarely supported by proper analysis of equity issues. Nevertheless, the commission has been an influential participant in the debate over the definition and application of equity in contemporary public policy. This is illustrated by the triumph of its long-argued normative definition of equity – based on the benefit (or contributor) principle; it became the norm and was adopted widely to justify the application of principles of full cost-recovery and user-pays to the provision of essential and public services. In addition, in its reports on the energy and water industries in the early 1990s, the commission made a seminal contribution to the theory of community service obligations. Its argument is that such obligations, if specifically identified and separately financed, are superior to internal cross-subsidies for addressing access and equity issues because they are transparent and enhance efficiency; this view has gained general currency in policy-making circles in Australia.

Table 14.1 Industry Commission inquiries

Year	Inquiry
Social Policy	
1992–93	Public housing
1993–95	Charitable organisations
Related Matters	
1990–91	Energy generation and distribution
1991–92	Water resources and waste water disposal
1991–93	Taxation and financial policy impacts on urban settlement
1992–94	Workers' compensation
1992–93	Impediments to regional industry adjustment
1992–94	Urban transport
1994–95	Work, health and safety
1994–96	Competitive tendering and contracting

Note: The dates are the year in which the reference was given and the year in which the inquiry was completed.

At a more fundamental level, the Industry Commission has been an intellectual contributor to the project of reformulating the meaning and place of citizenship in the Australian polity. As Brennan and others in this book argue, the dimensions of social citizenship, as enunciated by Marshall (1972) and other writers, have been progressively displaced by market-based consumerism during the 1990s. In each of its reports on essential services, the Industry Commission promulgated a specific set of values, backed up by proposals for policy change, which assigns commodity status to many essential services (such as energy and water) and which has served to weaken the conceptual nexus between provision of essential services and citizenship rights.

Competition and the Non-Government Welfare Sector

The Australian welfare system has long been characterised by features of a mixed economy, with public agencies supplemented by a strong, independent sector. Yet, despite the historical contribution of the non-government sector to the welfare of Australians and the growth in public finance directed towards the sector, relatively little was known of the non-government welfare sector in aggregate. It was partly for this reason that the federal government asked the Industry Commission to hold an inquiry into charitable organisations. Given the commission's reputation and record as an instrument of neoclassical economic surgery, the announcement of the inquiry sent a nervous shiver down the collective spine of the non-government welfare sector (NGOs). Anxiety about the focus and possible outcomes of the commission's investigation contributed to the unprecedented level of interest and involvement in the inquiry, as voluntary agencies sought to educate the commissioners about the unique qualities and complexities of the community services sector.

In the event, in the final report of the inquiry, the Industry Commission reached very positive conclusions about the worth and contribution of community social welfare organisations (as it describes NGOs) and the final report drew applause, as well as pleased surprise and relief, from the community services sector itself (ACOSS, *Impact*, November 1995). The report contains a number of positive proposals, including: establishing three-year funding cycles; providing greater recognition of, and financial provision for, the infrastructure costs of community organisations; and removing the taxation laws that have traditionally discriminated in favour of large, old-style benevolent organisations at the expense of newer and often more innovative agencies in the non-government welfare sector.

In these constructive recommendations, and the favourable conclusions drawn about the contribution and continuing importance of the non-government welfare sector, the micro-economic litany of the 1990s and the language and concepts of 'new public management' (Hood 1994) are much in evidence:

> Even though non-profit organisations are not driven by market values, the inquiry found that market-based mechanisms can be blended with the values of community social welfare organisations to improve efficiency and deliver quality services to the most vulnerable in Australian society and in other countries. For example, governments are increasingly contracting these organisations to provide services on their behalf to the community. Costs can be reduced and the quality of service to clients enhanced if the selection of service providers is made more contestable, transparent, open and accountable and is reviewed periodically. [IC 1995a: 27–8]

Throughout the report, the key words are: *competition*, *tendering*, *contestability*, *contracts*, *purchaser–provider splits*, *benchmarks*, *best practice*, *user pays*, and *private sector entry*. These are enunciated as prescriptions for the future. And with this, order is restored: the familiar template of the Industry Commission breaks through!

The Industry Commission's vision splendid of the competitive future is illustrated tellingly in the final chapter of the report (*Synthesis*). Summarising the 'four sets of objectives in the recommendations', it cites as objective one, the 'aim to strengthen the capacity of CSWOs [community social welfare organisations] to provide services to their range of clients using a mix of government, client and the organisation's own resources and to compete effectively where appropriate, with for-profit firms or government agencies'; and as objective four, the 'aim to increase the extent to which CSWOs can test themselves against each other and with both government and the for-profit providers *to determine whether there is scope for an enhanced role for other providers* in the provision of the range of welfare services funded by governments' (IC 1995a: 422–3, emphasis added).

The report treats as an article of faith – or at least, as an inevitability – the movement by governments out of direct service delivery, in favour of 'enabling' or 'steering' roles:

> The increased use of the sector as the delivery vehicle for human services has been accompanied by a reduction in direct service delivery by governments themselves. This is a worldwide trend. It delivers to governments the benefits of flexibility and cost effectiveness; it delivers to the sector the benefits of more assured funding and involvement in processes of social policy formulation; and most importantly, it delivers to service users greater diversity of service provision and a greater focus on individual welfare needs . . . Moreover this devolution is also coming to include the for-profit sector in the range of organisations eligible for providing services. [IC 1995a: 421]

The philosophical basis of the report could well explain the pains taken in its 400-odd pages to butter up the non-government sector. In a report that takes as its starting-point the assumption that governments should devolve service delivery to the non-government sector (as well as to the for-profit part of the mixed economy), it is not surprising to find that the sector is lauded beyond belief. There is more than a hint of flattering to deceive in all this.

For some welfare sector observers, the most surprising – and also, arguably, the most disingenuous – part of the final report is its discussion of welfare sector activities such as community development, independent policy analysis and advocacy (significantly, this was added after the community sector had commented on the draft report). The report makes considerable reference to the value of community development, advocacy and independent policy analysis; it suggests, quite reasonably, that the strict output-based performance measures that are advocated for the rest of the welfare service system are inappropriate in these areas.

Yet it is striking – if less surprising – that the report nowhere acknowledges the potential contradiction between market arrangements and government contracts, on the one hand, and fearless and disinterested (and publicly funded) policy advocacy and community action, on the other. In the world inhabited by the Industry Commission, there are no inherent tensions between economic rationalist prescriptions on social policy and collective community action and policy critique. In the real world of the mid-1990s – as experienced, for example, in Victoria – advocacy, independent analysis and community development were among the first casualties of the marketisation of welfare services.

The initial response of the federal government to the final report on charitable organisations, on the face of it, was less than a ringing endorsement of the report's conclusions: only three of the thirty-one recommendations were accepted in full. Yet the low-key government response is deceptive, and the report will almost certainly be more influential than this. A number of its key recommendations strike a chord that is in harmony with the neo-conservative times under the Howard federal government. In addition, the thrust of its recommendations on contestability and contracting-out is buttressed by the power and policy momentum of a government-wide – and virtually worldwide – project of marketisation and outsourcing.

Competition and the Public Sector

A year after commencing the inquiry into charitable organisations, the Industry Commission was asked to turn its attention to the public sector and to examine ways of extending the regime of competition and market testing in federal, state and local public sector agencies. Its final report into competitive tendering and contracting (CTC) was released in mid-1996.

In keeping with the commission's tradition, the report gives ample evidence of both productivity and prolixity. Its twenty-five recommendations can be summarised thus: 'Competitive tendering is about competition and hence it is intrinsically good, and while there is some evidence that problems can on occasion arise with CTC, in general these are relatively minor in the grand scheme of things, or alternatively they are amenable to correction.' So, intrinsic complications and difficulties notwithstanding, the Industry Commission argues, impresario-like, that competitive tendering 'will turn out all right on the night!'

In submissions and evidence to the inquiry, community sector organisations and the union movement highlighted issues such as:

- the variable nature of the data on CTC-derived cost savings
- the trade-off between reduced service costs and service quality
- the critical importance of effective contract regulation and monitoring
- the problems that may arise under the purchaser–provider split, such as the loss of policy intelligence and service delivery knowledge
- the inappropriateness of applying CTC indiscriminately across the public sector, and the community services in particular
- the problems for public accountability and user participation under regimes of competitive tendering
- the regressive employment effects of CTC – particularly on women and minority groups.

The report considers these issues in differing degrees of detail and understanding, but there is little analysis of the complexities of the competitive tendering and contracting process. The Industry Commission, in effect, concludes that there are no real barriers to applying CTC effectively, without exception, across the entire public sector.

The most controversial aspect of the politics of competitive tendering relates to whether it should be voluntary or compulsory. Significantly, the report does not recommend compulsory competitive tendering, as introduced in Victorian local government; although it leaves the door to compulsion temptingly ajar:

> Directives on the use of CTC need to be considered in the broader context of incentives for effective and efficient management in the public sector. Where public sector management systems are operating efficiently, it should not be

necessary to mandate the use of a particular management tool such as CTC. However, when these incentives are not operating, compulsory competitive tendering may be the best available option. [IC 1996: Recommendation 7]

The adoption of all or part of the recommendations contained in the final report by federal and state governments will substantially extend the use of competitive tendering and contracting throughout the public sector in Australia. Invariably, this will encompass the core areas of the welfare state, including health, community services and education.

The Competitive Model and the Welfare Sector

The drive to introduce greater competition into the welfare sector represents a neat paradox, for much of the historical and continuing work of the sector is directed at dealing with the casualties of competition and the fall-out from market failure in the general economy.

In the economy at large, competition is an important driver of efficiency, choice, innovation and economic growth. Yet to acknowledge the value of competition in the general economy is vastly different from admitting it into community services as some form of irresistible and guaranteed formula for success. By its very character, competition duplicates, in order to provide choice; competition excludes, in order to remove free-riders and to protect commercial secrets; and competition divides, in order to gain advantage and market share. But duplication, exclusion and division are directly at odds with the principles that should underpin the management and delivery of welfare services.

As has been the case with privatisation, the competition agenda is driven by a range of objectives. The objective of improving service quality is prominent in the rhetoric, but it occupies at best a secondary position on the hierarchy of objectives expressed in policy action; although the Pollyanna-like accounts of the new breed of public sector manager could persuade you otherwise. It would be unremarkable, but empirically sounder, to conclude that the major drive behind the public sector competition movement is the desire on the part of governments to reduce costs. In particular, they seek to reduce the input costs of production, as part of the quest for that Holy Grail of the late twentieth century – international competitiveness. But it is important to recognise that the push for competition is also motivated by deeper concerns. Competition theory is being used to remake government in the image of the market, and to encourage government to vacate the field of service provision altogether in many instances. In the language of the hunt so popular in British politics, competition is a stalking-horse for privatisation.

In the current policy environment, competition is indiscriminately applied to all areas of public sector activity, despite their distinct differences in purpose, technology, clientele and market environment. As indicated previously, the Industry Commission (1996) concluded – against the grain of the evidence – in its report, *Competitive Tendering and Contracting by Public Sector Agencies*, that no substantial barriers exist to the application of competitive tendering to the entire array of public sector services. The potential scope of the agenda for marketising public services is reflected in the commission's estimate, in the same report, that state governments could effectively increase their use of competitive tendering and contracting by almost 600 per cent. Across the nation, the core areas of social policy, including community services, health and education, are being progressively exposed to competitive regimes, even though the particular and unique characteristics of these sectors complicate and inhibit the use of market methods. The commodity or product paradigm and the unfiltered application of market principles are likely to prove dysfunctional, and even destructive, in the domain of social policy.

Markets, and the application of market theory, can be more imaginary than real. There are multiple examples of natural and contrived market failure in the contemporary private sector. The gap between competition as expressed in economic theory, and competition as realised in practice, is likely to be even greater when it is applied in the public sector.

One example of the failure of the theory is the assumption that greater diversity and choice will attend the introduction of competitive contracting in human services. But the dynamics of market forces regularly lead to the opposite outcome – concentration of market power and a net shrinking in the field of choice. Competition could remove much of the heterogeneity and diversity characterising the present system of community services in Australia, which was praised fulsomely by the Industry Commission in its report on charitable organisations. In the competitive future, large church-based NGOs, with their established infrastructure and legitimacy, will be in a much better position to compete for scarce public funds and government service contracts. They could well swallow up, or starve out, small community-based and community-managed service providers. This is particularly likely to be the case if their position is buttressed, as in Victoria and Western Australia, with government initiatives to rationalise and streamline – through amalgamation and defunding – parts of the community sector service system.

The drive towards contestability, competitive tendering and contracting-out generally overlooks, and in some cases dismisses completely, major distributional questions and regressive consequences for service users, employees and different regions of the country. John Quiggin made a similar point a few years back, when he argued that the Industry Commission 'normally takes no account of the effects of its policy recommendations on income distribution. Thus a policy which resulted in a large loss to low-income earners, but yielded a slightly larger increase in corporate profits (or to high-income salary earners) would normally be supported' (1993: 5).

Despite 200-odd years of experience of industrial capitalism, it is still necessary to remind policy-makers that, while the market under optimum conditions may deliver efficient outcomes, it patently does not deliver equitable ones. Studies of the social impact of the privatisation of public utilities in the United Kingdom (for example, Ernst 1994) show that privatisation of essential services produces regressive outcomes and deepens inequality. Research commissioned by the British Equal Opportunities Commission adds to the evidence – this time from the perspective of the workforce – that the marketisation of public sector services has distributionally adverse consequences: 'the differential between male, usually full-time, and female, usually part-time, manual workers has been exacerbated under CCT [compulsory competitive tendering] ... [and] many of the "savings" made under CCT of manual services have been achieved through the flexible use of the lowest-paid, part-time manual workers' (Escott and Whitfield 1995: 165). As Victorian local governments are finding out in the implementation of compulsory competitive tendering, managing the complex employment-related effects of 'restructuring for competition' in a way that does not increase inequity is like trying to square the circle.

The strategic implications of the demise of rural townships and depopulation – the hollowing of Australia that mirrors the hollowing of the state – are yet to be seriously confronted by federal and state governments. Privatisation, restructuring and the marketisation of public sector services are unlikely to contribute much to the revitalisation of rural economies. The evidence suggests, on the contrary, that these policies are likely to accelerate the process of rural decline (Tesdorf 1996). The contribution that the public sector makes to local and regional economies, through employment and through the multiplier effect of public sector spending, is often unacknowledged. In many rural towns, public sector workers are one-quarter or more of the employed workforce.

Arguments abound about the need for cultural change and the virtues of introducing private sector and competitive cultures in public and non-government organisations. Promoting a competitive culture across the public sector demands that organisations be split into service purchasers and service providers. It also requires the creation of separate business units. Although these structural changes may bring benefits, they are also likely to weaken planning and service development and produce an alien, atomised organisational environment, where staff no longer see themselves as being in the same organisation and regard one-time colleagues as potential competitors.

Research into the implementation of compulsory competitive tendering in Victorian local government (Ernst *et al.* 1997) has shown that the competitive culture undermines collaboration not only within the one organisation, but also in its external relations – in this case between local councils and other organisations (including other councils) and among outside agencies themselves, who have now become competitors for council work and council dollars. In the human services field, which centrally relies on co-operative relationships, collaboration, networking and co-ordination, this is leading to service failure through fracturing and fragmentation. The Industry Commission, in its *Inquiry into Charitable Organisations* (1995a: 401), argued that 'the discipline of competition ... is [not] antithetical to co-operation and collaboration. In fact, tendering can bring complementary parties together.' Interestingly, the report's example of collaborative tendering for contracts could be interpreted, under the framework of competition law and protocols of tendering practice, as collusive bidding and anti-competitive behaviour.

Markets are not democratic, nor obviously were they ever intended to be so. Therefore the transfer of functions from governments to pseudo-market forces leads to a significant shift in the meaning and locus of public accountability. Collective political accountability for service provision is displaced under market arrangements by an accountability relationship between the individual consumer and service provider. This may well strengthen the individual consumer orientation of the service agency – a useful gain in accountability at one level. But it may not: an analysis of competitive tendering in local government in Victoria by the Consumer Law Centre reveals major gaps in the ability of individuals to gain redress for service failure (Trifiletti 1996). Whatever the scope for consumerist gains, where service systems are managed by private contractors or corporatised government businesses, operating under general conditions of commercial secrecy, beyond the direct scrutiny of elected representatives and outside the scope of appellate bodies such as the Ombudsman and the Administrative Appeals Tribunal, there is a major loss of public and collective accountability.

Indeed, the development of the privatisation and competition movements and their policy ascendancy are a metaphor for the difficulties that democracy and equity encounter in the marketplace. Pervasive competition policy, like privatisation, owes much of its origin and its progress to the support of political and economic elites who stand to gain directly from the change process. Public engagement and debate on the issue – particularly among those groups most at risk from structural change – has not been sought; indeed, it has been assiduously avoided.

Conclusion

The Industry Commission has been an influential advocate of the widespread use of competition as an organising principle in essential service industries and across the public sector generally. However, there is a danger, in focusing on the role of one leading agent in the policy process, of overstating its degree of influence and autonomy as a policy actor. The Industry Commission has been active in, and created by, the development during the 1990s of an integrated and unified public policy approach to micro-economic reform (which has been documented in earlier chapters). But it is important to recognise that the influence of the commission has been mediated through government sanction and support for its central ideas. The Industry Commission has occupied an interesting and potent position in the policy development process because it has performed a special function for Australian governments. Its *modus operandi* of public inquiry, economic modelling and seemingly exhaustive factual analysis has given successive Australian governments the arguments, as well as the steel, to manage the politics of structural reform.

CHAPTER 15

Working Nation *and Beyond as Market Bureaucracy*
The Introduction of Competition Policy in Case-Management

Michael Wearing and Paul Smyth

In the declining years of the Roman Empire, the state decided to contract-out the policing of its boundaries to mercenary soldiers or barbarians. It was these undisciplined barbarians living off the resources of the Roman state who eventually fought against the Romans to claim their land, and contributed to the collapse of the Empire. This history lesson signals a warning for the competitive market-oriented basis of contracting-out, particularly in the delivery of services to unemployed people. The introduction of competition policy using competitive tendering and contracting-out principles marked a shift in Australian governmental relations with the community sector. In this chapter we characterise this shift as one from responsible bureaucratic delivery to competitive tendering and market or post-bureaucratic modes of social policy administration.

The 1994 White Paper of the federal Labor government, *Working Nation*, was a comprehensive statement on the issues of economic growth, employment and unemployment in Australia. It was framed within Labor's economic strategy of market-driven growth and international competitiveness, and couched in the rhetoric of a 'dynamic social democracy'. The White Paper outlined a plan for stimulating growth via support for industry, skilling the workforce, reforms to labour market assistance, creation of income-support incentives, and regional development strategies. The policies reflected the tensions within the government's overall platform discussed in earlier chapters. In particular, the policies for delivering labour-market programs reflected the ambiguities identified by Orchard in Chapter 7. Here, a degree of eclecticism will be shown which supports Orchard's view that administrative reform was seen as a technical, administrative matter with little inkling of possible conflict between certain modes of service delivery – competitive tendering, for example – and the document's stated social democratic objectives.

This chapter focuses on the policy implications of the competition model for the case-management of the long-term unemployed. In particular, it looks at the implications for the community sector. The model favours the withdrawal or minimisation of direct state involvement by contracting-out service delivery. In this approach, termed *market bureaucracy* or *post-bureaucracy*, competitive tendering, contracting-out and customer service are central to the reform process. The chapter argues that the model of case-management delivery is inadequate, and that issues such as pricing and quality of service are poorly thought through, especially for community agencies. Finally, some alternative strategies are suggested for more co-operative relationships between the state and non-government organisations than those adopted under *Working Nation* and pursued more fully by the Howard federal government.

The OECD Experience

There is currently extensive debate on the nature of social policy and administrative reform in OECD countries (see Considine 1995; Esping-Andersen 1990; Hughes 1994; Marsh 1995; Taylor-Gooby and Lawson 1993). This work provides insight into the trajectory of labour-market reform in Australia in the context of less centralised and more market-oriented social policies and social welfare delivery. In the non-profit sectors, in the United Kingdom and the United States especially, academics have detected a shift to what is described as the 'hollow (content-less) state' or 'post-bureaucracy' in the delivery of public and social services (Laffin 1995; Brennan 1996). This has also been located within debates about privatisation and voluntary ways of delivering services.

Frieder Naschold (1995, 1997) has shown that an idealised Anglo-American model based on the substitution of competitive markets is often presented as the 'one best development path'. In fact, he writes, there has been a limited plurality of pathways in the OECD, and he concludes from his survey that, although a 'return to the free market mechanism' might have been 'the hope of the 1980s, [it] might result in the likely disillusion of the 1990s' (Naschold 1995: 55). The basic problem with the model, as Naschold sees it, is that the conditions for effective market behaviour do not apply: the result is that steering degenerates into neo-Taylorist managerialism,[1] with the loss of those synergetic values created by co-operation between the different policy actors.

Naschold has six conclusions from his survey of the variety of OECD experience. First, it is necessary to develop a strategic leadership role within the state apparatus with effective linkages to community groups.

Second, the application of market mechanisms needs to take account of real-world contexts. It should distinguish between markets and competitive instruments, and between the use of markets as a means of dissolving the public sector and as a mechanism of social co-ordination. Market mechanisms must be complemented by, and integrated with, other modes of government regulation and control.

Third, although the trend towards government as a guarantor, rather than producer, of welfare is likely to continue, it would be a mistake to reduce public sector activities to core areas. In order to maintain its complementary role, Naschold argues, the public sector must retain, in addition to its undisputed regulatory role, some degree of in-house production. Experience at the local level, particularly among the most innovatory local authorities in the OECD, provides strong evidence in support of this point.

Naschold's fourth point relates to the third. As more functions are transferred to autonomous agencies or markets, the role of the top management is increasingly questioned. The value of strategic management in the chain of policy development is becoming a core concern in the OECD at the same time as large-scale devolution is decentring the policy process and creating co-ordination problems.

Naschold's fifth observation concerns an excessive or exclusive concern with management reforms, to the neglect of the labour process or work practices. New management forms, he emphasises, require different work practices to be effective.

Finally, the diversity of public sector change in the OECD highlights for Naschold the power of distinctive national social and political contexts to shape the direction of reform. Accordingly, he argues that the innovation process must be accompanied by an evaluation process located within the system. An effective policy development must allow policy actors at every organisational level to be involved in processing the experience and contributing to a collective evaluation.

Creating *Working Nation*

Working Nation itself offered no evidence of a decisive trend in the mode of administration of employment services. The need for a new partnership between government and community was a central thrust: 'Commonwealth Government programs alone will not be sufficient: action is needed from all branches of government, and from business, unions and communities' (Commonwealth of Australia 1994a: 2–3). If a new partnership was thought to be crucial, its institutional mechanism was to take a variety of forms. A corporatist conception of the relationship, in keeping with the social democratic rhetoric of the White Paper, appears to have underpinned the establishment of the National Employment and Training Task Force: it was 'established to promote partnerships between employers, unions and community groups. It will provide an opportunity for all parties to work co-operatively to resolve issues and assist in speedy implementation of employment strategies' (C of A 1994a: 118). A similar framework informed the creation of the Area Consultative Committees. *Working Nation* also established a special relationship between government and business with a range of 'employer support measures'; these were not replicated with other potential partners, as one might expect in a corporatist approach which recognises the contribution to employment creation of sectors other than employers. Finally, a different type of relationship again was proposed for the implementation of case management. Here, influenced by a predominantly Anglo-American trend towards welfare privatisation, the Employment Services Regulatory Authority was established to encourage and regulate competition in the provision of case management.

As we will see, the introduction of the competition model into *Working Nation* was a hasty, eleventh-hour affair, and scarcely constitutes evidence that the model represented the way of the future for social policy administration under Labor. Indeed, the ideologically odd mixture of institutional forms of the new partnership within *Working Nation* might be considered typical of the wider tension between social democratic and economic fundamentalist approaches which characterised the public policies of the Labor government generally. No such tensions appear to trouble the Coalition government. We seem to be witnessing the wholesale return to what the then president of the Australian Council of Social Service described as an 'out-moded and narrow economic orthodoxy which is no longer relevant to contemporary life' (Fitzgerald 1990). This reassertion of economic rationalism undoubtedly positions the competition model as the template for the administration of welfare services generally.

The Green Paper, Case-Management and the Principle of Complementarity

The proposals for case-management implementation contained in the Green Paper, *Restoring Full Employment*, were very different to what emerged in the subsequent White Paper. Unlike the latter, the Green Paper's proposals were thoroughly canvassed in the public consultations and enjoyed wide community support. As the Green Paper reported, although 75 per cent of job-seekers were satisfied with the services they received, it was generally accepted that there had been undesirable tendencies: to process clients rather than actively assist them; to be inflexible in the administration of programs; to be inflexible in what non-government agencies could offer; and to create confusion through the complexity of program structures (Committee on Employment Opportunities 1993: 143).

Building on a series of previous studies of practice in the Department of Education, Employment and Training (DEET), the Green Paper suggested a consolidation and extension of case-management as one way to overcome these tendencies. The Hilmer Report, *National Competition Policy* (1993), had already been released, with strong recommendations for the introduction of the competition model into welfare service delivery; it is noteworthy that the authors of the Green Paper did not discuss the possibility in relation to setting up the proposed case-management system. Indeed, in view of what they referred to as an already long history of reforming the Commonwealth Employment Service (CES), the presumption was thought to be against major change: it was 'important to acknowledge the need to resource Australia's public employment service properly and to avoid change for its own sake' (Committee on Employment Opportunities 1993: 138).

The Green Paper proposed to extend existing practice, which, in relation to the community sector, was built on the principle of complementarity. The CES, it observed, offered few labour-market programs itself, but had developed a system of contracting such services to agencies such as TAFE and Skillshare. This diversity of providers, it argued, provided a base on which to build a role that complemented that of the CES. This complementary role was understood primarily in terms of the non-government sector's particular abilities: to meet the needs of job-seekers with special needs more effectively; to establish better links with some job opportunities; to co-ordinate, through community contacts, the range of services often needed by job-seekers; and to help, through its community focus and profile, people who did not want to deal with government officials.

The sector's role could be expanded through greater use of existing large organisations and through the development of local partnerships made up of industry groups, local government and community organisations. Such providers could come from the for-profit sector, but the Green Paper thought that their role would be limited because of the small profits associated with finding low-skilled jobs and assisting the long-term unemployed. Existing contract arrangements with non-CES providers might be modified by use of more comprehensive contracts, allowing providers more autonomy and flexibility; contracts with large agencies who could sub-contract with local agencies; and a greater emphasis on payment by performance (CEO 1993:151–4).

Consistent with its emphasis on the essentially complementary role of non-CES providers, the Green Paper indicated that the role had inherent limits. In particular, there was a danger that involvement in high-volume service delivery would eliminate 'the characteristics that make them different and complementary to government agencies – such as their sense of mission, their advocacy role on behalf of disadvantaged people, and their capacity to innovate and be flexible'. In the case of for-profit providers, it was thought, there might be conflicts between the needs for profit and for accountability for use of public money (CEO 1993: 153).

The Green Paper offered a comprehensive review of the need for a case-management system and clearly supported the view that its administration would be enhanced by developing what it saw as the essentially complementary roles of both the public and non-government sectors. The mechanisms for developing this relationship were to build on existing practice: more resources for the public agency; consolidation of the roles of existing non-CES providers, providing them with a corporatist style mechanism for co-ordination; and more flexible funding arrangements with a greater emphasis on payment by outcomes. In doing so, the Green Paper was able to draw on a substantial body of supportive opinion from the community sector.

Working Nation, Case Management and 'Healthy' Competition

Although *Working Nation* endorsed much of the proposed case-management system, it proceeded to add to it a competitive model not obviously compatible with the Green Paper's framework of partnership based on complementarity. From the outset, it was clear that the authors of the White Paper did not accept the Green Paper's counsel against basic change; they declared 'fundamental reform' to be 'essential'. *Working Nation* continued to use the rhetoric of partnership – 'The Government will not work alone, but will harness the expertise and capacity of the community and private sectors' – but it was clear that the fundamental reform would involve an emphasis on 'healthy' competition (C of A 1994: 126–7).

Elements of competition had been, of course, part of the system of contracting-out of employment services by government to the non-government agencies for some time. Thus non-government providers of training programs competed on the basis of quality of provision for fixed-price contracts. This practice was endorsed by the Green Paper, within its framework which emphasised that some services are truly complementary to what a government agency can offer and suited to competitive tendering among those within the appropriate sector. *Working Nation*, by contrast, blurred the idea that government, for-profit and community providers have different roles to play. Not only would there be an element of competition for services deemed appropriate for contracting-out to non-government agencies, but these agencies would compete for the full range of services with the public agency itself.

To ensure that public and private agencies were treated the same in a competitive environment, a new public authority separate from DEET, the Employment Service Regulatory Authority, was to be established. It would regulate competition, accredit and develop the expertise of the non-CES providers, and provide advice on funding arrangements. Contracts were to be at a price no greater than that of the CES, and there was to be a measure of payment by outcomes. The competitive model would offer job-seekers a choice between CES and non-CES providers, although the extent of choice was limited. In the first year of operation only 10 per cent of case-management would be contracted out, rising to 30–40 per cent in later years if the capacity of the community and private sector providers proved adequate.[2]

Although the Green Paper's framework for case-management had encompassed elements of competition, the idea of 'healthy' competition informing *Working Nation* clearly recast the relationship between the public and private sectors in a fundamental way. The model of a partnership between complementary sectors was replaced by one of competition between sectors which were essentially the same. At least, this was the case in relation to the delivery of services. Clearly, the public sector, through the creation of the regulatory body, would have a new role as umpire of the competition, but how this body would relate to DEET and the non-government sectors in the wider policy process was not explained. As with the question about the future extent of non-CES service delivery, these questions were left to the process of implementation.

Rationale of the Competition Model

Because of the unheralded entry of healthy competition into the model of case-management in *Working Nation*, it is necessary to look beyond *Working Nation* for the rationale of its model. A report for the Department of Social Security in March 1994 presented arguments for 're-engineering the delivery of employment services', which included the introduction of a competition model. The report situated its proposals for administrative reform in the context of recent efficiency gains achieved in various commercial arenas through corporate restructuring, and set out to apply the lessons of the new private sector management practices to the proposed case-management system for the long-term unemployed.

Unlike the Green Paper, which saw the benefits of case-management – such as flexible programs and responsiveness to individual circumstances – as achievable through reform of existing structures, the DSS report proposed fundamental change. It said: 'It is essential that the paradigm ... shifts from one of client management to one of servicing a market. Only by taking a market perspective and a customer focus can the necessary specialisation and incentives be established to maximise the impact of Commonwealth expenditure on employment services' (DSS 1994: 43).

The merits of the 'market perspective', it said, were obvious, not only from the record of restructuring of private businesses but also from developments in the public sector. 'As microeconomic reform in the banking, telecommunications and power generation sectors has shown, the introduction of competition is the great driver of improved customer service and product innovation' (DSS 1994: 6, 54).

The DSS report argued that employment services needed to be established on a competitive model; this, it said was also the clear implication of the Hilmer Report, which had been ratified by the Council of Australian Governments in February 1994. Hilmer, according to the DSS report, had put forward a compelling case for breaking down government monopolies over welfare. Hilmer had stated: 'A further form of monopoly exists where budget-funded government services are provided within government, without being subject to a competitive tendering process.' Welfare and community services were examples, the Hilmer Report continued, and their competitive tendering could be expected to yield average cost savings 'in the order of 20 per cent'. Accordingly, all Australian governments should observe a set of principles which separated regulatory from commercial functions; natural monopoly from potentially competitive activities; and potentially competitive activities into a number of smaller, independent business units.

The DSS report proceeded to clarify the implications of the Hilmer Report for the administration of employment services. Thus, only certain functions were to be regarded as of an 'essentially public sector nature'. These included market segment analysis, resource allocation, registration and screening, explanation and payment of entitlement, reference to case-managers based on informed client choice, and monitoring. Other functions were categorised in terms of delivery of services for which there was 'no compelling argument' that they remain solely within the government arena; and functions of gathering and distributing information, which would be suited to a public agency but which could be accessed by private agencies on a user-pays basis. On the basis of this analysis, it was proposed that the first and third functions might be united in a new Employment Business Unit, while the remainder of the CES could be set up as a 'corporatised Government Business Enterprise'. The latter was important in order to ensure an 'arm's-length commercial interaction' between the resource and service providers. The DSS report also offered a series of strategies for phasing in the competitive model. Thus it was important to enlarge immediately the number of non-CES service providers; other items, such as the corporatisation of the remainder of the CES, might happen in stages (DSS 1994: 54–7).

Given the fundamental departures from the Green Paper recommendations, it is remarkable how little attention the DSS report gave to engaging with the proposals put forward by the authors of that document after their considerable public consultation. The Green Paper appears in the DSS report only as a caricature: a vision of a single government provider with a one-size-fits-all approach (DSS 1994: 54). It ignored the partnership model based on the complementarity of government and non-government providers in order to present the 'market perspective' as the *only* way to enhance program flexibility and responsiveness of services to individual circumstance. If the DSS report represents the reasoning behind the eleventh-hour inclusion of the competition model for case-management in *Working Nation*, then it was clearly quite unrelated to existing understandings of the role of the public sector and its relationship to the non-government sectors. In retrospect, its introduction without benefit of public debate must be seen as unfortunate, because it soon became apparent that a rationale for employment service delivery based on recent commercial practice and the Hilmer recommendation of competitive tendering was out of step with community sector thinking (see, for example, Cappo 1995; Cass 1995b; Thompson and Ball 1995; Ball 1995). Certainly, the rationale had been widely criticised by academics and others on conceptual and evidential grounds.

Competition and the Market Bureaucracy Model

Much of the discussion on the implementation of case-management is better understood within wider discussions of the competitive paradigm. Considine (1995, 1996) argues that federal administrative reforms are oriented to a market bureaucracy paradigm that values competition and smaller government as drivers of policy. In the United

States this approach is termed *post-bureaucracy*. Its central elements include: a focus on general responsiveness to clients and increased flexibility of service delivery; and, a reduction of government activity to a model of the delivery of goods and services (Barzelay 1992). These ideas are underpinned by public choice theory and agency theory.

Such ideas underlie the contractualist approach as it has been found in the public sector restructures of the Anglo-American countries (Osborne and Gaebler 1992; Barzelay 1992; Gore 1993). However, as others have argued, the arm's-length relationship of contractor and purchaser is fraught with difficulties, including cost hazards. For instance, there is uncertainty in terms of cost overruns; long-term contractors can get a lock on the contract by building up skills and expertise or assets; and there is the problem of 'bounded rationality', whereby service cultures tend to become subordinate to the reform framework handed down to them (that is, service providers lock into the assumptions and develop opportunism in gaining resource advantages) (see Alford and O'Neil 1994: ch. 1).

Critical accounts of the rise of market bureaucracy in Anglo-American countries highlight two influences: the rise of 'new public management' or managerialism; and the theoretical antecedents of the administrative reforms (Alford and O'Neil 1994; Hughes 1994). In countries such as the United Kingdom, New Zealand and Canada, the development of new public management was associated with financial management reforms which included a shift of focus to outputs, program-based organisation structures, performance control and generalist management expertise. The theoretical foundations for managerialism were provided by texts such as *Reinventing Government* by Osborne and Gaebler, and a variety of others, such as the literature on Total Quality Management, which drew on the ideologies of the private sector (see Chapters 7 and 8). In Australia, the Greiner–Fahey governments in New South Wales and the Kennett government in Victoria drew on many of these ideas to reshape administration in the competitive and post-bureaucratic mould (Wearing 1995; Brennan 1996).

The Welfare Sector, Public Policy and the Australian Way

In this final section, we offer some general reflections on the long-term significance for the welfare sector of the imposition of the competition model on the case-management system for the long-term unemployed. Space precludes documentation of the initial response but suffice it to say that it was akin to the reaction of consternation and surprise at the announcement of the Industry Commission inquiry into charitable organisations referred to in Chapter 14 by Ernst. As Cass, Roe and

Whiteford point out in Chapters 2, 4 and 13, social welfare under Labor had been a social democratic counter-theme to the economic rationalism that had increasingly taken hold in economic policy. In the Australian social welfare context, what the DSS report introduced as market competition had previously been associated only with the more extreme advocates of economic rationalism. Before the Hilmer Report, the only published advocacy of competitive tendering of government welfare services in Australia had come from the right-wing think-tank, the Centre for Independent Studies (Smyth 1995: 51–4).

To this extent, we see the future of the competition model in the welfare sector as linked to the fate of economic rationalism on the wider public policy stage. In this regard, it should be recognised that the Hilmer vision of administrative reform reflected a period in Australian public policy when, as Hugh Emy noted in 1993, economic rationalism appeared to be like a 'juggernaut without brakes'. It was a time when, he writes: 'the state and the market were conceptualised as implicitly antagonistic to one another: the size and activities of the state were usually presented as an obstacle to the efficient development of the market' (Emy 1993: 29–31). The role of government was cast in a wholly negative way. It was there merely to police market rules and repair market failures. In 1993, those like Emy who saw a need to move beyond this antagonistic logic and take a more positive approach to the role of government were hampered by the lack of a substantial body of alternative economic theory within the Australian public policy community. The same could not be said today.

Other chapters canvass the elements of such an economic policy alternative, while Part III discusses the possibilities of going beyond market bureaucracy in the context of public sector reform generally. To these views we would add a welfare sector perspective and emphasise that the Coalition faces a very different policy environment to that of the former government. There are three features in that environment which we believe will shape the coming contest over welfare sector administration.

Many would agree with Considine that, in time, the introduction of market bureaucracy will be seen as 'a form of "house cleaning" ... as a half-way house in the search for alternatives to the cumbersome, mass institutions of the previous order' (1996: 77). The Green Paper acknowledged the weaknesses of the earlier welfare administration, and elements of the market approach will undoubtedly be a part of the future order. As Naschold (1995) indicates, there is a wide acceptance within the OECD of the merits of a 'rational' use of competitive instruments in public administration. At the same time, as Ernst shows in Chapter 14, the recent experience of compulsory competitive tendering in Australia suggests it is not an approach which will be sustainable across the board in the welfare sector.

A second important effect of the introduction of the competition model, as Brennan shows in Chapter 8, has been the emergence of the non-government, not-for-profit organisations as a key element in any new administrative regime. The themes of social capital and civil society have produced vigorous writing that attempts to chart a new and independent role in terms such as *sense of mission, flexibility, innovation* and *advocacy* (for examples, see Cox 1995; Latham 1998; and the journal, *The Third Sector*). The sector has been thrust into this prominence by the market bureaucracy approach; it is therefore ironic that – as Brennan and Ernst show in Chapters 8 and 14 – the model is seen as inimical to the sector's independence and integrity as a genuine third sphere. The unfolding debate over the role of the sector, in relation to both the market and the state, will be a vital ingredient in any future form of welfare administration.

The third, and perhaps most crucial, development is the growing reappraisal of the role of the government sector. We highlight two aspects. The first arises from a variety of critiques of market bureaucracy as a model of management. These parallel the findings of Naschold (see above) and highlight issues such as the need for strategic leadership by government agencies and, by implication, the retention of significant in-house production of services. Supporters of an enhanced role for non-government organisations also emphasise that such roles depend upon an 'articulate administrative apparatus potentially available only in the state' (Porter 1990: 34). The second aspect is not managerial effectiveness, but the underlying values we place on government. In an analysis which parallels Nevile's exposure in Chapter 11 of the libertarian values masquerading as economic science, Yeatman (1997) shows how similar values have been disguised within the instrumental discourse of the competition model with its orientation towards managerial efficiency (see also Chapter 7). The model, she shows, radically individualises the relationship between government and individuals, displacing any notion of a body politic within the democratic enterprise. Such extremism, we believe, will prove incompatible with an Australian Way of welfare administration.

These three key features of the current policy environment suggest to us that the market bureaucracy is rightly seen as a half-way house in the emergence of a new form of welfare administration. From being an unexpected, contentious, eleventh-hour, bureaucratic intrusion into *Working Nation*, the competition model has developed as the template for the Coalition government's approach to welfare administration generally. The policy future is not clear. There is undeniably enthusiasm for the market bureaucracy model in the current federal government. The problem for the Coalition is that we are no longer living in the 1980s. The policy environment has changed substantially. In the long term, the government may have to come to terms with a present in which policy communities look for a more nuanced approach to the roles and interrelationships of state, markets and civil society.

Notes

We would like to thank Jo Barakett and Merrin Thompson for their advice and assistance in the preparation of this chapter.
 1 Taylorism is a form of industrial organisation known as scientific management. It features the separation of the conception and execution of tasks and the fragmentation of the production process, features which heighten managerial control. Naschold suggests that the marketisation of public services leads to a smiliar reduction in worker discretion and control at the workplace.
 2 The measures outlined here were implemented by the Labor government; but the marketisation of employment services has been pursued more radically by the Howard government (see Goodman 1997).

References

Aaron, H. 1978. *Politics and the Professors: The Great Society in Perspective*, Washington, DC: Brookings Institute.
Aaron, H. 1992. 'The Economics and Politics of Pensions: Evaluating the Choices', in *Private Pensions and Public Policy*, Paris: OECD.
Abo Call. 1938. 'Our Historic Day of Mourning and Protest', April, p. 19.
Adams, R. G. 1958. *Political Ideas of the American Revolution*, 3rd edn, New York: Barnes and Noble.
Akyuz, Y. 1995. 'Taming International Finance', in J. Michie and J. Grieve Smith (eds), *Managing the Global Economy*, Oxford University Press.
Alexander, J. 1995. 'Modern, Anti, Post and Neo', *New Left Review*, 210: 63–101.
Alford, J. 1993. 'Towards a New Public Management Model: Beyond "Managerialism" and its Critics', *Australian Journal of Public Administration*, 52, 2: 135–48.
Alford, J., and O'Neill, D. (eds). 1994. *The Contract State: Public Management and the Kennett Government*, Deakin University Press.
Allen, Judith. 1994. *Rose Scott: Vision and Revision*, Oxford University Press.
Allum, P. 1995. *State and Society in Western Europe*, Cambridge: Polity Press.
Amin, A. (ed.). 1994. *Post-Fordism: A Reader*, Oxford: Blackwell.
AMWU (Australian Manufacturing Workers Union). 1997. *Rebuilding Australia: Industry Development for More Jobs*, Sydney: AMWU.
Anderson, John. 1945. 'Introductory Essay', in W. H. C. Eddy (ed.), *Prospects of Democracy*, Sydney: Consolidated Press, pp. 7–12.
Anderson, M., and Blandy, R. 1992. 'What Australian Economics Professors Think', *Australian Economic Review*, 4: 17–40.
Angell, I. 1995. 'Winners and Losers in the Information Age', *LSE Magazine*, Summer: 10–12.
Arblaster, Anthony. 1984. *The Rise and Decline of Western Liberalism*, Oxford: Blackwell.
Argy, F. 1995. *Financial Deregulation: Past Performance, Future Promises*, Sydney: CEDA.
Argy, F. 1996. 'The Integration of World Capital Markets: Some Economic and Social Implications', *Economic Record*, 15: 1–19.

Armstrong, P., Glyn, A., and Harrison, J. 1991. *Capitalism Since 1945*, Oxford: Blackwell.
Arndt, H. W. 1956. *Labour and Economic Policy*, Chifley Memorial Lecture, Carlton: Melbourne University ALP Club.
Aschauer, D. A. 1989. 'Is Public Expenditure Productive?', *Journal of Monetary Economics*, 23: 177–200.
Aschauer, D. A. 1992. 'Infrastructure, Productivity and Growth: Fair Dinkum?', in BIE Infrastructure Forum, *The Private Provision of Economic Infrastructure*, Canberra: AGPS.
Aspromorgous, T. 1995. 'The Green Paper in the Wider Context of Employment Policy: An Overview', in T. Aspromorgous and M. Smith (eds), *The Pursuit of Full Employment in the 1990s*, Department of Economics, University of Sydney.
Aspromorgous, T., and Smith, M. (eds). 1995. *The Pursuit of Full Employment*, Department of Economics, University of Sydney.
Atkinson, A., Rainwater, L., and Smeeding, T. 1995. *Income Distribution in OECD Countries*, Paris: OECD.
Atkinson, T. 1993. 'Participation Income', *Citizen's Income Research Group Bulletin*, 16 (July), pp. 7–10.
Australia Institute. 1997. *Towards a Professional Australian Public Service: Response to a Discussion Paper by Mr Peter Reith*, Background Paper no. 6, Canberra: Australia Institute.
Australian Bureau of Industry Economics (BIE). 1995. *Australian Industry Trends*, no. 22, Canberra: AGPS.
Australian Business Foundation. 1997. *The High Road or the Low Road? A Report on Australia's Industrial Structure*. Melbourne: ABF.
Australian Catholic Social Welfare Commission. 1995. 'Is Inequality an Inevitable Outcome of Enterprise Bargaining?', *ACSW Journal*, 4, 1.
Australian Council of Social Service. 1997. *For a Future that Works: Budget Priorities Submission, 1997–98*, Sydney.
Australian Dictionary of Biography, vol. 8, 'Deakin, Alfred' (R. Norris).
Australian Dictionary of Biography, vol. 12, 'Unaipon, David' (Philip Jones).
Australian Urban and Regional Development Review. 1995. *Investing in Infrastructure: Proceedings of a Conference organised by Australian Urban and Regional Development Review, August 1994*, Workshop Papers no. 5, Canberra.
Bagguley, P. 1992. 'Social Change, the Middle Class and the Emergence of "New Social Movements"', *Sociological Review*, 40, 1: 26–48.
Bagguley, P. 1995. 'Middle-class Radicalism Revisited', in T. Butler and M. Savage (eds), *Social Change and the Middle Classes*, London: University College London Press.
Baldock, C. 1988. 'Public Policies and the Paid Work of Women', in C. Baldock and B. Cass (eds), *Women, Social Welfare and the State*, Sydney: Allen and Unwin, pp. 20–53.
Baldwin, P. 1990. *The Politics of Social Solidarity: Class Bases of the European Welfare State, 1875–1975*, Cambridge University Press.
Ball, C. 1995. 'Reviewing Progress and Future Directions in Employment and Growth', Paper presented to the Mission Employment Services National Conference, Sydney.
Barbalet, J. M. 1989. 'Social Movements and the State: The Case of the American Labour Movement', in C. Jennett and R. Stewart (eds), *Politics of the Future*, Melbourne: Macmillan.

Barbalet, J. M. 1996a. 'Social Emotions: Confidence, Trust and Loyalty', *International Journal of Sociology and Social Policy*, 16, 9–10: 75–96.
Barbalet, J. M. 1996b. 'Citizenship, Trust and Loyalty', Paper presented to the Conference on Citizenship, Community and Development, University of Wollongong, 1–2 November.
Barber, B. 1994. *Strong Democracy: Participatory Politics for a New Age*, University of California Press.
Barker, G. 1991. 'Elegance without Relevance', *Age*, 11 October.
Barr, N. 1990. *The State of Welfare: The Welfare State in Britain since 1974*, Oxford: Clarendon Press.
Barr, N. 1992. 'Economic Theory and the Welfare State: A Survey and Reinterpretation', *Journal of Economic Literature*, 30 (June): 741–803.
Bartlett, W. *et al.* (eds). 1994. *Quasi-Markets in the Welfare State: The Emerging Findings*, Bristol: School for Advanced Urban Studies (SAUS) Publications.
Barzelay, M. 1992. *Breaking through the Barriers: A New Vision for Managing Government*, Berkeley: University of California.
Battin, T. 1991. 'What is This Thing Called Economic Rationalism?', *Australian Journal of Social Issues*, November: 294–307.
Battin, T. 1993. 'A Break from the Past: The Labor Party and the Political Economy of Keynesian Social Democracy', *Australian Journal of Political Science*, 28, 2: 221–41.
Battin T. 1996. 'Explaining the Breakdown of Keynesianism in Australia: An Approach in Political Economy', PhD thesis, University of New England, Armidale.
Battin, T. 1997. *Abandoning Keynes: Australia's Capital Mistake*, London: Macmillan.
Bean, Clive. 1991. 'Are Australian Attitudes to Government Different?', in F. G. Castles (ed.) 1991.
Beck, Ulrich. 1994. 'The Reinvention of Politics: Towards a Theory of Reflexive Modernisation', in U. Beck, A. Giddens and S. Lash (eds), *Reflexive Modernisation*, Cambridge: Polity Press.
Beilharz, P. 1994. *Transforming Labor: Labour Tradition and the Labor Decade in Australia*, Cambridge University Press.
Beilharz, P., Considine, M., and Watts, R. 1992. *Arguing About the Welfare State*, Sydney: Allen and Unwin.
Bell, S. 1993. *Australian Manufacturing and the State: The Politics of Industry Policy in the Post-War Era*, Cambridge University Press.
Bell, S. 1995. 'The Collective Capitalism of Northeast Asia and the Limits of Orthodox Economics', *Australian Journal of Political Science*, 30: 264–87.
Bell, S. 1997a. *Ungoverning the Economy: The Political Economy of Australian Economic Policy*, Oxford University Press.
Bell, S. 1997b. 'Globalisation, Neoliberalism and the Transformation of the Australian State', *Australian Journal of Political Science*, forthcoming.
Bentham, Jeremy. 1973. 'Of the Principle of Utility', in Bikhu Parekh (ed.), *Bentham's Political Thought*, London: Croom Helm.
Berger, S., and Dore, R. (eds). 1995. *National Diversity and Global Capitalism*, Cornell University Press.
Bernard, M. 1994. 'Post-Fordism, Transnational Production and the Changing Global Political Economy', in R. Stubbs and G. R. D. Underhill (eds), *Political Economy and the Changing Global Order*, London: Macmillan.
Bhaduri, A., and Steindl, J. 1985. 'The Rise of Monetarism as a Social

Doctrine', in P. Arestis and T. Skouras (eds), *Post-Keynesian Economic Theory: A Challenge to Neo-Classical Economics*, Sussex: Wheatsheaf Books, 56–78.
BIE (Bureau of Industry Economics). 1995. *Beyond the Firm: An Assessment of Business Linkages and Networks in Australia*, Canberra: AGPS.
Birrell, R. 1995. *A Nation of Our Own*, Melbourne: Longman.
Blackwell, J. 1992. 'Changing Work Patterns and their Implications for Social Protection', Paper presented to the International Conference on Beveridge and Social Security, University of York, UK.
Blau, F., and Kahn, L. 1992. 'The Gender Earnings Gap: Learning from International Comparisons', *AEA Papers and Proceedings*, 82, 2: 533–8.
Blendell-Wignell, A. (ed.). 1992. *Inflation, Disinflation and Monetary Policy*, Sydney: Reserve Bank of Australia.
Block, F. 1977. *The Origins of International Economic Disorder*, University of California Press.
Bollen, J. D. 1972. *Protestantism and Social Reform in New South Wales, 1890–1910*, Melbourne University Press.
Bolton, Geoffrey. 1996. *The Oxford History of Australia, vol. 5: 1942–1996: The Middle Way*, Oxford University Press.
Boorstin, Daniel J. 1953. *The Genius of American Politics*, University of Chicago Press.
Borrus, M., Weber, S., and Zysman, J. 1992. 'Mercantilism and Global Security', *The National Interest*, Fall: 21–9.
Boston, J., and Uhr, J. 1996. 'Reshaping the Mechanics of Government', in F. Castles, R. Gerritson and J. Vowles (eds), *The Great Experiment: Labour Parties and Public Policy Transformation in Australia and New Zealand*, Sydney: Allen and Unwin.
Boston, J., et al. (eds). 1991. *Reshaping the State: New Zealand's Bureaucratic Revolution*, Oxford University Press.
Bradbury, B. 1993. 'Male Wage Inequality Before and After Tax: A Six-Country Comparison', Discussion Paper no. 42, Social Policy Research Centre, University of New South Wales.
Brain, P. 1992. *Financing the Development of Manufacturing Industry*, Melbourne: NIEIR.
Brennan, D. 1994a. *The Politics of Australian Child Care: From Philanthropy to Feminism*, Cambridge University Press.
Brennan, D. 1994b. 'Social Policy', in Judith Brett *et al.*, Developments in Australian Politics, Melbourne: Macmillan.
Brennan, D. 1996. 'Reinventing Government', in A. Farrar and J. Inglis (eds), *Keeping It Together: State and Civil Society in Australia*, Sydney: Pluto Press, pp. 2–17.
Brennan, G. 1993. 'Economic Rationalism: What Does Economics Really Say?', in S. King and P. Lloyd (eds), *Economic Rationalism: Dead End or Way Forward?*, Sydney: Allen and Unwin.
Brigden, J. 1929. *The Australian Tariff: An Economic Enquiry*, Melbourne University Press.
Broom, L., and Jones, F. L. 1976. *Opportunity and Attainment in Australia*, Australian National University Press.
Bryson, L. 1994. 'The Welfare State and Economic Adjustment', in S. Bell and B. Head (eds), *State, Economy and Public Policy in Australia*, Oxford University Press.
Burgess, J., and Green, R. 1997. *Structural Change and Employment Growth in Australia*, Melbourne: Brotherhood of St Laurence.

Butlin, N. G. 1987. 'Human or Inhuman Capital? The Economics Profession, 1916–1987', Australian National University Working Papers in Economic History no. 91, September.
Cairns, J. F. 1957. 'The Welfare State in Australia', PhD thesis, University of Melbourne.
Camilleri, J. A., and Falk, J. 1992. *The End of Sovereignty?*, Aldershot: Edward Elgar.
Canberra Bulletin of Public Administration. 1994. *Reinventing Government: Papers from AIC/RIPAA (ACT Division) Conference*, Sydney.
Capling, M. A., and Galligan, B. 1992. *Beyond the Protective State: The Political Economy of Australia's Manufacturing Industry Policy*, Cambridge University Press.
Cappo, D. 1995. 'Introduction', in *Proceedings of the National Summit on Employment Opportunities and Case Management*, Canberra: Australian Catholic Social Welfare.
Carroll, J., and Manne, R. (eds). 1992. *Shutdown: The Failure of Economic Rationalism and How to Rescue Australia*, Melbourne: Text Publishing Company.
Carter, J. 1993. 'Social Equality in Australia', in P. Saunders and S. Shaver (eds), *Theory and Practice in Australian Social Policy: Rethinking the Fundamentals*, Social Policy Research Centre, University of New South Wales, Reports and Proceedings, no. 111.
Carter, Stephen L. 1993. *The Culture of Disbelief*, New York: Anchor Books.
Carver, L. 1996. 'Competition Policy and Consumer Outcomes', in A. Farrar and J. Inglis (eds), *Keeping It Together: State and Civil Society in Australia*, Sydney: Pluto Press, pp. 114–29.
Cass, B. 1988. *Income Support for the Unemployed in Australia: Towards a More Active System*, Canberra: AGPS.
Cass, B. 1995a. 'Overturning the Male Breadwinner Model in the Australian Social Protection System', in P. Saunders and S. Shaver (eds), *Social Policy and the Challenges of Social Change*, Social Policy Research Centre, University of New South Wales, Reports and Proceedings, no. 122, pp. 47–66.
Cass, B. 1995b. 'Unemployment and Active Employment Policies', in *Proceedings of National Summit on Employment Opportunities*, Canberra: Australian Catholic Welfare Commission.
Cass, B. 1998. 'The Social Policy Context', in P. Smyth and B. Cass (eds), *Contesting the Australian Way: Government, Society and Market Forces*, Cambridge University Press, Sydney.
Cass, B., and Freeland, J. 1994. 'Social Security and Full Employment in Australia: The Rise and Fall of the Keynesian Welfare State and the Search for a Post-Keynesian Consensus', in J. Hills *et al.* (eds), *Beveridge and Social Security*, Oxford: Clarendon Press.
Castles, F. G. 1985. *The Working Class and Welfare: Reflections on the Political Development of the Welfare State in Australia and New Zealand, 1890–1980*, Sydney: Allen and Unwin.
Castles, F. G. 1989. *Australian Public Policy and Economic Vulnerability*, Sydney: Allen and Unwin.
Castles, F. G. 1991a. *Australia Compared: Policies and Politics*, Sydney: Allen and Unwin.
Castles, F. G. 1991b. 'On Sickness Days and Social Policy', Discussion Paper no. 25, Public Policy Program, Australian National University.
Castles, F. G. 1994. 'The Wage Earners' Welfare State Revisited', *Australian Journal of Social Issues* 29, 1: 120–45.

Castles, F. G. 1997. 'The Institutional Design of the Australian Welfare State', *International Social Security Review*, 50, 2: 25–41.
Castles, F. G. (ed.). 1991. *Australia Compared: People, Policies and Politics*, Sydney: Allen and Unwin, pp. 133–5.
Castles, F. G., and Mitchell, D. 1992a. 'Three Worlds of Welfare Capitalism or Four?', *Governance*, 5, 1: 1–26.
Castles, F., and Mitchell, D. 1992b. 'Identifying Welfare State Regimes: The Links between Politics, Instruments and Outcomes', *Governance*, 5, 1.
Chapman, B. 1994. 'Long-term Unemployment: The Case for Policy Reform', *Social Security Journal* (June).
Civics Expert Group. 1994. *Whereas the People . . .: Civics and Citizenship Education*, Canberra: AGPS.
Cohen, J. 1982. *Class and Civil Society: The Limits of Marxian Critical Theory*, Amherst: University of Massachusetts Press.
Cohen, J. 1985. 'Strategy or Identity: New Theoretical Paradigms and Contemporary Social Movements', *Social Research*, Winter: 663–73.
Cohen, Joshua, and Rogers, Joel. 1995. 'Secondary Associations and Democratic Governance', in Erik Olin Wright (ed.), *Associations and Democracy*, London: Verso.
Cohen, S., and Zysman, J. 1987. *Why Manufacturing Matters: The Myth of the Post-Industrial Economy*, New York: Basic Books.
Collins, H. 1985. 'Political Ideology in Australia: The Distinctiveness of a Benthamite Society', in S. R. Graubard (ed.), *Australia: The Daedalus Symposium*, Sydney: Angus and Robertson.
Commission for the Future of Work. 1996a. *A Future that Works for All of Us*, Commission for the Future of Work, Sydney.
Commission for the Future of Work. 1996b. *A Future that Works: Goals and Strategies for Australia*, ACOSS Paper no. 78, Sydney.
Commission of Inquiry into Poverty. 1975. *First Main Report*, Canberra: AGPS.
Committee on Employment Opportunities. 1993. *Restoring Full Employment: A Discussion Paper*, Canberra: AGPS.
Commonwealth of Australia. 1945. *Full Employment in Australia*, Canberra: Government Printer.
Commonwealth of Australia. 1994a. *Working Nation: Policies and Programs*, Canberra: AGPS.
Commonwealth of Australia. 1994b. *Working Nation: White Paper on Employment and Growth*, Canberra: AGPS.
Connell, R. W. 1991. 'The Money Measure: Social Inequality of Wealth and Income', in J. O'Leary and R. Sharp (eds), *Inequality in Australia: Slicing the Cake, The Social Justice Collective*, Melbourne: William Heinemann.
Considine, M. 1988. 'The Corporate Management Framework as Administrative Science: A Critique', *Australian Journal of Public Administration*, 47, 1: 4–18.
Considine, M. 1990. 'Managerialism Strikes Out', *Australian Journal of Public Administration*, 49, 2: 166–78.
Considine, M. 1994. *Public Policy: A Critical Approach*, Melbourne: Macmillan.
Considine, M. 1995. 'Bureaucracy in Fours: Frameworks of Administrative Reform in the Anglo-American Democracies', unpublished paper, Department of Political Science, University of Melbourne, 25 pp.
Considine, M. 1996. 'Market Bureaucracy', in A. Farrar and J. Inglis (eds), *Keeping It Together: State and Civil Society in Australia*, Sydney: Pluto Press, pp. 76–91.

Considine, M., and Painter, M. 1997. 'Introduction', in M. Considine and M. Painter (eds), *Managerialism: The Great Debate*, Melbourne University Press.
Coombs, H. C. 1944. *The Special Problems of Planning*, Melbourne University Press.
Coombs, H. C. 1984. 'John Curtin: A Consensus Prime Minister?', *Arena*, 69: 46–59.
Cooper, R., and John, A. 1995. 'Coordinating Coordination Failures in Keynesian Models', in G. Mankiw and D. Romer (eds), *New Keynesian Economics*, Cambridge, Mass.: MIT Press.
Corry, D., and Glyn, A. 1994. 'The Macroeconomics of Equality, Stability and Growth', in A. Glyn and D. Miliband (eds), *Paying for Inequality: The Economic Costs of Social Injustice*, London: Rivers Oram Press.
Cox, Eva. 1995. *A Truly Civil Society: 1995 Boyer Lectures*, Sydney: ABC Books.
Crawford, J. G. 1959. 'The Role of Government and the Place of Planning', in *The Industrial Development of Australia, Symposium*, University of New South Wales, pp. 43–51.
Creedy, J. 1992. *Income, Inequality and the Life Cycle*, Aldershot: Edward Elgar.
Crouch, C., and Pizzorno, A. (eds). 1978. *The Resurgence of Class Conflict in Western Europe Since 1968*, London: Macmillan.
Cryle, D. 1989. *The Press in Colonial Queensland*, University of Queensland Press.
Danziger, S., and Gottschalk, P. (eds).1993. *Uneven Tides: Rising Inequality in the 1980s*, New York: Russell Sage.
Davidson, Alastair. 1997. *From Subject to Citizen: Australian Citizenship in the Twentieth Century*, Cambridge University Press.
Davis, G. 1997. 'Toward a Hollow State? Managerialism and its Critics', in M. Considine and M. Painter (eds), *Managerialism: The Great Debate*, Melbourne University Press.
De Maria, W. 1990. 'Better than Beveridge? The Start of the National Welfare Scheme in Australia', *Royal Australian Historical Society Journal*, 76, 2 (October): 140–52.
De Maria, W. 1992. 'Discounting in Paradise: The Inglorious Start to the 1943 National Welfare Scheme', *Royal Australian Historical Society Journal*, 78, 1–2 (June): 17–29.
Department of Social Security. 1994. *From Client to Customer: An Approach to Re-engineering of Employment Services*, Canberra.
Dickey, Brian. 1987. *No Charity There: A Short History of Social Welfare in Australia*, Sydney: Allen and Unwin.
Dodgson, M. 1996. 'Technology and Innovation: Strategy, Learning and Trust', in P. Sheehan, P. B. Grewal and M. Kumnick (eds), *Dialogues on Australia's Future*, Centre for Strategic Economic Studies, Victoria University, Melbourne.
Dow, G. 1992. 'The Economic Consequences of Economists', *Australian Journal of Political Science*, 27, 2: 258–81.
Dow, G. 1996. 'Full Employment and Social Democratic Institutions', in T. Battin and G. Maddox (eds), *Socialism in Contemporary Australia*, Melbourne: Longman.
Dowrick, S. 1991. 'Has the Pattern of Australian Wages Growth Been Unique?', in F. G. Castles (ed.) 1991.
Dowrick, S. 1995. 'A Review of New Theories and Evidence on Economic Growth: Their Implications for Australian Policy', Discussion Paper no. 275, Centre for Economic Policy Research, Australian National University.

Drucker, P. 1986. 'The Changed World Economy', *Foreign Affairs*, 64: 768–91.
Duckett, R. 1985. 'The Emergence of Pensioner Groups in New South Wales: The Making of an Association', BA (Hons) thesis, Macquarie University.
Duncan, Bruce. 1991. *The Church's Social Teaching: From 'Rerum Novarum' to 1931*, North Blackburn, Vic.: Collins Dove.
Duncan, T. 1993. 'New Ways to Kill the Goose: Sectoral Clashes After Protectionism', in C. James, C. Jones and A. Norton (eds), *A Defence of Economic Rationalism*, Sydney: Allen and Unwin.
Duverger, Maurice. 1964. *Political Parties. Their Organization and Activity in the Modern State* (trans. Barbara and Robert North), London: Methuen, 3rd edn.
Dyster, B., and Meredith, D. 1991. *Australia in the International Economy in the Twentieth Century*, Cambridge University Press.
Eardley, T., et al. 1996. *Social Assistance in OECD Countries*, vols 1–2, Research Reports nos. 46 and 47, UK Department of Social Security, London: HMSO, and Paris: OECD.
Eatwell, J. 1995. 'The International Origins of Unemployment', in J. Michie and J. Grieve Smith (eds), *Managing the Global Economy*, Oxford University Press.
Eatwell, J. (ed.). 1996. *Global Unemployment: Loss of Jobs in the '90s*, New York: M. E. Sharpe.
Economic Planning Advisory Commission. 1994. *Shaping Our Future: National Strategies Conference*, Canberra: AGPS.
Economist. 1994a. 5–11 November, pp. 19–23.
Economist. 1994b. 'For Richer, For Poorer', 5 November.
Edwards, A., and Magarey, S. (eds). 1995. *Women in a Restructuring Australia*, Sydney: Allen and Unwin.
Eichner, A., and Kregel, J. 1975. 'An Essay on Post-Keynesian Theory: A New Paradigm in Economics', *Journal of Economic Literature*, 13: 1293–1314.
Eisinger, P. 1990. 'Do the American States Do Industrial Policy?', *British Journal of Political Science*, 20: 509–35.
Elias, N. 1987. 'The Retreat of Sociologists into the Present', *Theory, Culture and Society*, 4, 2–3: 223–47.
Emy, H. V. 1993. *Remaking Australia: The State, the Market and Australia's Future*, Sydney: Allen and Unwin.
Emy, H. V., and Hughes, O. E. 1991. *Australian Politics: Realities in Conflict*, Melbourne: Macmillan.
Encel, S. 1970. *Equality and Authority*, Melbourne: Cheshire.
Encel, S. 1988. 'Public Administration: Then, Now and in the Year 2000', *Australian Journal of Public Administration*, 47, 3: 231–40.
EPAC. 1995. *Income Distribution in Australia: Recent Trends and Research*, Canberra: AGPS.
Ernst, J. 1994. *Whose Utility? The Social Impact of Public Utility Privatization and Regulation in Britain*, Buckingham: Open University Press.
Ernst, J., Glanville, L., and Murfitt, P. 1997. *Breaking the Contract? The Implementation of Compulsory Competitive Tendering in Victoria*, Melbourne: Outer Urban Research and Policy Unit.
Escott, K., and Whitfield, D. 1995. *The Gender Impact of CCT in Local Government*, Manchester: Equal Opportunities Commission.
Esping-Andersen, G. 1990. *The Three Worlds of Welfare Capitalism*, Cambridge: Polity Press.

Evatt Foundation. 1995. *Unions 2001: A Blueprint for Trade Union Activism*, Evatt Foundation, Sydney.
Evatt, H. V. 1942. *Post-War Reconstruction: The Case for Greater Commonwealth Powers*, Canberra: AGPS.
Eyerman, R. 1984. 'Social Movements and Social Theory', *Sociology*, 1: 71–82.
Fagan, R. H., and Webber, M. 1994. *Global Restructuring: The Australian Experience*, Oxford University Press.
Falkingham, J., and Harding, A. 1996. 'Poverty Alleviation versus Social Insurance Systems: A Comparison of Lifetime Redistribution', Discussion Paper no. 12, NATSEM, University of Canberra.
Fitzgerald, T. 1990. *Between Life and Economics: 1990 Boyer Lectures*, Sydney: ABC.
Fraser, N. 1992. 'Rethinking the Public Sphere: Towards a Critique of Actually Existing Democracies', in Craig Calhoun (ed.), *Habermas and the Public Sphere*, Cambridge, Mass.: MIT Press.
Fraser, N., and Gordon, L. 1994. 'Dependency Demystified: Descriptions of Power in a Keyword of the Welfare State', *Social Politics*, 1, 1: 4–31.
Freeden, Michael. 1970. 'Review', *Journal of Modern History*, 48, 3: 549.
Freeland, J. 1995. 'The White Paper and Labour Market Programs: A Critical Analysis', in T. Aspromorgous and M. Smith (eds), *The Pursuit of Full Employment*, Department of Economics, University of Sydney.
Freeman, C. 1994. 'The Economics of Technical Change', *Cambridge Journal of Economics*, 18: 463–514.
Friedman, F. A. 1962. *Capitalism and Freedom*, Chicago: Phoenix Books.
Fukuyama, F. 1995. *Trust: The Social Virtues and the Creation of Prosperity*, London: Hamish Hamilton.
Gabay, A. 1992. *The Mystic Life of Alfred Deakin*, Cambridge University Press.
Garrett, G. 1993. 'The Politics of Structural Change: Swedish Social Democracy and Thatcherism in Comparative Perspective', *Comparative Political Studies*, 25, 4: 521–47.
Garrett, G., and Lange, P. 1991. 'Political Responses to Interdependence: What's Left for the Left?', *International Organisation*, 45: 539–64.
Garton, S. 1990. *Out of Luck: Poor Australians and Social Welfare, 1788–1988*, Sydney: Allen and Unwin.
Garton, S. 1996. *The Cost of War*, Oxford University Press.
Gelbach, J. B., and Pritchett, L. H. 1997. *Does More for the Poor Mean Less for the Poor? The Politics of Tagging*, World Bank, mimeo.
Genoff, R. 1997. 'Manufacturers Need Fewer Impediments', *Australian Financial Review*, 17 February.
Genoff, R., and Green, R. (eds). 1998. *Manufacturing Prosperity: Ideas for Industry, Technology and Employment*, Sydney: Federation Press.
Gersuny, C. 1994. 'Industrial Rights: A Neglected Facet of Citizenship Theory', *Economic and Industrial Democracy*, 15: 211–26.
Giblin, L. F. 1943. 'Reconstruction: A Pisgah View', *Australian Quarterly*, 15, 3 (September): 5–17.
Giblin, L. F. 1945. 'Financing Full Employment', Economic Papers no. 5, Sydney, pp. 59–67.
Gilbert, M. 1981. 'A Sociological Model of Inflation', *Sociology*, 15: 185–209.
Gill, F. 1995. 'Microeconomic Aspects of Unemployment and the Complex Web of Macro and Micro Roots', in T. Aspromorgous and M. Smith (eds), *The Pursuit of Full Employment*, Department of Economics, University of Sydney.

Gill, S. R. 1989. *American Hegemony and the Trilateral Commission*, Cambridge University Press.
Gill, S. R., and Law, D. 1989. 'Global Hegemony and the Structural Power of Capital', *International Studies Quarterly*, 33: 475–99.
Gillespie, James. 1992. *The Price of Health*, Cambridge University Press.
Gilpin, R. 1987. *The Political Economy of International Relations*, Princeton University Press.
Glezer, L. 1982. *Tariff Politics*, Melbourne University Press.
Glyn, A. 1995. 'Social Democracy and Full Employment', *New Left Review*, 211: 33–55.
Goldsmith, W. W., and Blakely, E. J. 1992. *Separate Societies: Poverty and Inequality in US Cities*, Temple University Press.
Goldthorpe, J. 1978. 'The Current Inflation: Towards a Sociological Account', in F. Hirsch and J. Goldthorpe (eds), *The Political Economy of Inflation*, London: Martin Robertson.
Goodman, J. 1997. 'New Deals and Privatising Unemployment in Australia', *Journal of Political Economy*, 40: 27–43.
Gore, A. 1993. *From Red Tape to Results: Creating a Government that Works Better and Costs Less*, Washington, DC: US Government Printing Office.
Gornick, J., and Jacobs, G. 1994. 'A Cross-National Comparison of the Wages of Part-Time Workers: Evidence from the United States, United Kingdom, Canada and Australia', LIS Working Paper no. 113, Luxembourg: CEPS/INSTEAD.
Gottschalk, P. 1993. 'Changes in Inequality of Family Income in Seven Industrialised Countries: Responses to Growing Earnings Inequality', *AEA Papers and Proceedings*, 83, 2: 136–42.
Gourevitch, P. 1986. *Politics in Hard Times*, Cornell University Press.
Gowa, J. 1984. 'State Power, State Policy: Explaining the Decision to Close the Gold Window', *Politics and Society*, 13: 91–117.
Gramsci, A. 1971. *Selections from the Prison Notebooks*, New York: International Publishers.
Gray, J. 1993. *Beyond The New Right: Markets, Government and the Common Environment*, London and New York: Routledge.
Gray, J. 1994. 'Why Tories Should Vote Labour', *The Times*, 24 June.
Green, G., Coder, J., and Ryscavage, P. 1992. 'International Comparisons of Earnings Inequality for Men in the 1980s', *Review of Income and Wealth*, 38, 1: 1–15.
Green, R. 1996a. 'Reconnecting with the Workplace: How Labor Can Win Again', *Australian Quarterly*, December.
Green, R. 1996b. 'How Manufacturing Can Help Young People to Get High-Wage Jobs', in J. Spierings, I. Voorendt and J. Spoehr (eds), *Jobs for Young Australians: Selected Papers of an International Conference*, Adelaide: Social Justice Research Foundation, pp. 72–86.
Green, R. 1997. 'Globalising Steel', *Australian Options*.
Green, R., and Genoff, R. 1993. 'Introduction', in R. Green and R. Genoff (eds), *Making the Future Work: Crisis and Change in the South Australian Economy*, Sydney: Allen and Unwin.
Gregory, R. 1997. 'The Peculiar Tasks of Public Management: Toward Conceptual Discrimination', in M. Considine and M. Painter (eds), *Managerialism: The Great Debate*, Melbourne University Press.

Gregory, R. G. 1993. 'Aspects of Australian Living Standards: The Disappointing Decades', *Economic Record*, 69: 61–76.
Groenewegen, P., and McFarlane, B. 1990. *A History of Australian Economic Thought*, London: Routledge.
Gruen, F. H. 1989. *Australia's Welfare State: Rearguard or Avant Garde?*, Discussion Paper no. 212, Centre for Economic Policy Research, Australian National University.
Habermas, J. 1981. 'New Social Movements', *Telos*, 49: 5–31.
Habermas, J. 1991. [1962] *The Structural Transformation of the Public Sphere*, Cambridge, Mass.: MIT Press.
Hall, P. (ed.). 1989. *The Political Power of Economic Ideas: Keynesianism Across Nations*, Princeton University Press.
Hall, Peter A. 1992. 'The Movement of Keynesianism to Monetarism: Institutional Analysis and British Economic Policy in the 1970s', in S. Steinmo, K. Thelen and F. Longstreth (eds), *Structuring Politics*, Cambridge University Press, pp. 90–113.
Hampden-Turner, C., and Trompenaars, F. 1993. *The Seven Cultures of Capitalism*, New York: Doubleday.
Hancock, W. K. 1961. [1930] *Australia*, Brisbane: Jacaranda Press.
Harding, A. 1995. 'Equity, Redistribution and the Tax-Transfer System', in M. Hogan *et al.* (eds), *Equity and Citizenship Under Keating*, University of Sydney, Department of Government.
Harding, A., and Mitchell, D. 1992. 'The Efficiency and Effectiveness of the Tax-Transfer System in the 1980s', *Australian Tax Forum*, 9, 3: 277–303.
Harris, S. E. (ed.). 1948. *The New Economics*, London: Robson.
Hartz, Louis. 1955. *The Liberal Tradition in America*, New York: Harcourt, Brace and World.
Hasluck, Paul. 1952. *The Government and the People, 1939–1941*, Canberra: Australian War Memorial.
Hayden, W. G. 1975. In *Commonwealth Parliamentary Debates*, 19 August, p. 53.
Hayek, F. A. 1949. *Individualism and Economic Order*, London: Routledge and Kegan Paul.
Hayward, J., and Page, E. (eds). 1995. *Governing the New Europe*, Cambridge: Polity Press.
Heilbroner, R. L. 1979. 'Inflationary Capitalism,' *New Yorker*, 8 October.
Helleiner, E. 1994a. *States and the Reemergence of Global Finance: From Bretton Woods to the 1990s*, Cornell University Press.
Helleiner, E. 1994b. 'From Bretton Woods to Global Finance: A World Turned Upside Down', in R. Stubbs and G. R. D. Underhill (eds), *Political Economy and the Changing Global Order*, London: Macmillan.
Henderson, R. F., Harcourt, A., and Harper, R. J. A. 1970. *People in Poverty: A Melbourne Survey*, Melbourne: Cheshire.
Hewitt, M. 1993. 'Social Movements and Social Need: Problems with Postmodern Political Theory', *Critical Social Policy*, 37: 52–74.
Hilmer Report, see National Competition Policy Review.
Hirsch, F. 1978. 'The Ideological Underlay of Inflation', in F. Hirsch and J. Goldthorpe (eds), *The Political Economy of Inflation*, London: Martin Robertson.
Hirst, J., and Thompson, G. 1996. *Globalization in Question: The International Economy and the Possibilities of Governance*, Cambridge: Polity Press.

Hirst, P. 1994. *Associative Democracy*, Cambridge: Polity Press.
Hirst, Paul. 1996. 'Democracy and Civil Society', in Paul Hirst and Sunil Khilnani (eds), *Reinventing Democracy*, Oxford: Blackwell.
Hobsbawm, E. 1994. *Age of Extremes: The Short Twentieth Century, 1914–1991*, London: Michael Joseph.
Holmwood, J. 1996. 'Abject Theory', *Australian and New Zealand Journal of Sociology*, 32, 2: 86–108.
Hood, C. 1994. *Explaining Economic Policy Reversals*, Buckingham: Open University Press.
Hughes, O. E. 1994. *Public Management and Administration*, Melbourne: Macmillan.
Hume, L. J. 1994. 'Foundations of Populism and Pluralism: Australian Writings on Politics to 1860', in Geoff Stokes (ed.), *Australian Political Ideas*, University of New South Wales Press, pp. 22–76.
Hunter Economic Development Corporation (HEDC). 1997. *Hunter Region: Towards a Sustainable Future*, Discussion Paper for Jobs Summit, Newcastle: HEDC.
Hutton, W. 1995. *The State We're In*, London: Vintage.
Hutton, W. 1997. 'Free Market Needs Governance', *Sydney Morning Herald*, 29 October.
Industry Commission. 1992. *Annual Report 1991–92*, Canberra: AGPS.
Industry Commission. 1994. *Annual Report 1993–94*, Canberra: AGPS.
Industry Commission. 1995a. *Charitable Organisations in Australia*, Report no. 45, Melbourne: AGPS.
Industry Commission. 1995b. *Annual Report 1994–95*, Canberra: AGPS.
Industry Commission. 1995c. *The Growth and Revenue Implications of Hilmer and Related Reforms*, Melbourne.
Industry Commission. 1996. *Inquiry into Competitive Tendering and Contracting by Public Sector Agencies*, Melbourne.
Ingles, D. 1981. *Statistics on the Distribution of Income and Wealth in Australia*, Research Paper no. 14, Development Division, Department of Social Security, Canberra.
International Labour Office. 1993. *Labour Statistics*, Geneva.
Irving, Helen. 1994. 'Who Were the Republicans?', in David Headon, James Warden and Bill Gammage (eds), *Crown or Country: The Traditions of Australian Republicanism*, Sydney: Allen and Unwin, pp. 69–79.
James, C., Jones, C., and Norton, A. (eds). 1993. *A Defence of Economic Rationalism*, Sydney: Allen and Unwin.
Jenkins, S. 1996. *Accountable to None*, London: Penguin Books.
Johnson, C. 1986. 'Institutional Foundations of Japanese Industrial Policy', in C. Barfield (ed.), *Politics of Industrial Policy*, Washington, DC: American Enterprise.
Jones, F. L. 1975. 'The Changing Shape of the Australian Income Distribution, 1914–15 to 1968–69', *Australian Economic History Review*, 15: 21–34.
Jones, M. A. 1990. *The Australian Welfare State*, 3rd edn, Sydney: Allen and Unwin.
Junankar, P., and Kapuscinski, C. 1992. 'The Costs of Unemployment in Australia', *EPAC Background Paper No. 24*, Canberra: AGPS.
Kakwani, N. 1980. *Income Inequality and Poverty: Methods of Estimation and Policy Applications*, New York: Oxford University Press.
Kalecki, M. 1943. 'Political Aspects of Full Employment', *Political Quarterly*, 14: 322–31.

Kangas, O., and Palme, J. 1992. *Class Politics and Institutional Feedbacks: Development of Occupational Pensions in Finland and Sweden*, Stockholm: Swedish Institute for Social Research.

Kaptein, E. 1993. 'Neo-Liberalism and the Dismantling of Corporatism in Australia', in H. Overbeek (ed.), *Restructuring Hegemony in the Global Political Economy*, London: Routledge.

Katzenstein, P. J. 1985. *Small States in World Markets: Industrial Policy in Europe*, Cornell University Press.

Keating, M. 1989. 'Quo Vadis? Challenges of Public Administration', *Australian Journal of Public Administration*, 48, 2: 123–31.

Keating, M. 1993. 'The Influence of Economists', in S. King and P. Lloyd (eds), *Economic Rationalism: Dead End or Way Forward?*, Sydney: Allen and Unwin, pp. 57–81.

Keating, M. 1995. 'Public Service Values', *Australian Quarterly*, 67, 4: 15–25.

Keating, P. J. 1992. *One Nation: Statement by the Prime Minister*, Canberra: AGPS.

Kelly, Paul. 1992. *The End of Certainty: The Story of the 1980s*, Sydney: Allen and Unwin.

Kewley, T. H. 1969. *Australia's Welfare State*, Melbourne: Macmillan.

Kidd, Benjamin. 1893. *Social Evolution*, London: Macmillan.

King, S., and Lloyd P. (eds). 1993. *Economic Rationalism: Dead End or Way Forward?*, Sydney: Allen and Unwin.

Kingston, Beverley. 1988. *Oxford History of Australia*, vol. 3: *Glad Confident Morning: 1861–1901*, Oxford University Press.

Kolberg, J. (ed.). 1992. *The Study of Welfare State Regimes*, New York: M. E. Sharpe.

Korpi, W., and Palme, J. 1994. 'The Strategy of Equality and the Paradox of Redistribution', Paper presented to the UK Social Policy Association Conference, University of Liverpool.

Kramer, R. M. 1994. 'Voluntary Agencies and the Contract Culture: Dream or Nightmare?', *Social Service Review*, 68, 1: 33–60.

Kurzer, P. 1993. *Banking and Business: Political Change and Economic Integration in Western Europe*, Cornell University Press.

La Nauze, J. A. 1965. *Alfred Deakin: A Biography*, Melbourne University Press, 2 vols.

Laffin, M. 1995. 'The Bureaucracy Compared: Past and Future Trends', in G. Davis and P. Weller (eds), *New Ideas, Better Government*, Sydney: Allen and Unwin, pp. 38–54.

Lamare, J. W., and Vowles, J. 1996. 'Party Interests, Public Opinion and Institutional Preferences', *Australian Journal of Political Science*, 31, 3: 321–45.

Landt, J., Percival, R., Schofield, D., and Wilson, D. 1995. *Income Inequality in Australia: The Impact of Non-cash Subsidies for Health and Housing*, Discussion Paper no. 5, NATSEM, University of Canberra.

Lang, J. D. 1850. *The Coming Event; or the United Provinces of Australia*, Sydney: D. L. Welch.

Langmore, J., and Quiggin, J. 1994. *Work for All*, Melbourne University Press.

Latham, M. 1998. *Civilising Global Capital*, Sydney: Allen and Unwin.

Layard, R. 1977. 'On Measuring the Redistribution of Lifetime Income', in M. S. Feldstein and R. P. Inman (eds), *The Economics of Public Services*, London: Macmillan.

Lewis, J. 1992. 'Gender and Welfare Regimes', *Journal of European Social Policy*, 2, 3: 159–71.

Lewis, J. 1993. 'Developing the Mixed Economy of Care: Emerging Issues for Voluntary Organisations', *Journal of Social Policy*, 22, 2: 173–92.
Liberal and National Parties. 1991. *Fightback: Taxation and Expenditure Reform for Jobs and Growth and Jobsback*, Canberra: Coalition Parties.
Lind, M. 1992. 'The Catalytic State', *The National Interest*, 27: 3–12.
Lind, M. 1995. *The Next American Nation: The New Nationalism and the Fourth American Revolution*, New York: Free Press.
Lindsay, A. D. 1943. *The Modern Democracy State*, Oxford University Press.
Lipietz, A. 1992. *Towards a New Economic Order*, Cambridge: Polity Press.
Lipietz, A. 1994. 'Post-Fordism and Democracy', in A. Amin (ed.), *Post-Fordism: A Reader*, Oxford: Blackwell, pp. 338–58.
Lustiger-Thaler, H., and Maheu, L. 1995. 'Social Movements and the Challenge of Urban Politics', in Louis Maheu (ed.), *Social Movements and Social Classes: The Future of Collective Action*, London: Sage Studies in International Sociology/ISA.
Lydall, H. 1968. *The Structure of Earnings*, Oxford University Press.
MacDermott, T. 1997. 'Industrial Legislation in 1996: The Reform Agenda', *Journal of Industrial Relations*, 39, 1 (March): 52–76.
Macintosh, Maureen. 1993. 'Creating a Developmental State: Reflections on Policy as Process', in G. Albo, D. Langille and L. Panitch (eds), *A Different Kind of State? Popular Power and Democratic Administration*, Oxford University Press.
Macintyre, S. F. 1983. 'Labour, Capital and Arbitration, 1890–1920', in B. Head (ed.), *State and Economy in Australia*, Oxford University Press.
Macintyre, Stuart. 1989. *The Labour Experiment*, Melbourne: McPhee Gribble.
Mackay, H. 1993. *Reinventing Australia: The Mind and Mood of Australia in the 90s*, Sydney: Angus and Robertson.
Maddox, Graham. 1996. *Religion and the Rise of Democracy*, London: Routledge.
Magarey, Susan. 1985. *Unbridling the Tongues of Women: Catherine Helen Spence. A Biography*, Sydney: Hale and Iremonger.
Manning, I. et al. 1997. *Economic Growth and Employment*, Melbourne: Brotherhood of St Laurence.
Marceau, J., Manley, K., and Sicklen, D. 1997. *The High Road or the Low Road? Alternatives for Australia's Future*, Sydney: Australian Business Foundation.
Marginson, S. 1992. *The Free Market: A Study of Hayek, Friedman and Buchanan and Their Effects on the Public Good*, Public Sector Research Centre, University of New South Wales.
Marglin, S. A., and Schor, J. B. 1990. *The Golden Age of Capitalism: Reinterpreting the Post-War Experience*, Oxford: Clarendon Press.
Markell, P. 1997. 'Contesting Consensus: Rereading Habermas on the Public Sphere', *Constellations*, 3, 3: 377–400.
Marsh, I. 1995. *Beyond the Two-Party System*, Cambridge University Press.
Marsh, Ian. 1989. 'Setting the Agenda in Australian Politics', *Australian Quarterly*, 61, 2: 229–41.
Marshall, D. D. 1996. 'Understanding Late Twentieth Century Capitalism: Reassessing the Globalisation Theme', *Government and Opposition*, 31: 193–215.
Marshall, T. H. 1972. 'Value Problems of Welfare Capitalism', *Journal of Social Policy*, 1: 15–32.
Matzner, E., and Streeck, W. 1991. *Beyond Keynesianism: The Socio-Economics of Production and Full Employment*, Aldershot: Edward Elgar.
May, M. 1995. 'Money Could Become a Taxing Problem for Governments', *The Times*, 1 September.

McClelland, A. 1994. 'Families and Financial Disadvantage', *Family Matters*, 37 (April): 28–33.
McCracken, P., et al. 1977. *Towards Full Employment and Price Stability*, Paris: OECD.
McGregor, D. 1960. *The Human Side of the Enterprise*, New York: McGraw Hill.
McLaughlin, E. 1991. 'Work and Welfare Benefits: Social Security, Employment and Unemployment in the 1990s', *Journal of Social Policy*, 20, 4 (October): 485–508.
McLean, I., and Richardson, S. 1986. 'More or Less Equal? Australian Income Distribution in 1933 and 1980', *Economic Record*, 62, 176: 67–81.
McRae, H. 1995. *The World in 2020*, London: HarperCollins.
Meehan, E. 1994. 'Equality, Difference and Democracy', in D. Miliband (ed.), *Reinventing the Left*, Cambridge: Polity Press.
Melleuish, G. 1995. *Cultural Liberalism in Australia: A Study in Intellectual and Cultural History*, Cambridge University Press.
Melucci, A. 1989. *Nomads of the Present: Social Movements and Individual Needs in Contemporary Society*, London: Hutchinson.
Melville, L. G. 1946. 'Some Post-War Problems', *Economic Record*, 22 (June): 4–22.
Mendelsohn, R. 1979. *The Condition of the People: Social Welfare in Australia, 1900–1975*, Sydney: George Allen and Unwin.
Métin, Albert. 1977. *Socialism without Doctrine* (trans. Russel Ward), Chippendale, NSW: Alternative Publishing Co-operative.
Miliband, D. (ed.). 1994. *Reinventing the Left*, Cambridge: Polity Press.
Mill, John Stuart. 1962. 'Bentham', in Mill, *On Bentham and Coleridge*, New York: Harper and Row.
Miller, J. D. B. 1959. *Australian Government and Politics*, 2nd edn, London: Duckworth.
Mishra, R. 1984. *The Welfare State in Crisis*, London: Harvester
Mishra, R. 1990. *The Welfare State in Capitalist Society*, London: Harvester.
Mishra, R. 1995. 'Social Policy and the Challenge of Globalisation', in P. Saunders and S. Shaver (eds), *Social Policy and the Challenges of Social Change*, Social Policy Research Centre, University of New South Wales, Reports and Proceedings no. 122.
Mitchell, D. 1992. 'Welfare States and Welfare Outcomes in the 1980s', *Social Security 50 Years after Beveridge, Volume A, Plenary Papers*, University of York.
Mitchell, D., and Dowrick, S. 1994. *Women's Increasing Participation in the Labour Force: Implications for Equity and Efficiency*, Discussion Paper no. 308, Centre for Economic Policy Research, Australian National University.
Mitchell, D., Harding, A., and Gruen, F. 1994a. *Targeting Welfare: A Survey*, Discussion Paper no. 316, Centre for Economic Policy Research, Australian National University.
Mitchell, D., Harding, A., and Gruen, F. 1994b. 'Targeting Welfare', *Economic Record*, 70, 10: 315–40.
Mitchell, Deborah. 1991. 'Comparing Income Transfer Systems: Is Australia the Poor Relation?', in F. G.Castles (ed.) 1991.
Moore-Wilton, M. 1996. 'Achieving Change and Growth in the Public Sector', *Canberra Bulletin of Public Administration*, 82: 34–42.
Mortimer D. 1997. *Going for Growth: Business Programs for Investment, Innovation and Export*, Canberra: Commonwealth of Australia.
Moses, John A. 1991. 'The "Ideas of 1914" in Germany and Australia: A Case of Conflicting Perceptions', *War and Society*, 9, 2: 61–82.

Moses, John A. 1994. 'Anzac Day as Religious Revivalism: The Politics of Faith in Brisbane, 1916–1939', in Mark Hutchinson and Stuart Piggin (eds), *Reviving Australia: Essays on the History and Experience of Revival and Revivalism in Australian Christianity*, Sydney: Centre for the Study of Australian Christianity, pp. 170–84.
Mottl, T. 1980. 'The Analysis of Counter Movements', *Social Problems*, 27, 5.
MTIA (Metal Trades Industry Association). 1997. *Make or Break: A Report by EIU Australia*, Sydney: MTIA.
Mulgan, G. 1994. *Politics in an Antipolitical Age*, Cambridge: Polity Press.
Murray, C. 1984. *Losing Ground*, New York: Basic Books.
Naschold, F. 1995. *The Modernisation of the Public Sector in Europe*, Labour Policy Studies no. 93, Helsinki: Ministry of Labour.
Naschold, F. 1997. 'The Work of Bureaucracy: Modernising the Public Sector', in P. James et al. (eds), *Work of the Future: Global Perspectives*, Sydney: Allen and Unwin.
National Commission of Audit. 1996. *Report to the Commonwealth Government*, Canberra: AGPS.
National Competition Policy Review. 1993. *National Competition Policy (Hilmer Inquiry)*, Canberra: AGPS.
NATSEM. 1994. *Income Distribution Report*, no. 1, University of Canberra.
Nevile, J. 1993. 'Comment on Carter', in P. Saunders and S. Shaver (eds), *Theory and Practice in Australian Social Policy: Rethinking the Fundamentals*, Social Policy Research Centre, University of New South Wales, Reports and Proceedings, no. 111.
Nevile, J. W. 1994. 'Economic Rationalism, On Throwing Out the Bathwater, but Saving the Baby', *Australian Quarterly*, 66, 1 (Autumn): 25–43.
Nevile, J. 1995. 'Deregulation and the Welfare of the Less Well Off', Paper presented to the Conference of Economists, University of Adelaide, September.
Nevile, J. W. 1996. 'The Future of Work', Centre for Applied Economic Research, Working Paper no. 3, University of New South Wales.
Niskanen, W. 1971. *Bureaucracy and Representative Government*, Chicago: Rand McNally.
O'Connor, Mark, et al. 1992. *Catholic Social Teaching*, North Blackburn, Vic.: Collins Dove.
O'Connor, M. 1973. *The Fiscal Crisis of the State*, New York: St Martin's Press.
O'Farrell, P. 1992. 'Bible Reading and Related Mental Furniture', *Australian Cultural History*, 11.
OECD. 1978. *Trends in Public Expenditure*, Paris.
OECD. 1992. *The Long-Term Unemployed and Measures to Assist Them*, OECD Occasional Paper no. 7, Paris.
OECD. 1993. *Employment Outlook*, Paris.
OECD. 1994a. *Economic Outlook*, Paris.
OECD. 1994b. *Jobs Study: Facts, Analysis, Strategies*, Paris.
OECD. 1995. *Economic Outlook*, Paris.
OECD. 1996a. *Employment Outlook*, Paris.
OECD. 1996b. *Technology and Industrial Performance*, Paris.
OECD. 1997. *National Innovation Systems*, Paris.
OECD. 1998. *Social Policy Implications of Income Distribution Trends*, Paris.
Offe, C. 1984. *Contradictions of the Welfare State*, London: Hutchinson.
Oliver, Dawn. 1993. 'Citizenship in the 1990s', *Politics Review*, 3: 1.
Osborne, D., and Gaebler, T. 1992. *Reinventing Government: How the Entrepreneurial Spirit is Transforming the Public Sector*, New York: Plume.

Palme, J. 1990. *Pension Rights in Welfare Capitalism: The Development of Old-Age Pensions in 18 OECD Countries, 1930–1985*, Stockholm: Swedish Institute for Social Research.
Panitch, L., and Miliband, R. 1992. 'The New World Order and the Socialist Agenda', *The Socialist Register 1992*, London: Merlin Press.
Partridge, P. H. 1945. 'The State and Democracy', in W. H. C. Eddy (ed.), *Prospects of Democracy*, Sydney: Consolidated Press, pp. 12–19.
Passmore, J. A. 1945. 'Majority Rule—Is that Democracy?', in W. H. C. Eddy (ed.), *Prospects of Democracy*, Sydney: Consolidated Press.
Paterson, J. 1988. 'A Managerialist Strikes Back', *Australian Journal of Public Administration*, 47, 4: 287–95.
Paterson, J. 1997. 'Mission, Strategy, Structure and Business Rules', Paper presented to Public Service and Merit Protection Commission, *Improving Public Service: Innovations Expo-Conference '97*, Canberra, February.
Paukert, F. 1973. 'Income Distribution at Different Levels of Development: A Survey of Evidence', *International Labour Review*, 108: 97–125.
Peck, J., and Jones, M. 1995. 'Training and Enterprise Councils: Schumpeterian Workfare State, or What?', *Environment and Planning*, 27: 1361–96.
Pederson, A. W. 1994. 'The Welfare State and Inequality: Still No Answer to the Big Questions', LIS Working Paper no. 109, Luxembourg: CEPS/INSTEAD.
Perry, J. 1994. 'Women, Work and Families: Implications for Social Security', in J. Disney and L. Briggs (eds), *Social Security Policy, Issues and Options*, Canberra: AGPS.
Perry, J. 1995. 'Twenty Payments or One? Alternative Structures for the Australian Social Security System', in P. Saunders and S. Shaver (eds), *Social Policy and the Challenges of Social Change*, Social Policy Research Centre, University of New South Wales, Reports and Proceedings no. 122.
Persson, T., and Tabellini, G. 1995. 'Is Inequality Harmful for Growth?', *American Economic Review*, 84, 3: 600–21.
Peters, B. G. 1996. *The Future of Governing: Four Emerging Models*, University of Kansas Press.
Peterson, A. 1989. 'Social Movement Theory', *Acta Sociologica*, 32, 4: 419–26.
Pickvance, C. 1995. 'Social Movements in the Transition from State Socialism', in Louis Maheu (ed.), *Social Movements and Social Classes: The Future of Collective Action*, London: Sage Studies in International Sociology/ISA.
Pierson, P. 1994. *Dismantling the Welfare State*, Cambridge University Press.
Piggin, Stuart. 1996. *Evangelical Christianity in Australia: Spirit, Word and World*, Oxford University Press.
Pike, Douglas. 1967. *Paradise of Dissent: South Australia, 1829–1857*, 2nd edn, Melbourne University Press.
Pixley, J. F. 1991. 'Wowsers and Pro-Woman Politics: Temperance against Australian Patriarchy', *Australian and New Zealand Journal of Sociology*, 27, 3: 293–314.
Pixley, J. F. 1992. 'Citizen, Client or Worker? State, Class and Welfare', in M. Muetzelfeldt (ed.), *State, Society and Politics in Australia*, Sydney: Pluto Press.
Pixley, J. F. 1993. *Citizenship and Employment: Investigating Post-Industrial Options*, Cambridge University Press.
Pixley, J. F. 1996. 'Economic Democracy: Beyond Wage Earners' Welfare', in J. Wilson *et al.* (eds), *The Australian Welfare State*, Melbourne: Macmillan Education.

Polanyi, K. 1957. *The Great Transformation*, Boston: Beacon Press.
Pons, X. 1994. *A Sheltered Land*, Sydney: Allen and Unwin.
Pontusson, J. 1992. 'At the End of the Third Road: Social Democracy in Crisis', *Politics and Society*, 20: 305–22.
Pontusson, J. 1995. 'From Comparative Public Policy to Political Economy: Putting Institutions in their Place and Taking Interests Seriously', *Comparative Political Studies*, 28, 1: 117–47.
Porter, M. 1990. *The Competitive Advantage of Nations*, New York: Free Press.
Portes, A., and Landolt, P. 1996. 'The Downside of Social Capital', *American Prospect*, 26: 16–21, 94.
Prezeworski, A. 1985. *Capitalism and Social Democracy*, Cambridge University Press.
Pringle, R. 1992. 'Financial Markets Versus Governments', in T. Banuri and J. B. Schor (eds), *Financial Openness and National Autonomy*, Oxford: Clarendon Press.
Purdy, D. 1994. 'Citizenship, Basic Income and the State', *New Left Review*, 208: 30–48.
Pusey, M. 1991. *Economic Rationalism in Canberra*, Cambridge University Press.
Putnam, R. D. 1993. *Making Democracy Work: Civic Traditions in Modern Italy*, Princeton University Press.
Putnam, R. D. 1995. 'Bowling Alone: America's Declining Social Capital', *Journal of Democracy*, 6: 65–78.
Putnam, R. D. 1996. 'The Strange Disappearance of Civic America', *American Prospect*, 24: 34–48.
Quiggin, J. 1993. *The Industry Commission Approach to Public Sector Reform*, Sydney: Evatt Foundation.
Quiggin J. 1996. *Great Expectations: Microeconomic Reform in Australia*, Sydney: Allen and Unwin.
Radice, H. 1984. 'The National Economy: A Keynesian Myth?', *Capital and Class*, 22: 111–41.
Raskall, P. 1980. 'Who's Got What in Australia? The Distribution of Wealth', in G. Crough, T. Wheelwright and T. Wilshire (eds), *Australia and World Capitalism*, Ringwood, Vic.: Penguin.
Raskall, P. 1992a. 'The Widening Income Gap', *Modern Times* (March): 9.
Raskall, P. 1992b. 'Inequality in Australia: What We Know and What We Don't', in P. Raskall and P. Saunders (eds), *Economic Inequality in Australia, vol. 1: Government and Redistribution, Study of Social and Economic Inequalities*, Monograph no. 1, University of New South Wales.
Raskall, P. 1992c. 'Plutoprosody Revisited: Trends in the Distribution of Income in Australia', *Social Policy Research Centre Newsletter*, 46 (September): 1–2.
Ravenhill, J. 1994. 'Australia and the Global Economy', in S. Bell and B. Head (eds), *State, Economy and Public Policy in Australia*, Oxford University Press.
Rawson, Don. 1958. 'Politics and Responsibility in Australian Trade Unions', *Australian Journal of Politics and History*, 4, 2 (November): 224–43.
Razeen, Sally R. 1994. 'The Social Market and Liberal Order: Theory and Policy Implications', *Government and Opposition*, 29, 4: 461–76.
Rees, S., Rodley, G., and Stilwell, F. (eds). 1993. *Beyond the Market: Alternatives to Economic Rationalism*, Sydney: Pluto Press.
Rees-Mogg, W. 1995. 'The End of Nations', *The Times*, 31 August.
Reeves, W. P. 1969. [1902] *State Experiments in Australia and New Zealand*, Melbourne: Macmillan.
Reich, R. 1992. *The Work of Nations*, New York: Vintage Books.

Reith, P. 1996. *Towards a Best Practice Australian Public Service: Discussion Paper*, Canberra: AGPS.
Reynolds, M., and Smolensky, E. 1977. *Public Expenditures, Taxes and the Redistribution of Income: The USA, 1950, 1961, 1970*, New York: Academic Press.
Richardson, S. 1979. 'Income Distribution and Poverty', in F. H. Gruen (ed.), *Surveys of Australian Economics*, vol. 2, Sydney: Allen and Unwin.
Ringen, S. 1987. *The Possibility of Politics*, Oxford: Clarendon Press.
Rodrik, D. 1995. 'Getting Interventions Right: How South Korea and Taiwan Grew Rich', *Economic Policy*, 20.
Roe, Jill. 1983. 'The End Is Where We Start From: Women and Welfare since 1901', in B. Cass and C. Baldock (eds), *Women, Social Welfare and the State*, Sydney: Allen and Unwin.
Roe, Jill. 1993. 'Social Policy and the Cultural Cringe', in P. Saunders and S. Shaver (eds), *Theory and Practice in Australian Social Policy: Rethinking the Fundamentals*, Social Policy Research Centre, University of New South Wales, Reports and Proceedings no. 113, pp. 107–20.
Roe, Jill. 1994. 'What has Nationalism offered Australian Women?', in A. Burns and N. Grieve (eds), *Contemporary Feminist Thought*, Melbourne: Oxford University Press.
Roe, Jill. 1997. '"We Won't Go Back": Notes from America', in Melanie Oppenheimer and Maree Murray (eds), *Proceedings of the 5th Women and Labour Conference*, Macquarie University.
Roe, Jill (ed.). 1976. *Social Policy in Australia: Some Perspectives, 1901–1975*, Stanmore: Cassell.
Rootes, C. 1995. 'A New Class? The Higher Educated and the New Politics', in Louis Maheu (ed.), *Social Movements and Social Classes: The Future of Collective Action*, London: Sage Studies in International Sociology/ISA.
Rosecrance, Richard N. 1964. 'The Radical Culture of Australia', in Louis Hartz et al. *The Founding of New Societies*, New York: Harcourt, Brace and World.
Ross, Lloyd. 1953. 'Comparative Labour Movements', *Australian Quarterly*, 25, 3 (September): 106–13.
Ryan, J. A. 1995. 'Bernhard Ringrose Wise', *Royal Australian Historical Society*, 81, 1 (June): 81–2.
Saunders, P. 1990. *Indirect Tax Reform and Low-Income Groups: An Assessment of Methods of Compensation*, Sydney: Australian Tax Research Foundation.
Saunders, P. 1993. 'Longer-Run Changes in the Distribution of Income in Australia', *Economic Record*, 69, 207: 353–66.
Saunders, P. 1994. *Welfare and Inequality*, Cambridge University Press.
Saunders, P. 1995. 'Market Incomes and the Trend to Inequality', in Commission for the Future of Work, *Proceedings of the Future of Work and Access to Incomes Seminar*, Sydney: ACOSS.
Saunders, P., and Fritzell, J. 1995. 'Wage and Income Inequality in Two Welfare States: Australia and Sweden', Discussion Paper no. 60, Social Policy Research Centre, University of New South Wales.
Saunders, P. and Hobbes, G. 1988. *Income Inequality in Australia: An International Comparative Perspective*, SWRL Discussion Paper no. 4, Kensington, NSW.
Sawer, M. 1996. 'Review of Melleuish', *Political Theory Newsletter*, 8, 1: 82–4.
Sawer, M., and Groves, A. 1994. 'The Women's Lobby: Networks, Coalition Building and the Women of Middle Australia', *Australian Journal of Political Science*, 29, 3: 435–59.
Sawyer, M. 1976. 'Income Distribution', *OECD Occasional Studies*, Paris: OECD.

Scharpf, F. W. 1987. *Crisis and Choice in European Social Democracy*, Cornell University Press.
Schor, J. B. 1992. 'Introduction', in T. Banuri and J. B. Schor (eds), *Financial Openness and National Autonomy*, Oxford: Clarendon Press.
Schroder, P. 1997. 'The Impact of the Coalition Government on the Public Service: Was Change Inevitable?', *Australian Journal of Public Administration*, 56, 2: 12–17.
Schwartz, H. 1994. 'Small States in Big Trouble: State Reorganisation in Australia, Denmark, New Zealand and Sweden', *World Politics*, 46: 527–55.
Schwartz, H. Forthcoming. 'Economic Rationalism in Canberra and Elsewhere: Public Sector Reorganisation in Social Democracies', in C. Lloyd (ed.), *Australian Institutions Transformed*.
Scott, J., and Saunders, K. 1993. 'Happy Days are Here Again? A Reply to David Potts', *Australian Studies*, 36 (March).
Self, P. 1993. *Government by the Market? The Politics of Public Choice*, London: Macmillan.
Sharp, R. 1991. 'Introduction', in J. O'Leary and R. Sharp (eds), *Inequality in Australia: Slicing the Cake, The Social Justice Collective*, Melbourne: William Heinemann.
Shaver, S. 1988. 'Sex and Money in the Welfare State', in C. Baldock and B. Cass (eds), *Women, Social Welfare and the State*, Sydney: Allen and Unwin, pp. 150–67.
Sheehan, P. 1996. 'Economics and the National Interest', in P. Sheehan, B. Grewal and M. Kumnick (eds), *Dialogues on Australia's Future*, Centre for Strategic Economic Studies, Victoria University, Melbourne.
Sheehan, P., Grewal, B., and Kumnick, M. (eds). 1996. *Dialogues on Australia's Future*, Centre for Strategic Economic Studies, Victoria University, Melbourne.
Sheehan, P., Pappas, N., and Cheng, E. 1994. *The Rebirth of Australian Industry*, Centre for Strategic Economic Studies, Victoria University, Melbourne.
Simpson, M., Dawkins, P., and Madden, G. 1995. 'The Patterns and Determinants of Casual Employment in Australia, 1984–1992', Paper presented to the 24th Conference of Economists, University of Adelaide.
Skidelsky, R. 1979. 'The Decline of Keynesian Politics', in C. Crouch (ed.), *State and Economy in Contemporary Capitalism*, London: Croom Helm.
Sklair, L. 1991. *The Sociology of the Global System*, Hemel Hempstead: Harvester Wheatsheaf.
Sloan, J. 1993. 'Labour-Market Reform: An Economist's Perspective', in S. King and P. Lloyd (eds), *Economic Rationalism: Dead End or Way Forward?*, Sydney: Allen and Unwin.
Smeeding, T., and Coder, J. 1993. 'Income Inequality in Rich Countries During the 1980s', LIS Working Paper no. 88, Luxembourg: CEPS/INSTEAD.
Smeeding, T. *et al.* 1992. 'Noncash Income, Living Standards and Inequality: Evidence from the Luxembourg Income Study', LIS Working Paper, Luxembourg: CEPS/INSTEAD.
Smelser, N. 1962. *Theory of Collective Behaviour*, New York: Simon and Schuster.
Smyth, P. 1994. *Australian Social Policy: The Keynesian Chapter*, University of New South Wales Press.
Smyth, P. 1995. 'Review Essay', *Just Policy*, 3: 51–4.
Speerings, J., Voorendt, I., and Spoehr, J. (eds). 1996. *Jobs for Young Australians: Proceedings of an International Conference*, Adelaide: Social Justice Foundation.

Ståhlberg, A.-C. 1985. *On Misleading Income Comparisons Between Societies With Social Insurance Sectors of Different Sizes*, Discussion Paper no. 18/1985, Stockholm: Swedish Institute for Social Research.
Ståhlberg, A.-C. 1986. *Social Welfare Policy: Nothing But Insurances?*, Report no. 6/1986, Stockholm: Swedish Institute for Social Research.
Stark, T. 1977. *The Distribution of Income in Eight Countries*, Background Paper no. 4, Royal Commission on the Distribution of Income and Wealth, London: HMSO.
State Government of Victoria. 1996. *Competitive Neutrality: A Statement of Victorian Government Policy*, Melbourne: Department of Premier and Cabinet.
Steindl, J. 1989. 'Reflections on Kalecki's Dynamics', in Mario Sebastiani (ed.), *Kalecki's Relevance Today*, London: Macmillan Press, pp. 309–13.
Steindl, J. 1993. 'Some Comments on the Politics of Full Employment', in S. Biasco, A. Roncaglia and M. Salvati (eds), *Markets and Institutions in Economic Development*, New York: St Martins, pp. 183–91.
Steketee, M. 1997a. 'Public Servant or Party Slave?', *Weekend Australian*, 5–6 April, p. 23.
Steketee, M. 1997b. 'The Incredible Shrinking Public Service', *Australian*, 7 April, p. 9.
Stern, Robert W. 1993. *Changing India: Bourgeois Revolution on the Subcontinent*, Cambridge University Press.
Stewart, J. 1997. 'A Recipe for Decline', *Canberra Bulletin of Public Administration*, 83: 22–4.
Stilwell, F. 1993. *Economic Inequality: Who Gets What in Australia*, Leichhardt, NSW: Pluto Press.
Stopford, J., and Strange, S. 1991. *Rival States, Rival Firms: Competition For World Market Shares*, Cambridge University Press.
Strange, S. 1995. 'The Limits of Politics', *Government and Opposition*, 30, 3: 291–311.
Stretton, H. 1980. 'The Corruption of the Intellectuals', Oscar Mendelson Lecture, Monash University.
Stretton, H. 1987a. *Political Essays*, Melbourne: Georgian House.
Stretton, H. 1987b. 'Tasks for Social Democratic Intellectuals: Address to Eighth Symposium of the Academy of the Social Sciences, 1984', in Stretton, 1987a.
Stretton, H. 1993. 'Whodunnit to Social Democracy?', *Overland*, 132: 50–64.
Stretton, H., and Orchard, L. 1994. *Public Goods, Public Enterprise, Public Choice*, London: Macmillan.
Sturgess, G. 1994. 'Virtual Government: An Australian Perspective on Reinventing Government', *Canberra Bulletin of Public Administration*, 77 (December): 43–8.
Sturgess, G. 1996. 'Virtual Government: What Will Remain Inside the Public Sector?', *Australian Journal of Public Administration*, 55, 3: 59–73.
Stzompka, P. 1993. *The Sociology of Social Change*, Oxford: Blackwell.
Taskforce on Regional Development 1993. *Developing Australia: A Regional Perspective*, Canberra: National Capital Printing.
Taylor-Gooby, P., and Lawson, R. 1993. 'Where We Go from Here: The New Order in Welfare', in P. Taylor-Gooby and R. Lawson (eds), *Markets and Managers: New Issues in the Delivery of Welfare*, Buckingham: Open University Press.
Tesdorf, P., and Associates. 1996. *Competitive Communities? A Study of the Impact*

of Compulsory Competitive Tendering on Rural and Remote Communities, Melbourne.
Thane, Pat. 1982. *Foundations of the Welfare State*, London: Longman.
Therborn, G. 1986. *Why Some Peoples are More Unemployed Than Others*, London: Verso.
Thomas, G. M., and Meyer, J. W. 1984. 'The Expansion of the State', *Annual Review of Sociology*, 10: 461–82.
Thompson, D., and Ball, C. 1995. 'Case Management: Five Issues in Danger of Being Overlooked', unpublished paper.
Thompson, David, and Tapper, Alan. 1993. 'Meet the Luckies . . . and the Unluckies', *Independent Monthly*, April, pp. 20–3.
Thompson, E. 1994. *Fair Enough: Egalitarianism in Australia*, University of New South Wales Press.
Thurow, L. 1993. *Head to Head: The Coming Economic Battle Among Japan, Europe and America*, Sydney: Allen and Unwin.
Times. 1995. 'OECD Statistics', 24 August.
Tingle, L. 1995. 'The Fall of the Mandarins', *Weekend Australian*, 29–30 July, pp. 21, 23.
Toohey, Brian. 1994. *Tumbling Dice*, Sydney: Reed Books.
Touraine, A. 1971. *The Post-Industrial Society*, New York: Random House.
Touraine, A. 1977. *The Self-Production of Society*, University of Chicago Press.
Touraine, A. 1981. *The Voice and the Eye*, Cambridge University Press.
Touraine, A. *et al*. 1983. *Anti-Nuclear Protest*, Cambridge University Press.
Travers, P., and Richardson, S. 1993. *Living Decently: Material Well-Being in Australia*, Oxford University Press.
Trifiletti, G. 1996. *Contracting Out: The Case for Consumer Rights in the Provision of Local Government Services*, Melbourne: Consumer Law Centre Vic. Ltd.
Turner, I. 1968. *The Australian Dream*, Melbourne: Sun Books.
United Nations. 1993. *Human Development Report 1993*, United Nations Development Program, Oxford University Press.
Van Parijs, P. (ed.). 1992. *Arguing for Basic Income*, Verso, London.
Vandenberg, A., and Tregenza, I. 1994. 'Rational Economics and the Public Sphere: An Essay in Retrieval', *Australian Journal of Political Science*, 29: 338–53.
Victorian Chamber of Manufactures (VCM). 1997. '1997: Crucial Time for Manufacturers', *VCM File*, 22, 1.
Vintila, P., Philimore, J., and Newman, P. (eds). 1992. *Markets, Morals and Manifestos*, Murdoch University, Institute for Science and Technology.
Wade, R. 1990. *Governing the Market: Economic Theory and the Role of Government in East Asian Industrialisation*, Princeton University Press.
Walker, E. R. 1947. *The Australian Economy in War and Reconstruction*, Oxford University Press.
Ward, Russel. 1978. *The Australian Legend*, Oxford University Press.
Waters, M. 1992. *Globalization*, London and New York: Routledge.
Watson, S. (ed.). 1990. *Playing the State: Australian Feminist Interventions*, Sydney: Allen and Unwin.
Watts, R. 1987. *The Foundations of the National Welfare State*, Sydney: Allen and Unwin.
Wearing, M. 1995. 'A Citizen's Republic? Australian Social Policy Towards 2000', *Social Policy Review*, 7: 213–29.
Webb, Elizabeth. 1995. 'Charities Do it Better: Community Sector Welfare

Organisations in the Australian Welfare State', BA (Hons) thesis, Department of Government, University of Sydney.
Weiss, L. 1997. 'Globalization and the Myth of the Powerless State', *New Left Review*, 225: 3–27.
Weiss, L. 1998. *The Myth of the Powerless State: Governing the Economy in a Global Era*, Cambridge: Polity Press.
Weiss, L., and Hobson, J. 1995. *States and Economic Development*, Cambridge: Polity Press.
Weller, P., and Davis, G. 1996. *New Ideas, Better Government*, Sydney: Allen and Unwin.
Wettenhall, R. 1997. 'Public Administration and Public Management: The Need for a Top-quality Public Service', in M. Considine and M. Painter (eds), *Managerialism: The Great Debate*, Melbourne University Press.
Wheelwright, T. 1990. 'Are the Rich Getting Richer and the Poor Poorer? If so, Why?', in A. Gollan (ed.), *Questions for the Nineties*, Sydney: Left Book Club Cooperative.
White, G. 1988. *Developmental States in East Asia*, London: Macmillan.
Whiteford, P. 1994. 'Income Distribution and Social Policy Under a Reformist Government: The Australian Experience', *Policy and Politics*, 24, 4: 239–55.
Whiteford, P. 1995a. 'Labour Market and Income Inequalities in Australia: A Comparative Review', in Commission for the Future of Work, *Proceedings of the Future of Work and Access to Incomes Seminar*, Sydney: ACOSS.
Whiteford, P. 1995b. 'The Use of Replacement Rates in International Comparisons of Benefit Systems', *International Social Security Review*, 48, 2/95: 3–30.
Whiteford, P. 1997. 'Measuring Poverty and Income Inequality in Australia', *Agenda*, Summer, 39–50.
Whiteford, P., and Kennedy, S. 1995. *Incomes and Living Standards of Older People: A Comparative Analysis*, Research Report no. 34, UK Department of Social Security, London: HMSO.
Whitfield, D. 1995. *The Costs of Competitive Tendering: An Economic and Social Audit for the UK*, Public Sector Research Centre, University of New South Wales.
Whitwell, G. 1995. 'Economic Policy', in S Fraser et al. (eds), *The Menzies Years*, Sydney: Hale and Iremonger, pp. 166–84.
Wilenski, P. 1980. 'The Left and the State Bureaucracy', *Australian Quarterly*, 52, 4: 398–414.
Wilenski, P. 1984. 'Small Government and Social Equity', *Politics*, 18: 7–25.
Wilenski, P. 1986. *Public Power and Public Administration*, Sydney: Hale and Iremonger.
Wilenski, P. 1988. 'Social Change as a Source of Competing Values in Public Administration', *Australian Journal of Public Administration*, 48, 3: 213–22.
Willetts, D. 1994. *Civic Conservatism*, London: Social Market Foundation.
Wise, B. R. 1892. *Industrial Freedoms: A Study in Politics*, London: Cassell and Co.
Wise, B. R. 1913. *The Making of the Australian Commonwealth*, London: Longmans Green.
Wolff, Robert Paul. 1990. 'Methodological Individualism and Marx: Some Remarks on Jon Elster, Game Theory and Other Things', *Canadian Journal of Philosophy*, 20, 4: 469–86.
Wrenn, R. 1982. 'Management and Work Harmonisation', *Insurgent Sociologist*, 11: 23–38.

Wrenn, R. 1985. 'The Decline of American Labour', *Socialist Review*, 81–2: 89–117.
Wright, C. 1995. *The Management of Labour*, Oxford University Press.
Yates, J. 1991. Australia's Owner-Occupied Housing Wealth and Its Impact on Income Distribution', Social Policy Research Centre, University of New South Wales, Reports and Proceedings no. 92.
Yeatman, A. 1987. 'The Concept of Public Management and the Australian State in the 1980s', *Australian Journal of Public Administration*, 46, 4: 339–53.
Yeatman, A. 1990. *Bureaucrats, Technocrats, Femocrats: Essays on the Contemporary Australian State*, Sydney: Allen and Unwin.
Yeatman, A. 1993. 'Corporate Managerialism and the Shift from the Welfare State to the Competition State', *Discourse*, 13, 2: 3–9.
Yeatman, A. 1997. 'The Reform of Public Management: An Overview', in M. Considine and M. Painter (eds), *Managerialism: The Great Debate*, Melbourne University Press.
Zimbalist, A. 1975. 'The Limits of Work Humanisation', *Review of Radical Political Economics*, 7: 50–9.

Index

Aaron, H. 202
Aboriginal people 144
  see also indigenous Australians
Aboriginal rights 75, 79
Academy of Social Sciences in Australia 2, 69
Accord (Prices and Incomes Accord) 2, 3, 46, 102, 141, 162, 178
accountability 126, 158, 188, 191, 226, 233
Adam Smith Institute 215
administration, principles of 126
Administrative Appeals Tribunal 226
advocacy 221, 239
affirmative action 26, 113
aged care 130
agency theory 237
agriculture policy 146
aid to families program (US) 70
alliances, historical 151
Anderson, M. 174
Angell, I. 34
anti-immigration policy 142
arbitration system *see* industrial arbitration
Argy, F. 164
aristocracy, hereditary 199
Arndt, Heinz 90
Asia 35, 192
  East 19, 146, 162, 186, 191, 193
  South-East 162
Audit Commission
  see National Commission of Audit
Australian Business Chamber 166
Australian Business Foundation 182, 186, 191, 193
Australian Chamber of Commerce and Industry (ACCI) 182

Australian Council of Social Service (ACOSS) 125, 231
Australian Council of Trade Unions (ACTU) 145
  see also trade unions
Australian Industrial Relations Commission (AIRC) 47, 101, 141, 143, 152
Australian Labor Party 2, 3, 90, 102, 104, 145, 152, 183
Australian Manufacturing Council 190, 191
Australian Manufacturing Workers' Union (AMWU) 182, 190
Australian Settlement 4–8, 10, 17, 20, 57–68, 77, 79, 81–4, 85, 89, 111, 139, 145, 151, 182
Australian Way 2–5 7–9, 10, 12–13, 38, 41, 49–54, 69–80, 81–93, 94, 111, 140, 197, 201, 215, 237–40
  middle way 4, 73, 81, 89, 90
  narrow way 74, 80
  flexible way 75
Austria 48
authoritarian rule 138
automotive industry 183
award system, Australia 41, 43, 47, 169
awards, industrial 122, 210

balance of payments 185, 187
Baldwin, P. 204
banking industry 132, 163, 186, 235
banking policy
  full employment and 87, 105
banking system, Australia 169
Barbalet, J. 148
Barber, Benjamin 135, 136
Barton, Edmund 57

265

Battin, T. 170
Beck, U. 148
Beilharz, P. 7, 72
Bell, S. viii, 10, 157-8
Bellamy, E. 58
benchmarking 112, 220
benefit outlays 181
benefits, basic 204
Benevolent Society 125
Benthamism 59-60
best practice 112, 191, 220
Bhaduri, A. 97
BHP Limited
 closure of Newcastle steelworks 183
Bible 58, 69, 76
Birrell, Robert 73
Blair, Tony 29
Blandy, R. 174
Bourdieu, P. 148
Brennan, D. vii, 11, 124-37, 239
Brennan, G.
Bretton Woods monetary order 159
Brigden Report 181
Britain *see* United Kingdom
Broom, L. 199
Bryce, J. 57
Buchanan 172, 173
budget deficit 48
budget maximisation 134
budget outlays 126
budgetary processes 113
budgeting 115, 117, 122
budgets 122, 131
 balanced 185
Bureau of Industry Economics (BIE) 192
bureaucracy 5, 111-23, 125
 democracy and 125
 modernisation of 128, 129
 see also market bureaucracy
bureaucratic government 115
bureaucratic model 128, 130, 150
bureaucratic processes 123
bureaucrats 114, 133
business 119, 128, 141, 161, 164, 168, 182, 230, 231
business costs 193
Business Council of Australia (BCA) 182
business programs 188, 189
business sector 162, 177

Cairns, J. 91
Canada 45, 48, 127, 197, 237
capital 32, 82, 97, 151, 159, 160, 161, 163, 164, 165, 185, 189
capital flight 161
capital formation 167
capital inflows 185, 193
capitalism 21, 24, 25, 26, 28, 29, 30, 31, 35, 81, 83, 86, 89, 157, 165, 198, 225
 collaborative 21
 communitarian 29, 30, 35
 democratic 25, 26, 30, 31
 economic rationalist 167
 free-market 25, 35
 global 31
 laissez-faire 30
 managed 168
 social market 28, 30
Carroll, J. 6
case management 228-40
Cass, B. viii, 3, 8, 38-67, 85, 86
Castles, F. 72, 81-4, 204
Centre for Independent Studies 238
charitable organisation sector 217
charities 125
Chifley Labor government 73, 94, 96, 102, 106
Chifley, J. B. 76, 96
child care 131, 134, 135
 public investment in 49, 53
child-care centres, closure 13
Childe 57
children's services 130, 132, 134
choice 223, 224
churches 149
citizen entitlements 75
citizens 131
citizenship 30, 51, 52, 71, 136, 137, 218
 participatory 127
 social 218
citizenship rights 23
civil rights movement (US) 140
civil society 7, 11-12, 22, 25, 38, 41, 43, 50, 54, 85, 118, 123, 124-37, 142, 144, 239, 240
Clark, D. 134
Clark, M. 58, 69
class 26, 79, 119, 140, 148, 151, 152, 198
Clinton Administration (US) 127
Clinton, W. 193
Coalition government, Australia *see* Greiner-Fahey government, NSW; Howard Liberal-National Coalition government; Kennett government, Victoria; Menzies Liberal-Country Coalition government
cognitive elite 34
Cohen, J. and Rogers, J. 124
Cold War 89
collective action 148
collective bargaining 52

collective behaviour 140
collective goods 29
collective interests 131, 136
collectivism 29, 59, 61, 62, 67, 72, 120, 172
Collins, H. 59–60
commodity export sectors 163, 167, 186
commodity prices 159
Commons, J. R. 186
Commonwealth Bank of Australia 87, 169
Commonwealth Employment Service (CES) 232, 234
Commonwealth government 127, 134, 230
Commonwealth of Australia 71, 77, 145
community 25, 62, 125, 126, 131, 132, 136, 221, 230
community care 130
community development 221
community networks 124
community organisations 126, 133, 135, 231, 232
community participation 113
community sector 228, 229, 232, 233, 236
community service obligations 218
community services 88, 124–37, 219, 223, 235
community social welfare organisations (CSWOs) 219, 220, 222
community-managed services 135
comparative advantage 24, 70, 186
competition 117, 121, 129, 130, 132, 135, 144, 145, 173, 192, 217, 220, 227, 234, 238
 international 82, 119, 160, 161, 163
 non-government welfare sector and 219–21
 public sector and 221–3, 226
 resource intensive 192
competition model 232–40
competition policy 36, 227, 228
 case management and 228–40
 national 4, 126, 232
competitive advantage 24, 25, 29, 32, 35, 181, 186, 187, 188, 189, 192, 193
competitive settlement 139
competitive tendering 5, 11, 218, 220, 222, 224, 228, 229, 234, 235, 236, 238
 see also compulsory competitive tendering (CCT)
competitiveness 145, 148, 181, 182, 183
 international 187, 216, 223, 228

compulsory competitive tendering (CCT) 225, 226, 238
Conciliation and Arbitration Commission 101, 152, 171
Conciliation and Arbitration Court 71, 180
conflict, industrial 159
consensus 183
consensus management 139
consensus politics 58
consensus tradition 8
conservatism 57, 59, 63
 civic 29
Constitution of Australia 60
constitutional change 105
consumer confidence 166
consumer groups 126, 133
consumerism 219
consumers 132, 134, 135, 136
 rational 143
consumption 191
consumption tax 204, 208
contestability 224
contracting out 112, 121, 122, 130, 220, 224, 228, 229, 233
Coombs, H. C. 88, 90, 119, 125
Coombs Royal Commission 113, 125
cooperation 192
corporate sector 33
corporatisation 130, 178, 217, 236
corporatism 139, 231, 232
cost-effectiveness 220
cost minimisation 193
cost of living 197
cost reduction 162, 164, 216, 223
Council of Australian Governments (COAG) 127, 235
courts 128
Cox, Eva 124, 135
Crawford Report 181
credit-rating agencies, international 138, 151
cultural cringe 9
culture war 26
current account deficit 158, 185
Curtin, J. 67
Curtin Labor government 73, 96
customer focus 130
customer service 229, 235
customer–supplier chains 189
cyberspace 34–5
Czechoslovakia 198

Davies, A. F. 111
Day of Mourning 79
Deakin, A. 57, 60, 76–7, 78, 145
 see also liberalism, Deakinite

INDEX

debt
  foreign 46, 159
  government 161
decentralisation 111, 114, 120
  of management authority 120
  of service delivery 117, 137
  political 29
decommodification 39, 40
deficit financing 111
deindustrialisation 167
demand 101, 102, 103, 104, 166, 185
demand management 158, 180, 181, 185
democracy 9, 23, 25, 26, 30, 58, 65, 67–8, 71, 79, 120, 124, 128, 138–53, 227
  associative 124
  Australian 65, 67–8, 74, 79, 152, 197, 198
  corporatist 23
  economic 88, 91, 92
  liberal 138, 146, 147, 151
  pluralist 25
democratisation 115, 121
Department of Employment, Education and Training (DEET) 232, 233
Department of Social Security (DSS) 234
deregulation 46, 50, 135, 163, 180, 217
  economic 7
  financial 35, 46, 116, 165, 169, 177, 178
  in UK 29
  in US 27
  of employment contracts 38
  of industrial relations 46
  of labour market 3, 40, 43, 46, 54, 176, 177
  of markets 32, 33, 138
  of wages system 47, 54
  power of governments and 178
design, investment in 189
development
  policy 118
  state 111
  sustainable 184, 192
  technology 193
  urban 51, 113
developmentalism 139, 146
discrimination, prevention of 128, 135
distribution 85, 160
  see also income distribution
diversity 224
Dow, G. 101
Downing, W. 199
Downs, A. 143
downsizing 34, 183, 191
Drucker, P. 34
Dyster, B. 86

earnings distribution 210
Eatwell, J. 94
economic crisis 157
economic decline 144
economic development 22, 124, 146, 149
  domestic defence model 158–62
  Keynesian full-employment model *see* full employment
  'low road' to 167
  models 157–68
economic fundamentalism 128
economic growth 43, 45, 46, 84, 178, 180, 182, 185, 193, 205, 216, 223, 228
  interventionist approach to 183
  slow 165
economic management 86, 87
economic performance 124, 161
economic policy 1, 6, 83, 84, 86, 94, 97, 104, 141, 144, 152, 157, 169
  governments and 142
  inappropriate 177
  interventionist 193
  neoclassical 142
  social policy and 4, 5, 6, 7, 9, 94–5, 96, 106, 119
  welfare policy and 7, 83
economic rationalism 2, 3, 4, 6, 10, 11, 12, 17, 36, 66, 84, 89, 112, 115, 117, 118, 121, 122, 123, 126, 158, 161, 162–8, 169–79, 217, 221, 231, 238
  as microeconomic agenda 173
  as political program 172–3
  definition of 170–2
  economic restructuring and 162–4
  mainstream economics and 174–7
  outcomes of 164–8
  unemployment and 177–9
economic regeneration 149
economic restructuring 157–68
economic sectors, globally-oriented 163
economics
  evolutionary 186, 188
  institutionalist 185, 188
  Keynesian *see* Keynesian economic policy
  neoclassical 12, 25, 114, 148, 172, 184, 215, 216, 219
  mainstream 174–9
  normative 174
  positive 174, 176
economies of scale 192
economy 127, 157
  Australian 180
  government regulation of 175
  structural adjustment in 181

education 40, 45, 46, 47, 50, 51, 60, 62, 87, 88, 113, 135, 145, 208, 223, 224
  employment and 40, 46, 47, 50, 51
  tertiary 134
  training and 40, 46, 47, 50, 51, 52, 53, 54, 194
effectiveness 120, 130, 207
efficiency 113, 117, 120, 123, 130, 207, 216, 223, 239
egalitarianism 58, 88, 197, 199, 200, 204
elaborately transformed manufactures 24, 185, 185, 188, 189, 190, 192
elite consensus 17–20, 24, 35
employees 191
  public 133
employers 151, 231
employment 3, 38, 39, 40, 45, 46, 53, 54, 69–70, 178, 180, 187, 190, 193, 225, 228
  casual 44, 45, 48, 50
  education and 40, 46, 50, 51
  full-time 45, 48, 69–70
  generation of 184
  insecurity of 167
  part-time 44, 45, 48, 53
  security of 46, 94, 193
  temporary 44
  training and 40, 46, 50, 51
  see also full employment; self-employment; underemployment
employment benefits 44, 53
employment growth 46, 50, 53
employment policy 40, 42, 50, 51, 86, 87
Employment Services Regulatory Authority (ESRA) 231, 234
employment services, administration of 230
Emy, H. viii, 4, 6–8, 10, 17–37, 84, 128, 148, 238
Encel, S. 199, 202
enterprise bargaining 38, 47, 52, 145, 162, 169, 178, 179, 190
entrepreneurialism 130
environment 19, 31, 171
environmental movement 142, 149
environmentalists 147
equal opportunities 191
Equal Opportunities Commission (UK) 225
equal remuneration for work of equal value 53
equality 5, 28, 197, 205
  gender 50, 66
  in Australia 199
  racial 66
  see also inequality

equity 113, 120, 123, 128, 135, 136, 218
  see also gender equity
Ernst, J. viii, 11, 215–27, 238, 239
Esping-Andersen, G. 39, 40, 209
ethical state theory 77
ethnic identity 26
ethnic minorities 198
Europe 30, 35, 44, 45, 59, 82, 140, 162, 193, 197
  Eastern 162
European Human Rights Convention 24
European Union 24, 47
exceptionalism, Australian 92
exchange rate
  floating of 169
  movements of 182
  overvalued 185
expenditure
  public 126, 131
  private 210
export assistance 183
exports 185, 190

families
  income distribution and 206
  indigenous 42
  low-income 42, 49
  sole parent 42
  women and 40, 48, 53, 54
family allowance 71
family policy 42, 142
federalism 60, 78
Federation, Australian 58, 73, 74, 78, 152
feminism 78, 79, 140, 141, 151, 152
feminist groups 135
feminist movement 142, 149
finance 187
finance capital 149, 185
financial interests 163
financial sector 165, 166, 177, 178
financial systems 193
Finland 200
fiscal consolidation 183
fiscal equalisation 145
fiscal policy 50, 162, 164, 181
Fitzgerald, Tom 116
flexibility 43, 75, 115, 118, 120, 137, 192, 201, 220, 233, 236, 237, 239
flexible specialisation 188
Fordism 81, 89
Fortress Australia 82, 84
fragmentation 142
France 44, 66, 186, 198, 200
franchising 130
Fraser, B. 178
free enterprise 90, 140

INDEX

free market 4, 7, 13, 17, 20, 22, 29, 30, 88, 96, 105, 146, 148, 162, 164, 180, 186, 229
free trade 28, 61–2, 74, 77, 159, 193
free-traders 145
freedom
 individual 176
 negative concept of 116
freedom of association 151
freedom of contract 78
freedom of information 113
Freeland, J. 85, 86
Friedman, M. 172, 173
Fukuyama, F. 25–6, 148
full cost-recovery principle 218
full employment 4, 5, 10, 38, 42, 43, 47, 50–1, 54, 162, 164, 168, 169, 184
 Keynesianism and 4, 10, 85–91, 96–8, 100, 102, 104–7, 158, 159, 179, 181
 see also employment
full-employment investment boards 106
functionalism 139–40, 142, 146, 147

Gabay, A. 77
Gaebler, T. 127–30, 135
Galbraith, J. K. 186
Gelbach, J. 204
gender equity 43, 79
George, H. 58
Germany 27, 30, 146, 162, 186, 192
Gini coefficient 199, 207
global marketplace 129
globalisation 1, 7, 9, 10, 17–18, 20, 21, 22, 24, 26, 27, 30–5, 43, 49, 84, 93, 99, 104, 129, 138, 142, 144, 152, 163, 166, 188
goods and services 131, 170–1
Gore Report 127
Gore, Al 127
governance 30, 163, 164
 corporate 183
 developmental model 144–7
government
 accountability in 120
 activities 182
 alliances with business 141
 as guarantor of welfare 230
 as service industry 129
 business and 231
 central 113
 contemporary 215
 control of economic policy and 142
 core business 54, 125
 distinctiveness 122
 federal 225
 Industry Commission and 227
 inefficiency in 114
 intervention by 175
 local 232
 limited 116, 173
 market-oriented 149
 minimal 171, 172, 177
 national 118, 119
 processes 122
 redistributive role of 135
 restructuring of community services and 124–37
 role 117, 239
 size 162
 service provision and 223
 social movements and 140, 146, 147
 smaller 237
 state 225
 see also reinventing government
government funding 127
government spending 102, 103
Gramsci, A. 151
Gray, J. 28–9
Great Depression 12, 64, 83, 87, 202
Greece 44
green bans 141
Green, R viii, 10, 180–94
Green, T. H. 77
Greiner–Fahey government, NSW 237
gross domestic product (GDP) 160, 161
Gruen, F. 69

Habermas, J. 141, 143
Hancock, K. 8, 57, 63
Hanson, P. 143
Hasluck, P. 85
Hawke, R. J. L. 46, 64, 66, 67
Hawke–Keating Labor government
 Australian Industrial Relations Commission and 152
 deregulation and 116
 economic policy 13, 18, 36, 46, 96, 110, 139
 economic rationalism 4, 228–40
 employment policy 228–40
 governance and 144
 non-profit sector and 132
 public sector reform 11, 111, 112, 115, 116, 119, 125, 136–7,
 role of government 5
 social corporatism 12
 social policy 46, 66, 72, 96, 231
 social welfare 238
 unemployment 104
 wages policy 162
 see also Australian Labor Party; Hawke, R. J. L.; Keating, P. J.
Hayden, W. 64, 98, 102–3
Hayek, F. 172, 173

INDEX

health 208, 223, 224
health care system 128
health insurance 71, 74
health policy 40, 43, 49, 113
health services 127
Higgins, H. B. 57
Hilmer Report 232, 235, 238
Hirst, P. 124
Hobbes, T. 57
Hobsbawm, E. 31, 32, 35
Hobson, J. 22-3, 146
Holman, W. A. 57
Holmwood 142
Holt, H. 199
home and community care 130
home ownership, private 41, 42, 210, 211
homeless youth services 130
Horne, D. 58
household size 206
housing 208
  public 217
housing policy 40, 49, 50, 87, 113,
Howard Liberal–National Coalition government
  Australian Industrial Relations Commission and 152
  economic policy 139, 144
  economic rationalism and 12-13, 36, 169
  elite consensus and 17
  industrial relations 52, 53
  industry policy 182
  market bureaucracy 229, 238
  non-profit sector and 132
  public sector reform 111, 112, 115, 121, 122, 125, 126
  social policy 231
  social protection and 46
  welfare administration 239-40
Howard, J. 46
Hughes, W. M. 57
human rights 140
human rights movement 149
human services 135, 137, 220, 226
Hungary 198
Hunter Valley 192
Hunternet 192
Hutton, W. 29, 35, 44, 94, 168
hysteresis 177

identity politics 26
immigration controls 71, 158
immigrants 212
imperial benevolence 64, 66
import substitution 181, 185
income 171
citizens' 51
household 206
market 207
minimum income guarantee 51
participation 51-2
see also inequality
income distribution 38, 39, 40, 101-5, 175, 176, 184, 197-213, 225
  equality of 197
  inequality of 171
  international comparisons 198-9
income redistribution 39, 123, 204-10
income share 101, 102
income stream 210
income support 42, 45, 48, 50
  redistributive system of 9
  residual system of 54, 82, 88
  policy 51-52
incomes policy 172
India 162
indigenous Australians 212
individual employment contracts 38, 47, 53
individual freedom 114
individualism 25, 61-3, 66, 120, 172
industrial arbitration 79, 83, 152, 158, 182
  compulsory 180
Industrial Arbitration Act 1901 77
industrial awards 122
see also award system
industrial relations 38, 50, 52
  legislation 52
  policy 38, 50, 52-3, 54, 193
  reform 181
  see also Workplace Relations Act 1996
Industrial Relations Commission
  see Australian Industrial Relations Commission
industrial sector 165, 166, 186
industrialisation 22
industries
  high-technology 182, 193
  low-technology 182
  strategic 192
industry clusters 182, 189, 191, 192
Industry Commission 181, 183, 215-27
  social policy and 217-19
industry development 192, 228
industry groups 232
industry policy 24, 50, 87, 105, 145, 146, 148, 163, 167, 168, 180-94
industry protection 7, 41, 64-5, 181
see also protectionism
industry-sector working parties 190, 191
inefficiency 166

inequality 9, 20, 26, 27, 30, 31, 35, 39, 40, 51, 93, 139, 166, 168
  Australian 197–214, (new view) 200–3, (problems of measurement) 206–13, (traditional view) 197–9, (welfare state and) 203–6
  gender 38, 47, 53–4, 152
  income 40, 43, 47, 54, 101, 165, 171, 197–214
inflation 46, 87, 88, 91, 98, 99, 100, 101, 102, 103, 104, 139, 159, 160, 162, 163, 164, 165, 166, 172, 177–9
information society 129
infrastructure 50, 186, 219
  economic 87, 91
  educational 189
  knowledge 187
  public sector investment in 167
  transport 189
innovation 186, 187, 189, 191, 192, 193, 223, 235, 239
innovation networks, local and regional 182, 192
innovation systems, national 182–3
insecurity 31, 167, 168
institutional reform 138–53
institutions
  democratic 142, 198
  economic 199, 201
  educational 129
  environmental 140
  financial 162
  public 138
interest rates
  changes in 169
  rate of economic growth and 177
  reducing 185
International Monetary Fund 138, 151, 163, 178
international pressures 163
international trade 91
internationalisation 17–19, 38, 67
investment 105, 106, 111, 116, 161, 183, 185, 186, 188, 190, 191, 192
  foreign 158
  patterns of 166
  private 160, 185, 210
  public 160
investment policy 40
Ireland 200
Ireland, P. 70
Italy 146, 200

Jackson Report 181
James, C. 6
Japan 26, 29, 44, 48, 146, 162, 186, 193, 198, 200
job creation 85, 180, 181

jobs
  high-skilled 45, 49, 50, 188
  low-paid 53, 187
  low-skilled 45, 49, 232
  'Mickey Mouse' 101
  part-time 167
  quality of 182, 188
Jones, F. 199, 202
justice 30, 136
  distributive 54
  see also social justice

Kakwani, N. 199
Kalecki, M. 101, 105, 159
Kaptein, E. 162
Karpin Report 194
Keating, M. 120
Keating, P. J. 7, 18, 46, 64, 66, 67, 137, 144
  see also Hawke–Keating Labor government
Kelly, P. 7, 63–7, 72, 81, 111
Kennett government, Victoria 121, 127, 128, 237
Kennett, G. 130
Keynesian economic policy 4, 10, 12, 41, 50, 69, 74, 81–93, 94–107, 111, 161, 184, 185, 193, 217
Kidd, B. 77
King, S. 6
Ku Klux Klan 140

Labor government *see* Chifley Labor government; Curtin Labor government; Hawke–Keating Labor government; Whitlam Labor government
Labor *see* Australian Labor Party
labour 32, 30, 151, 159, 160, 164, 167, 181, 185, 188, 197
  disciplined 164
  high-wage 158
  itinerant 152
  problem, the 159, 160
labour force participation rate 45, 49, 212
  women's 45, 49
labour force, quality of 70
labour market 3, 38, 40, 43, 44, 45, 50, 52, 160
  access 39
  deregulation 3, 40, 43, 46, 54, 165, 169, 176, 177
  fragmentation 191
  globalisation and 3, 49
  imperfections in 184
  reform 229
  structural adjustment 181
  two-tier 44

INDEX

labour market policy 40, 41, 87
labour market programs 45, 50, 52, 82, 193, 228
labour movement
   Australian 8, 58, 50, 63, 90, 91, 141, 152
   US 151
labour regulation 139
labour tradition 72
labourism 73
laissez-faire 139
Lang, J. D. 57
Langer, A. 74
Langmore, J. 86, 88
Latin America 162
Left, the 29, 50, 97, 100, 105, 113, 118, 120, 201
legal institutions 113
Lewis, J. 40
Liberal government *see* Howard Liberal–National Coalition government; Kennett Coalition government, Victoria; Menzies Liberal–Country Party Coalition government
liberal nationalism 26, 28
Liberal Party of Australia 2, 62, 135
liberalism 73, 92, 106
   Australian 57–68, 77, 90
   Benthamite 59–60
   cultural 61–3, 69
   Deakinite 8, 11, 67, 73, 90
   economic 2, 7, 51
   market 144, 170, 172
   neoclassical 21, 26, 28, 32, 99, 103
   rights-based 25
libertarianism 4, 25, 54, 58, 92, 114, 123, 175, 179, 239
Lind, M. 26–8
Lipietz, A. 89
living wage 47, 62, 69, 88
Lloyd, P. 6
Locke 57
low-income earners 132
loyalty 148
Lydall, H. 198
Lyotard, F. 143

Maastricht agreement 24
MacDermott, T. 47
Macintyre, S. 137
Mackay, H. 20
macroeconomic policy 86, 87, 97, 98, 99, 102, 105, 120, 158, 162, 165, 168, 177, 193
Maddox, G. viii, 5, 7–8, 57–68, 81, 89, 145, 152
Madison 57

Magarey, S. 78
male breadwinner model 41, 42, 45, 53
   modified 42
management 115, 117, 118, 160, 191, 194
   corporate 117
   devolved 115
   of public institutions 118
   program 117
   strategic 230
   Taylorist principles of 160
managerialism 111, 112, 115, 117, 120, 144, 229, 237
Manne, R. 6
manufacturing 186
manufacturing sector, Australia 43, 44, 158, 163, 165
   industry policy and 180–94
   export performance 186
   see also elaborately transformed manufactures
manufacturing technology 192
market bureaucracy 229–40
market economies 35, 119
market failure 171, 172, 175, 176, 223, 224, 238
market forces 22, 24, 29, 40, 92, 157, 158, 224, 226
market fundamentalism 28
market language 145
market mechanisms 135, 185, 215, 230
market model 4, 29, 112, 148, 215
market outcomes 40
market wage 103
market 5, 7, 8, 12, 18, 19, 20, 24, 28, 32, 38, 40, 41, 43, 46, 69, 84, 85, 88, 92, 118, 123, 138, 143, 146, 157, 170, 171, 172, 176, 188, 223, 238, 239
   impediments to operation 181
   managed 7
   performance 185
   reducing government intervention in 173
   self-regulating 82
   strong 30
   structure 185
   state and *see* state
marketing 187, 189
markets 22, 29, 31, 50, 121, 123, 129, 158, 167, 224, 226, 240
   access 189
   competitive 229
   deregulated 32
   financial 49, 161, 163, 164, 168, 177, 178
   global 129, 180, 182, 193
   private 114
Marsh, I. 145
Marx, K. 58

274   INDEX

Marxism 95, 99, 140
Matzner, E. 84
McLean, I. 202
McRae, H. 34
Medibank 74
Medicare 74
Melbourne, poverty in 199
Melleuish G. 61–2
Melucci, A. 142, 146
Mendelsohn, R. 199
Menzies Liberal–Country Coalition government 74, 83, 111
Menzies, R. G. 83
Meredith, D. 86
Metal Trades Industry Association (MTIA) 182, 190
Métin, A. 58
microeconomic policy 86, 87, 105, 116
microeconomic reform 19, 119, 120, 122, 162, 169, 177, 178, 180–4, 216, 217, 227, 235
microeconomic system 158
microeconomy 185
middle class 27, 28, 140, 161, 162, 167, 199, 205
Mill, J. S. 62
minimum wage 41, 70, 82, 88, 171, 184
Mishra, R. 1
Mitchell, D. 204
mixed economy 13, 73, 74, 75, 88, 89, 90, 95, 96, 98, 99, 101, 118, 121, 221
modernisation 140
monetarism 97, 102, 103, 104
monetary policy 87, 104, 159, 169, 172, 177, 181
monetary regulations 164
monopolies 173
Montesquieu 57
Mortimer Report 183, 184, 188, 189, 191, 194
multiculturalism 26, 64, 70, 144
multinational corporations 32, 140
mutual support 124

Naschold, F. 229–30, 238, 239
National Commission of Audit 127, 132
National Economic Development Strategy 182
National Employment and Training Task Force 231
National Organisation of Women (US) 70
National Party of Australia 2
national savings strategy 51
nationalism 73, 139
neighbourhood associations 124

neocorporatism 24, 30, 46
neoliberalism 2, 6, 12, 23, 26, 40, 43, 46, 54, 95, 97, 157, 163
   see also economic rationalism
neomercantilism 31
Netherlands 44, 48, 202
Nevile, J. viii, 10, 49, 169–79, 200, 239
new contractualism 5, 237
new feudalism 27, 33, 35
new growth theory 186, 188
New Labour (UK) 29, 34, 96
New Protection policies 82, 86, 152
New Right, the 28, 114, 126
New Social Movement thesis 141–2
New Zealand 43, 44, 46, 54, 74, 112, 121, 127, 145, 171, 237
   income inequality 197–201
newly industrialising countries (NICs) 188
Niskanen 134
Nixon, R. 184
non-government organisations (NGOs) 125, 143, 219, 224, 225, 232, 239
non-government sector 124, 137, 219–21, 233, 236
non-profit organisations 129, 134
non-profit sector 229
Norway 200

O'Connor, James 141
oil-price shocks 99, 100, 158
Ombudsman 226
One Nation Party 143, 144
Orchard, L. ix, 11, 111–23, 125
order 30
Organisation for Economic Cooperation and Development (OECD) 21, 43, 44, 45, 47, 48, 49, 97, 100, 103, 159, 160, 161, 163, 165, 167, 182, 188, 192, 198, 202, 203, 209, 212, 229, 230, 238
Organisation of Petroleum Exporting Countries (OPEC) 97, 99, 159
organisational learning 189
Osborne, D. 127–30, 135
overclass 26, 67

parent–teacher groups 124
Parsons, T. 14
pastoral industry 151, 152
Paterson, J. 120
Paukert, F. 198
pensioners 132
pensions
   invalid 71
   old age 71, 75
   state 77

INDEX

performance measures 221
Peters, B. Guy 123
Phillips curve interpolation 99
Pixley, J. 8, 11, 81, 138–53
planning 91
Polanyi, K. 40
policy development 227, 230
policy management 128
policy prescriptions 174, 175, 176
policy settlements 157–68
political economy 13, 17, 24, 43, 35, 81, 82, 138, 157, 158, 162, 163
political processes 82
political thought, Australia 57–68, 89
  Australian Settlement and 59, 63–8
  Benthamite characteristics 59–60
  collectivist influences 60, 62–3, 67
  influence of religion 60, 66–7
  liberalism and 59–63
  major figures in 57–8
  paternalism and 64–6
  positivism and 60
positivism 60, 69, 116
post-modernism 142, 143
post-bureaucracy 237
  see also market bureaucracy
postwar reconstruction 73, 86–7, 95, 98, 111
poverty 9, 28, 31, 42, 43, 51, 83, 171, 175, 198, 199, 200, 201, 203, 204
  child 200
poverty indexes 207
power generation sector 235
prisons 128
Pritchett, L. 204
private enterprise 21, 130, 149, 171
private sector 21, 23, 36, 111, 117, 122, 126, 129, 130, 131, 163, 167, 224, 225, 234, 235
  for-profit 126, 220, 232, 233
  not-for-profit 126, 129, 239
private sector entry 220
privatisation 21, 27, 46, 72, 112, 121, 122, 128, 137, 143, 149, 169, 217, 223, 225–7, 229, 231
production 161, 171
  mass 188
production values 33
productivity 160, 205
  growth in 167
Productivity Commission 190
profit restoration 164
program budgeting 111
Progress Foundation 215
protectionism 31, 60, 61, 63, 74, 77, 83, 84, 145, 162, 163
protest 151

public administration 11–12, 111, 113, 117, 126, 215
  market thinking in 136
  modernisation 128
  post-bureaucratic model 120, 121
  reform, Australia 3, 111, 115, 117, 120
public choice theory 112, 114, 115, 116, 120, 138, 142–4, 146, 148, 150, 237
public enterprise 217
public finance 219
public good, the 144
public goods 28, 118, 135, 136, 143, 171, 177
public interest 121, 133
public opinion 172, 173
public opinion polls 128
public policy, Australian 1, 4, 5, 10, 11, 40, 48, 81, 83, 88, 91, 92, 111, 115, 118, 120, 126, 170, 216, 217, 237–40
public sector 11, 23, 36, 125, 126, 127, 132, 133, 135, 167
  competition and 221–7
  reform of, Australia 111–23, 125, 217
  US 128, 129
public sector management 123
public service, Australia 4
  employment contracts in 122
  ethos 123
  generalists in 114, 117
  impartiality in 122
  performance assessment in 122
  permanency of tenure in 113, 121, 122
  reform 4, 112, 120
  structure 127
  'Westminster heresy' and 121
  Westminster principles in 122
public services 72, 126, 229
public spending
  increase in 201
  reduction of 111, 139, 185
public sphere 138, 139, 140, 143, 149, 150, 152
public utilities 218
public value 121
public works 88
public–private partnerships 130
purchaser–provider split 133, 220, 225–6
Pusey, M. 6, 116, 118
Putnam, R. 124, 147–8

Qantas 169
quasi-state, the 32
Quiggin, J. 80, 88, 216, 225

race, politics of 26, 79
racism 64, 144
Raskall, P. 200
rational choice theory 30
Rawls, J. 57
Reaganism 144
recession 160, 165, 185
reconciliation 143
redistribution 39, 40, 41, 83, 84, 85, 118, 203, 204–10
  see also income redistribution
redundancy 112
Rees, S. 6
Rees-Mogg, W. 34
reform
  administrative 238
  bureaucratic 111–23
  democratic 138
  economic 7
  management 230
  market-based 168
  social 201
  structural 182, 227
regional development 29, 50, 51, 191–4, 228
regional technology networks 189, 191, 192
regionalisation 113
regulation 128
  financial 158
rehabilitation services 134
Reich, R. 33, 34, 47
reinventing government 21, 112, 115, 124–37, 215, 237
religious thought, Australia 66–8, 70, 72, 76–7
republicanism, Australian 1, 66
research and development 87, 183, 186, 188, 192
Reserve Bank 167, 178
resource allocation 133, 184
resources production 186
returned soldiers 75
Richardson, S. 198, 202
Right, the 50, 118, 120, 201
rightsizing 34
Roe, J. ix, 2, 8, 12, 69–80, 81, 89
Rosencrance, R. N. 59
Ross, L. 90
ruling elites 147

Saunders, P. 49
savings, private 208, 210
Sawyer, M. 198
Scandinavia 200, 202
schools, public 128
Schumpeter, J. 186
Schwartz, H. 119

Scott, R. 78
secularism 60, 67, 77
security, economic 175
  see also economic development; industry development; regional development
self-employment 45
service delivery 129, 130, 132, 233
  direct 220
  devolution 221
  flexibility 235, 237
service delivery organisations 126
service industries 33, 44, 45, 227
service providers 132, 232–3, 237
service quality 223
service sector 165, 186
services
  continuity 135
  government 129, 149
  international trade in 185
  jobs growth in 187
  marketisation 225
  private provision 131, 134, 226
  public provision 33, 127, 130, 131, 134, 136, 226, 239
  trade in 158
short-termism 35, 142, 166, 178
Silicon Valley 186
skill formation 181, 191
skills
  low 45, 49, 167
  high 45, 49, 50
  new 192
  workforce 189, 228
Skillshare 232
Sloan, J. 174
small and medium-sized firms 166
small government 27, 33
Smelser, N. 140
Smyth, P. ix, 6, 74, 81–93
social capital 25, 26, 30, 31, 124, 126, 136, 148, 239
  trust and 25, 31
social change 140, 141
social cohesion 128, 135, 139, 144, 149
social contract 10, 86, 88, 179
social corporatism 2, 3, 12, 139
social Darwinism 61
social democracy 71, 90, 91, 95, 112, 113–14, 115–18, 119, 121, 123, 201, 228
social insurance 203, 205
social justice 38, 84, 127, 142, 151, 152, 180, 202
social market model 23
social movements 11–12, 138–53
  civil society and 11
  future role 149–53

INDEX

location 147–9
sociology 140–2
social participation 124
social policy
  Australian 6, 12, 38–54, 69, 72, 74, 77, 81, 82, 83, 85, 88, 89, 106, 113, 124, 130, 198, 215, 216
  formulation 220
  Industry Commission and 215–27
  liberal 79
  redistribution and 83, 84
  role 85, 229
  safety-net in 12
  US 70
social protection 40, 41, 43, 47, 95, 201, 202
social security
  Australian system 39, 40, 44, 46, 47, 48, 49, 51, 53–4, 70, 71, 75, 82, 85, 92, 96, 133, 171, 203, 204, 208, 209, 215
  employer contributions to 208
social services 74
social structure 151
social transfers 40, 206, 209
social wage 3, 38, 52, 71, 82, 86, 103, 104, 105, 171
social welfare 238
  delivery 229
social workers 133
socialism 57, 61, 62–3, 81, 86, 89, 90, 96, 172
  colonial 111
  democratic 90, 92, 95, 96, 126
socialist Keynesians 106
society 127, 139
  industrial 151
sole-parenting benefit 69, 70, 71
South Korea 146, 186
Soviet Union, former 162
Spain 44
special-interest groups 114, 131–4, 145–9
Spence, C. H. 78
Spence, W. G. 57
stagflation 159
stakeholders 139
standard of living 139, 206
  reduction in 144
Stark 198
state experiments 71
state intervention 85, 157
state paternalism 7, 64–5
state power 139, 150
state reform 111
state 7, 8, 13, 18, 20–4, 26, 30, 32, 35, 41, 43, 78, 50, 65, 69, 71, 85, 96, 118, 123, 124, 125, 127, 139, 140, 143, 146, 147–51, 164, 171

accountable 140
authoritarian 65, 148, 149
bureaucratic 149
contract 2, 4
corporatist 82
developmental 11, 18, 23, 139, 144, 147, 149, 150
enabling 191
executive 29
fiscal crisis of 161
hollow 121, 122, 225, 229
interventionist 62, 144, 147
liberal 71
market and 20, 22, 24, 40, 46, 69, 139, 157, 158, 238, 239–40
market-oriented 149
nanny 21
non-government organisations and 229
partnership 21
paternalist 7, 62, 65, 111
police 144
protective 84
self-limiting 149, 150
size 163
social citizenship 23
special interest 21
strong 21, 146
weak 33, 35, 147
welfare burden of 166
steering versus rowing 112, 129–33
Steindl, J. 97
Steketee, M. 122
Strange, S. 34
Streeck, W. 84
Stretton, H. 58, 99, 116
strikes 159, 160
structural adjustment 181
students' movement 140
Sturgess, G. 129
Stzompka, P. 150
superannuation 50, 71, 106, 210
supply 185
sustainability 18, 30, 153, 193
Sweden 48, 91, 146, 198, 199, 200, 201
Switzerland 200

TAFE 232
Taiwan 146, 186
Tariff Board 181
tariff protection 82, 83, 84, 92, 158, 180, 181
tariff reductions 169, 178, 183, 190
tariffs 182, 184
tax burden 26, 161
tax credits 135
tax revenue 181

tax-benefit systems 39, 40, 43, 48, 49, 53, 54, 204
  redistribution via 49, 54
tax-transfer systems 207
taxation 27, 28, 38, 40, 49, 87, 111, 161, 205, 219
  accounting of 209–10
  Australian system of 9, 42, 48, 49, 50, 75, 203, 204, 211
  direct 210
  high 162, 201
  limiting power of 114
  low 133, 171
  minimisation 33
  redistributive system 49, 53, 54, 74
  regressive 28
  US system 27
  see also consumption tax
taxation policy 46
taxation reform 169
technological change 30, 35, 49, 178, 180, 185
technologies 182, 188
  new 187, 192
telecommunications sector 235
Telstra 169
textile, clothing and footwear industry 183
Thatcher, M. 176
Thatcherism 28, 29, 112, 139, 144
think-tanks
  free market 215
  right-wing 238
Tory Party (Conservative Party, UK) 28, 29
Total Quality Management (TQM) 237
Touraine, A. 141, 151
tourism sector 167
trade deficit 190
trade policy 163
trade unions 27, 38, 41, 46, 52, 53, 60, 75, 78, 101, 102, 105, 119, 124, 133, 140, 141, 145, 148, 152, 160, 162, 184, 191, 230, 231
  see also Australian Council of Trade Unions (ACTU); Australian Manufacturing Workers' Union (AMWU); labour movement; union movement
trade, terms of 181, 186
training 40, 46, 47, 50, 181
  education and 40, 46, 47, 50, 194
  employment and 40, 46, 47, 50, 53, 54
transnational agreements 163
transnational corporations 32

transport policy 40
trickle-down effect 33, 205
trust 25, 26, 28, 139, 148, 149
  market and 28
  social capital and 25, 26
Turner, H. G. 197
Turner, I. 198
two-party system 145
Tyson, L. 193

Unaipon, D. 79
underclass 33, 34, 199
underemployment 43, 46
unemployed, the 146, 150
  long-term 232, 235, 237
unemployment 3, 9, 10, 11, 19, 38, 39, 40, 42–6, 48–54, 75, 86, 95, 98, 101, 103–5, 139, 160, 165, 166, 168, 170, 176, 185, 188, 228
  economic costs 181
  fear of 178
  growth in 177
  high 164, 183
  inflation and 104, 172
  involuntary 175
  long-term 43, 45, 50, 229
  reduction 178
  short-term 45
  structural 178
  youth 52
union movement 149, 222
unionisation 160
unions see trade unions
United Kingdom 2, 4, 21, 24–30, 46, 48–9, 54, 64, 66, 74, 91, 112, 124, 136, 188, 237
  civil service reforms 112
  democracy 74
  economic problems in 21
  interest groups 146
  income distribution 197–200, 209
  income inequality 202
  market model 4
  non-profit sectors 229
  neoliberalism 43, 46, 54
  New Fabianism 91
  new ideas in 24–30
  notions of the state 21
  poverty in 199
  provision of services 136
  racism 64
  reinventing government 127
  republicanism 66
  social protection 43
  wage differentials 48–9
  unemployment 176, 201
United Nations 9, 200

INDEX

United States of America 4, 9, 21, 24–30, 43, 45, 46, 47, 48–9, 54, 64, 66, 112, 193, 215, 236–7
  Brazilianisation of 27
  conceptions of the state 21, 24–30, 71, 127–33, 149
  democracy 74
  deregulation of labour market 176
  economic problems 21
  equality and 197
  income distribution 47, 171, 202, 209
  income inequality 202
  interest groups 146
  market model 4
  neoliberalism 43, 46, 54
  new political theories 24–30
  non-profit sectors 229
  poverty 199
  productivity 167
  racism in 64
  reinventing government 127–33
  Republican policies 70
  republicanism 66
  social movements 147, 151
  social protection 43–70
  unemployment 201
  wage differentials 48–9
  welfare 9, 70
urban transport 218
user-pays principle 218, 220, 236
utilitarianism 60

value judgements 175, 176
value-added manufactures 24, 158
value-adding industries 182
values
  ecological 28, 30
  ethical 120
  social 30, 120
Veblen, T. 186
Victoria 121, 127, 128, 224
  local government 225, 226
Victorian Chamber of Manufactures 166
Victorian Commission of Audit 127
Victorian government *see* Kennett Coalition government, Victoria
Vietnam War 99
Vintilla, P. 6
voluntary associations 130
voluntary organisations 171
voting
  compulsory 74
  effective 79
  preferential 74
  proportional 79, 145

voucher systems 130, 135, 136
  class-based 53
  market 49
  wage 49, 152

wage arbitration 7, 64–5, 145, 152
wage costs 188
wage decline 103
wage demands 103, 159
wage fixation 3, 5, 38, 41, 42, 43, 47, 49, 52, 152, 211
  collective bargaining and 52
wage increases 103, 159
wage system, Australia 12, 43, 54, 82, 86
wages 47, 48, 71, 102, 104, 145, 181
  award 171
  bargaining and 102, 160
  below-average 167
  centralised fixation 3, 5, 38, 41, 42, 43, 47, 49, 52, 152, 178
  cuts in 178, 185
  determination 40, 88, 122
  differentials in 45, 48–9
  growth in 45, 103
  inflation and 177–9
  low 167, 192
  market 38, 145, 171
  real 104
  see also living wage; minimum wage
wages policy 46, 88
Walker, E. R. 90
Ward, R. 58, 59, 198
wealth creation 33, 88, 161
wealth distribution 161, 206
wealth, private 210, 211
Wearing, M ix 228–40
Webb, B. and S. 197
Weiss, L. 22–3, 146
welfare 39, 40, 70, 145
  active versus passive 85
  administration of 238–9
  business 183
  failure 82
  government monopolies on 235
  middle class 203, 209, 210
  social 3, 85
welfare need 39
welfare organisations 125, 135, 145
welfare outcomes 39, 210
welfare payments 165
welfare policy 1, 66, 137
  economic policy and 83
welfare regimes 39, 40
welfare rights 39, 145
welfare sector 125, 129, 215–27, 237–40
  competitive model and 219–27

welfare services 134
  delivery 232
welfare spending 201, 204, 206
welfare state 4, 11, 28, 39, 41, 67, 73, 80, 96, 198, 207–9, 211, 218, 223
  Keynesian 81–93, 143
  New Fabian models of 90
  small 210
  social movements and 141
  Swedish models 90
  wage earners' 3, 81, 82, 84
welfare system
  Australian 3, 9, 12, 40, 82, 95, 204, 219
  egalitarianism and 11
  redistributive outcomes 3
  residualism in 3, 40
  US 9
  universalism in 3
Wentworth, W. C. 199
Western Australia 224
Wheelwright, E. 200
White Australia policy 7, 64, 73, 82
Whiteford, P. ix, 5, 9, 197–214
Whitlam, E. G. 64
Whitlam Labor government 82, 84, 102, 105, 106, 111, 112, 113, 125
Wilenski, P. 113, 117, 119, 123, 125, 161
Wise, B. R. 77–8
women 40, 48, 49, 53, 54, 70, 71, 151
  family responsibilities and 40, 48, 53, 54, 152
  votes for 79, 151
  wage differentials and 49
  work and 40, 48, 49, 53, 54, 152

women's movement 140, 146
women's organisations 124, 152
women's refuges 130
women's rights 144
work 39, 40
  caring 40, 41, 46, 51, 52, 54
  conditions 71, 144, 152, 159, 211
  intensification 191
  leave arrangements and 53
  non-market 40, 41, 51, 54
  paid 51, 54
  unpaid 51, 53
  welfare and 39, 40
  women and 40, 48, 49, 53, 54
  see also employment; employment benefits
work for the dole scheme 5
work incentives 201
work organisation 160
worker militancy 159, 160
workers 141, 143, 159
  highly skilled 190
workers' compensation 218
workers' rights 152
working class 82, 91, 159
working hours 53
Working Nation: White Paper on Employment and Growth, 1994 11, 46, 86, 230–6
working poor 212
Workplace Relations and Other Legislation Amendment Act 1996 47, 53

xenophobic movements 142

Yeatman, A. 120